A Companion to Muslim Ethics

The Institute of Ismaili Studies

MUSLIM HERITAGE SERIES, 2

General Editor: Amyn B. Sajoo

This series explores vital themes in the civilisations of Islam – including the nature of religious authority, ethics and law, social justice and civil society, the arts and sciences, and the interplay of spiritual and secular lifeworlds. In keeping with the Institute's mandate, the series is informed by the plurality of communities and interpretations of Islam, as well as their locus in modernity and tradition.

A Companion to Muslim Ethics

Edited by
AMYN B. SAJOO

I.B. Tauris *Publishers*
LONDON • NEW YORK
in association with
The Institute of Ismaili Studies
LONDON

Published in 2010 by I.B.Tauris & Co. Ltd
6 Salem Road, London W2 4BU
175 Fifth Avenue, New York, NY 10010
www.ibtauris.com

in association with The Institute of Ismaili Studies
210 Euston Road, London NW1 2DA
www.iis.ac.uk

Distributed in the United States and Canada Exclusively by Palgrave Macmillan,
175 Fifth Avenue, New York, NY 10010

ISBN: 978 1 84885 595 3

A full CIP record for this book is available from the British Library
A full CIP record for this book is available from the Library of Congress

Library of Congress catalog card: available

Typeset in Minion Tra for The Institute of Ismaili Studies
Printed and bound in Great Britain by CPI Antony Rowe, Chippenham, Wiltshire

FSC
www.fsc.org
MIX
Paper from
responsible sources
FSC® C013604

The Institute of Ismaili Studies

The Institute of Ismaili Studies was established in 1977 with the object of promoting scholarship and learning on Islam, in the historical as well as contemporary contexts, and a better understanding of its relationship with other societies and faiths.

The Institute's programmes encourage a perspective which is not confined to the theological and religious heritage of Islam, but seeks to explore the relationship of religious ideas to broader dimensions of society and culture. The programmes thus encourage an inter-disciplinary approach to the materials of Islamic history and thought. Particular attention is also given to issues of modernity that arise as Muslims seek to relate their heritage to the contemporary situation.

Within the Islamic tradition, the Institute's programmes promote research on those areas which have, to date, received relatively little attention from scholars. These include the intellectual and literary expressions of Shi'ism in general, and Ismailism in particular.

In the context of Islamic societies, the Institute's programmes are informed by the full range and diversity of cultures in which Islam is practised today, from the Middle East, South and Central Asia, and Africa to the industrialized societies of the West, thus taking into consideration the variety of contexts which shape the ideals, beliefs and practices of the faith.

These objectives are realised through concrete programmes and activities organized and implemented by various departments of the Institute. The Institute also collaborates periodically, on a programme-specific basis, with other institutions of learning in the United Kingdom and abroad.

The Institute's academic publications fall into a number of inter-related categories:

1. Occasional papers or essays addressing broad themes of the re-lationship between religion and society, with special reference to Islam.
2. Monographs exploring specific aspects of Islamic faith and cul-ture, or the contributions of individual Muslim thinkers or writ-ers.
3. Editions or translations of significant primary or secondary texts.
4. Translations of poetic or literary texts which illustrate the rich heritage of spiritual, devotional and symbolic expressions in Muslim history.
5. Works on Ismaili history and thought, and the relationship of the Ismailis to other traditions, communities and schools of thought in Islam.
6. Proceedings of conferences and seminars sponsored by the In-stitute.
7. Bibliographical works and catalogues which document manu-scripts, printed texts and other source materials.

This book falls into category two listed above.

In facilitating these and other publications, the Institute's sole aim is to encourage original research and analysis of relevant issues. While every effort is made to ensure that the publications are of a high academic standard, there is naturally bound to be a diversity of views, ideas and interpretations. As such, the opinions expressed in these publications must be understood as belonging to their au-thors alone.

Contents

*It is not piety that you turn your faces to the East
and to the West.
True piety is this ... to give of one's substance,
however cherished,
to kinsmen, orphans, the needy, the traveller, beggars, and to ransom
the slave, to perform the prayer, to pay the alms.
And they who fulfil their contracts, and endure with fortitude
misfortune, hardship and peril, these are they who are true
in their faith ...*

Quran, 2:177

*Generosity is not just giving money from excess,
but rather sharing with the poor.*

Proverb on Samanid bowl (ninth/tenth centuries), cited in Oya
Pancaroğlu, 'Serving Wisdom', *Studies in Islamic and Later Indian
Art from the Arthur M. Sackler Museum*
(Cambridge, MA, 2002), pp. 61–62

About the Contributors

Charles Butterworth is emeritus professor of Government and Politics at the University of Maryland, specialising in Islamic political thought. He has taught over the years across the Middle East and in 2008 was Distinguished Visiting Professor at the American University of Cairo. His books span the works of Ibn Rushd on Aristotle, translations of works by al-Farabi, al-Razi, Ibn Rushd and Maimonides, and the political thought of Frantz Fanon and Jean-Jacques Rousseau. Butterworth gave a series of lectures in 2000 at the Institut du Monde Arabe in Paris on the origins of political philosophy in Islam. He is past-president of the American Council for the Study of Islamic Societies and of the Société Internationale pour l'Étude de l'Histoire de la Philosophie et la Science Arabe et Islamique. His chapter in this volume builds on his contribution to the *Cambridge Companion to Arabic Philosophy* (2005).

Abdallah Daar is professor of Public Health Sciences and of Surgery at the University of Toronto, and director of Ethics and Commercialization at the McLaughlin-Rotman Centre for Global Health in Toronto. He was awarded UNESCO's Avicenna Prize for Ethics of Science in 2005. Daar serves on the bioethics committees of the Human Genome Organization and UNESCO. He is a fellow of the Islamic World Academy of Sciences, the Royal Society of Canada and the Academy of Sciences of the Developing World.

Ramin Jahanbegloo is professor of Political Science and a research fellow in Ethics at the University of Toronto. He was the Rajni

Kothari Professor of Democracy at the Centre for the Study of Developing Societies in New Delhi in 2006–7, having earlier served as head of Contemporary Studies of the Cultural Research Centre in Tehran. His books include *Conversations with Isaiah Berlin* (1992), *Gandhi: Aux sources de la nonviolence* (1999), *Penser la nonviolence* (2000), *Iran: Between Tradition and Modernity* (2004), *India Revisited: Conversations on Contemporary India* (2007), *The Clash of Intolerances* (2007) and *The Spirit of India* (2008). Jahanbegloo was awarded the 2009 Peace Prize of the United Nations Association in Spain, in recognition of his work on non-violence, both as a philosophy and political strategy and the promotion of freedom of thought and dialogue among cultures.

Zayn Kassam is associate professor and former chair in Religious Studies at Pomona College in Claremont, California, where she specialises in Islam. She holds two Wig Awards for Distinguished Teaching at Pomona College, as well as an American Academy of Religion Excellence in Teaching Award, and has lectured widely on both sides of the Atlantic. Kassam is the author of *Introduction to the World's Major Religions: Islam* (2006), and is at work on a feminist theology in Islam. She has published articles on a range of issues relating to the status of women, mysticism and ecology in Islam, as well as on the teaching of Islam in diverse settings.

Mohamed Keshavjee is a leading scholar and trainer in the field of alternative dispute resolution (ADR), and a lawyer with many years of experience in Canada and Kenya. He joined the Secretariat of His Highness the Aga Khan at Aiglemont, France in 1980, and directs community training programmes on family and commercial mediation for Muslim communities across the world. Keshavjee has served on the Steering Committee of the World Mediation Forum, and was a keynote speaker in 2009 at the Council of Europe's 7th International Family Mediation Conference in Strasbourg, France. He also lectures on ADR and Islamic Law at The Institute of Ismaili Studies, where he is a member of the Board of Governors.

Ahmed Al-Khitamy lectures in Bioethics at Sultan Qaboos University in Oman, and at the Oman Medical College. He has a particular interest in the role of religious scholars in East and South African Islam. An earlier version of his chapter here with Daar appeared as 'Bioethics for Clinicians: Islamic Bioethics', in the *Canadian Medical Association Journal* (2001).

Seyyed Hossein Nasr is University Professor of Islamic Studies at George Washington University. He has taught at Harvard, Princeton and Tehran universities, and was the first Aga Khan Professor of Islamic Studies at the American University of Beirut in 1964–65. Nasr's more than thirty books and numerous articles on themes in Islamic philosophy, ecology, science and spirituality have been translated into several languages. Among the best known of his works are *Science and Civilization in Islam* (1968), *Ideals and Realities of Islam* (1988), *Man and Nature: The Spiritual Crisis of Modern Man* (1997) and *The Heart of Islam: Enduring Values for Humanity* (2002). Nasr's chapter here is abridged from his 'Islam, the Contemporary Islamic World, and the Environmental Crisis', in Richard Foltz et al. eds., *Islam and Ecology: A Bestowed Trust*, pp. 85–105, by permission of the Harvard Center for the Study of World Religions, © 2003, President and Fellows of Harvard College.

Eric Ormsby is professor and senior research associate at The Institute of Ismaili Studies. He was previously director of libraries at McGill University, Montreal and director of the university's Institute of Islamic Studies. His publications include *Ghazali: The Revival of Islam* (2007), and articles on Islamic philosophy, theology and mysticism. From 1975 to 1983, Ormsby was Curator of Islamic Manuscripts at Princeton University and co-authored (with Rudolf Mach) the *Handlist of Arabic Manuscripts (New Series) in the Princeton University Library* (1987). He is a frequent contributor of essays and reviews on literature, history and philosophy to *The New York Times Book Review*, the *Times Literary Supplement*, *The New Criterion* and the *Wall Street Journal*, among others. Ormsby is currently working on a translation of Nasir-i Khusraw's last work, the *Jami' al-hikmatayn*.

Amyn B. Sajoo is resident scholar at Simon Fraser University's Centre for the Comparative Study of Muslim Societies and Cultures in Vancouver. He has held visiting appointments at Cambridge and McGill universities, as well as The Institute of Ismaili Studies. Earlier, he served with the Canadian Department of Justice in Ottawa, and as Canada-ASEAN Fellow at the Institute of Southeast Asian Studies in Singapore. Sajoo is the author of *Muslim Ethics: Emerging Vistas* (2009) and *Pluralism in Old Societies and New States* (1994); his edited works include *A Companion to the Muslim World* (2009), *Muslim Modernities: Expressions of the Civil Imagination* (2008) and *Civil Society in the Muslim World* (2002). He is a frequent contributor to the news media on both sides of the Atlantic.

Reza Shah-Kazemi is a research associate at The Institute of Ismaili Studies, where he serves as managing editor of *Encyclopaedia Islamica*. He has lectured internationally in the areas of Quranic studies, Sufism, Shiism and comparative mysticism. Shah-Kazemi's publications include *Paths to Transcendence: According to Shankara, Ibn Arabi and Meister Eckhart* (2006), *Justice and Remembrance: An Introduction to the Spirituality of Imam Ali* (2006) and *The Other in the Light of the One: The Universality of the Qur'an and Interfaith Dialogue* (2006). Among his forthcoming works are *Tolerance and the Spread of Islam* and *Common Ground: Spiritual and Moral Affinities between Islam and Buddhism*.

Fahmida Suleman is a curator at the British Museum's Middle East Department in London. She was formerly a research associate at The Institute of Ismaili Studies, where she lectured on Islamic art and material culture. Suleman is the editor of *Word of God, Art of Man: The Qur'an and its Creative Expressions* (2007), and her writing spans the full range of Muslim art history, including entries on Ceramics, Gifts and Gift Giving, and *Kalila wa Dimna* in *Medieval Islamic Civilization: An Encyclopaedia* (2006). She is currently editing *People of the Prophet's House: Art, Architecture and Shi'ism in the Islamic World*, a volume that stems from a 2009 conference co-sponsored by the British Museum and The Institute of Ismaili Studies.

Rodney Wilson is director of the University of Durham's Centre for Islamic Finance. He was a visiting professor in 2009 at the Qatar Foundation's Faculty of Islamic Studies in Doha. Wilson chairs the academic committee of the Institute of Islamic Banking and Insurance in London, and is consultant to the Islamic Financial Services Board on its Sharia Governance Guidelines. He has published widely on Islamic finance and corporate governance of Islamic financial institutions, and recently completed a paper for the Kuwait Programme of the London School of Economics on *Islamic Finance in the Gulf Co-operation Council*. Wilson has conducted training sessions for financial institutions in Abu Dhabi, Bahrain, Kuwait, London, Riyadh, Shanghai and Singapore.

List of Illustrations

Plate section located between pages 76 and 77

Acknowledgements

This *Companion* and the Muslim Heritage Series have a host of movers and makers. First among these are the authors whose chapters shape how the 'Muslim world' in its plurality and fertility of thought, practice and expression emerges for the reader. Their willingness to cast and recast complex ideas into narratives that are accessible and imaginative while upholding the integrity of scholarship is what this venture is ultimately about.

Stalwart support for this project has come from Farhad Daftary at the Institute of Ismaili Studies, first as head of research and publications, then as co-director of the Institute. Kutub Kassam's creative input has extended far beyond his technical editing skills, to a sharing of ideas that have enriched all aspects of the endeavour. Nadia Holmes and Patricia Salazar have unfailingly brought skill and patience to the editorial process. Eva Sajoo wore multiple hats, with a critical eye to the text, ideas and images while serving as a companion of the best kind along the journey.

The Centre for the Comparative Study of Muslim Societies and Cultures at Simon Fraser University facilitated much of the work on this volume. I extend deep appreciation to the director, Professor Derryl MacLean, and to Ellen Vaillancourt as co-ordinator.

For their generosity in granting permission for the use of various textual and figural resources, our thanks go to a host of cultural and educational institutions as noted at assorted points in this *Companion*. Our readers will doubtless be as grateful for the results.

Amyn B. Sajoo
Vancouver

Note on Dates

In the spirit of this Series, as set forth in the introduction to the *Companion to the Muslim World,* the life-dates for all major figures that appear in the text have been provided. This allows the reader a fuller appreciation of the figures and their roles in the larger picture of history, than if death-dates alone were provided. It is true that in many instances, the precision of life-dates for early figures may yet be somewhat uncertain. However, the dates offered in the text are judged to be the most widely cited among scholars at this point in time.

Introduction:
Roots and Branches

Amyn B. Sajoo

Why should I act ethically? How does this require me to act in a given situation – and what tells me that I have it right? These questions sit at the heart of most faith traditions, and Islam is no exception. Much of the Quran and the traditions linked to it are about these questions. Schools of law, philosophy and theology in classical Islam grappled mightily with them. In our time, the challenges of modernity have plenty to do with the answers we offer. This second volume in the Muslim Heritage Series is about the roots of Islam's ethical framework and how its teachings have branched out in the social and religious lives of Muslims past and present. We look too at how these roots and branches might give sustenance for journeys that lie ahead.

Taking ethics seriously means coming to terms with the real world where our sense of right and wrong plays out. Societies have devised complex theories about what is right and what is good, in keeping with Socrates' advice that the unexamined life is not worth living. Faith traditions at their best want philosophy to face the details of daily life – and daily life to face the tests of philosophy. Otherwise, we have what Abdolkarim Soroush calls an 'ethics of the gods' which is beyond the reach of mortals. Such an ethics may serve well enough in mythology or metaphysics. But like all communities of faith, the Muslim umma came into being not as an abstract ideal but an effort to live out its values as everyday reality.

'Let there be among you', proclaims the Quran, 'a community

that calls to the good (*al-khayr*), bidding virtue (*maruf*) and forbidding vice (*munkar*)' (3:104). Rooted in *arafa*, that which is known or familiar, *maruf* signifies the transparency of the virtues. They are accessible to all who care to make the effort, with an abundance of guidance from scripture; which also means there is no easy escape from responsibility. It is not the Prophet Muhammad alone for whom Quranic ethics is attainable, but all persons 'possessed of minds' (40:53–4). Belief is constantly coupled with 'good works' (e.g. 2:25), so the practice of ethics is central to one's identity as a member of the umma.

This chapter is a sketch of the ethical venture of Islam from its beginnings to the continuities that make up the rest of this volume. If ethics governs all of one's life, secular and religious, then values and principles must constantly be interpreted to reach an appropriate result. Does this make ethics into law that is binding in the name of a community of virtue? If law and ethics are so closely related, where does this leave one's choice about how to live the good life? Without choice, can there be responsibility for one's actions? If ethics is not binding in the same way as law, how has the difference played out in principle and practice? Islam's foundational phase had much to say on these matters, and history offers a rich array of interpretations of that teaching.

Roots

As the primary guide for Muslims, the Quran sets the tone for its moral universe in holding believing men and women as 'protective friends' who advocate the good (9:71). Belief is attached to behaviour, the individual to the community and, as noted earlier, the 'good' should be familiar to all. Justice, beneficence and charity are defining values, as against behaviour that brings shame or blame (16:90). Yet scripture is ultimately about character rather than abstract values.

There are over 200 references in the Quran to the sense of divine presence or *taqwa* that shapes the believer's conduct toward fellow human beings and God. It is what motivates one's integrity and forbearance in the face of adversity (2:177). Such forbearance or *hilm*, derived from one of the scriptural names of the divine, *al-Halim* (the Forbearing One), is essential not only in moral character but in the overall teaching:

> In a certain sense the Koran as a whole is dominated by the very spirit of *hilm*. The constant exhortation to kindness (*ihsan*) in human relations, the emphasis laid on justice *(adl)*, the forbidding of wrongful violence (*zulm*), the bidding of abstinence and control of passions, the criticism of groundless pride and arrogance – all are concrete manifestations of this spirit of *hilm*.[1]

This applies no less to how one 'forbids vice'; doing so in ways that violate this spirit of *hilm* can make the response itself a vice, whatever the righteous tone.

Virtue rests on choices that are made in light of the Revelation and the capacity for discernment with which human beings are endowed. Believers are those 'whom God has guided, and they are the possessors of minds' (39:17–18). This is not unique to Muslims: 'Formerly We gave guidance to Moses, and bequeathed to the Israelites the Book as guidance and a reminder to men possessed of minds' (40:53–4). Yet humans are seen as inclined to wayward passion or *al-hawa*, the kind of arbitrary behaviour that leads to egoism, error and worse. The story of Adam and Eve is perhaps the most dramatic instance; Adam finally comes to terms with his heedlessness, and is able to gain redemption (2:31–8).

Humans are not held accountable for wrongs without prior guidance. 'We never punish until we have sent a Messenger' (17:15), who serves as a 'reminder' of truths and virtues. Further, there is an abundance of 'signs' or *ayat* in nature (2:164, 10:5–6, 3:190) as well as in the Revelation which is evidence of its purpose, to be discerned by those with reason or *aql*. That *ayat* is also the term for verses in the Quran only underscores the fullness of this communication. Time and again, humans are exhorted to use

---

[1] Toshihiko Izutsu, *God and Man in the Koran: Semantics of the Koranic Weltanschauung* (Tokyo, 1964), p.216; see also his *Ethico-Legal Concepts in the Qur'an* (Montreal, 2002).

their senses and wits in discerning what should be obvious. Muhammad emerges as an exemplar heedful of the signs, and willing to use good sense in daily encounters. After all, he is called on to make quick judgements in the spirit of the scripture without the benefit of 'commands' for each situation. He chides preachers and the flock for treating animals without proper sensitivity; he is unhappy with a companion for wasting water during ablutions; he comforts a sick woman who has habitually abused him; and gives lavish praise for the charity of a farmer who shares a few dates. When told of the pious qualities of a Muslim, he interrupts with, 'But how is his reason?' As the praise continues to flow, he repeats 'How is his reason?' until the message gets through.

Broadly, it is 'exalted character' (68:4) that the Quran commends in Muhammad, just as it does in recounting the struggles of Abraham, Moses, Jesus, Joseph and Mary. This is cast as a *human* striving, and the more heroic for that. In this, Muhammad combines what Max Weber famously saw in *The Sociology of Religion* (1922) as the two alternative roles of prophets – 'ethical' figures conveying the will of God, or 'exemplary' figures who taught by their own actions. Hence, the believer is urged to 'strive, as in a race in all virtues' (5:48). Commentators often note that the Quran is not a textbook of law or religious doctrine, where systems of conduct and belief are laid out in an analytical framework. It is a call to human betterment in which the lyrical language of the text is 'a rich and subtle stimulus to religious imagination'.[2]

To the questions 'What should I do?' and 'Why should I do it?', the reply is an appeal to what one can discern from the evidence of creation and the record of man's encounter with the Creator. The appeal is to an intuitive sense of what is right and good, with broad guiding principles and examples. There are reminders of the limits of human knowing and wisdom, and the folly of ignoring this. 'We offered the Trust to the heavens, the earth and the mountains; but they refused to undertake it'; 'foolish' man, on the other

---

[2] George Hourani, *Reason and Tradition in Islamic Ethics* (Cambridge, 1985), p.56.

hand, accepted (33:72). Humans have the burden that goes with choosing what they do. 'Let him who will, believe, and let him who will, reject' (18:29) makes the choice stark.

But one is accountable only for one's own actions (2:286). The weight of individual action is tied to one's intention, in the light of *taqwa*, the consciousness of divine presence; but the constant stress on reason or *aql* means that choices must be informed and thoughtful. Poor choices are tied to a heedless attitude that fuels 'appetites unchecked by knowledge' (6:119). Good choices come from a character that cultivates the virtues of mind, body and spirit, for there are countless practical situations that require sound judgement, compared to the specific 'rules' about what to do.

Knowledge, even from scripture, needs reasoned engagement of intellect and faith. 'The Quran speaks only if you ask it to speak', observed Ali b. Abi Talib (c. 598–661), companion, cousin and son-in-law of the Prophet.[3] It was from engagement with scripture that we got the body of practical ethics we know as the sharia, and its more juristic offshoot, the *fiqh*. Since there are limits to what mortals can know, humility is called for, along with divine grace without which, finally, 'there is no light' (24:40). So with knowledge and reason, coupled with the grace of a higher wisdom, one may grasp the teaching and what it implies. The need for such grace is unsurprising: the point is not only to edify but to urge good choices. It brings us back to character-in-action as the core of the teaching, and the community as a vehicle through which it is to be realised.

The Setting

Traits of character or *akhlaq* as the essence of Muslim ethics was an idea at home in the social setting of the Revelation. A pre-Islamic social code of dignity was shared by the peoples of Arabia and the surrounding region, binding personal honour to that of

---

[3] Fazlur Rahman, 'Law and Ethics in Islam', in R.G. Hovannisian, ed., *Ethics in Islam* (Malibu, CA, 1985), p.14.

the family and the tribe or community. This was *adab*, which prized the cultivation of civility and refinement – but also courage, generosity and hospitality to the stranger. *Adab* came from *maduba*, a nourishing feast, which evolved into the sense of a proper disposition of the mind and self (*adab al-nafs*). A person with *adab* would know the value of a generous display of gratitude to a benefactor, for example, since a moral debt must be suitably repaid. One may see an extension of this ethic in the believer's gratitude to God in the Quran, which serves to bind together the community.

If *adab* called for steady cultivation, *akhlaq* was an innate or habitual leaning to virtue. The two terms were intimately bound, evoking a disciplined way of being and living. In this regard, they were close to a Mediterranean body of thought, notably that of the Greeks. The Hellenic *ethikos* stood for custom, and in the writings of Plato, Aristotle and Plotinus which were to deeply influence Muslim thinkers, the ideal was to nurture familiar traits of character. This could lead to excellence and happiness or *eudaimonia*; it required learning to steer a middle way, 'the golden mean', in making moral choices. These views were themselves shaped by Egyptian, Indian and Perso-Zoroastrian ideas. In any case, the pursuit of the golden mean also became a virtue for the Muslim umma as seekers of a 'balanced path' (2:143).

Many of these cultural influences were absorbed through the theologies and practices of the various Jewish and Christian communities of the region. After all, there was routine contact not only with priests and rabbis but also ordinary members of those diverse communities whose traditions had crystallised around specific monotheistic tenets. Their legitimacy as the 'religion of Abraham' was affirmed in the Quran (2:130), and Muhammad brought but a 'confirmation of prior scriptures' (12:111). The 'people of the book' (*ahl al-kitab*), then, shared the essential values from which Muslim ethics were to develop. A key aspect of these Abrahamic values was reciprocity, also found in other great traditions: treat others as you would expect them to treat you (Matthew 7:12, Leviticus 19:18). Muhammad was to put it thus: 'None of you [truly] believes until he wishes for his brother what he wishes for himself.'[4]

Some of the practices that were associated with pre-Islamic ways were less than salutary. These included infanticide, the abuse of slaves and prisoners of war, loose marriage arrangements, quick recourse to violence in resolving disputes, and highly exploitative commercial dealings. True, such practices could be the subject of local reproof and correction. For instance, the Quraysh clans in Mecca formed an alliance (*hilf al-fudul*) to make their city a 'fair trade area' by ensuring that if anyone were wronged in commerce, the alliance would side with the victim regardless of the offender. When a local merchant of the Sahm clan of the Quraysh failed to pay a visiting Yemeni of the Zubayd clan his due, the alliance leaned on the Sahmi to do the proper thing.[5] But such responses were ad hoc and driven by practicality, usually tied to the notion of 'honour'.

Individuals mattered less than the group; both were ranked by status based on descent and power. Women were entirely unequal in law, whether in inheritance, legal capacity or marriage. Polygamy, concubinage, unrestricted divorce and segregation were common. There were Egyptian and other Arab tribes, some of them matrilineal, that treated women better. Infanticide came from Greek times and was approved by Roman law, notably when it came to females. Judeo-Christian reforms left intact a world-view with the support of theology in which women were morally and socially inferior. This is evident in Augustine's writings, and even more in those of Tertullian (c. 160–220), 'father of Latin Christianity', on women: '*You* are the Devil's gateway. *You* are the unsealer of the forbidden tree. *You* are the first deserter of the divine Law. *You* are she who persuaded him whom the Devil was not valiant enough to attack. *You* destroyed so easily God's image,

---

[4] *An-Nawawi's Forty Hadith*, tr. E. Ibrahim and D. Johnson-Davies (Cambridge, 1997), hadith 13; also cited in *Sahih Bukhari*, Book 2:6:13.
[5] Michael Cook, *Commanding Right and Forbidding Wrong in Islamic Thought* (Cambridge, 2000), p.565.

man. On account of *your* desert, that is death, even the Son of God had to die.'[6]

Such was the ethos of the eastern Mediterranean world where Muhammad was tasked to deliver the Quranic message. There were practices that had to promptly cease and some that would take longer, yet others that would stand as discouraged. Many of the ways of *adab* and Judeo-Christian teaching were given fresh meaning. Charity, courage and generosity were raised to a plane of commitment to serve the welfare of the umma, whose solidarity extended to Christians and Jews in the Constitution of Medina (623). Membership in the community ranked above tribe or social class. Familial roles such as those of parents, spouses, guardians and siblings entailed specific ethical duties; and there were special duties toward orphans, the disabled, the poor and travellers. Again, this nourished an ethic of solidarity.

But moral accountability was made firmly *individual*. The language of the Quran stresses this not only in matters of faith but also of social obligation, as does the Prophet when he calls even his companions to account for their actions. Equality becomes a premier value and is affirmed as a universal ethic: 'We created you from a single [pair] of a male and a female, and made you into nations and tribes that you may know each other. Verily, the most honoured of you in the sight of God is he who is the most righteous of you' (49:13). Individual virtue is linked with a duty of care toward the Other. Muhammad appealed to a social conscience in asserting, 'the best Islam is that you feed the hungry and spread peace among those whom you know and those you do not know'.[7]

---

[6] Rosemary Ruether, 'Misogynism and Virginal Feminism in the Fathers of the Church', in R. Ruether, ed., *Religion and Sexism: Images of Women in the Jewish and Christian Traditions* (New York, 1974), p.157; see also James Brundage, *Law, Sex, and Christian Society in Medieval Europe* (Chicago, 1987), pp.85–6.

[7] Cited in *Sahih Bukhari*, Book 2:5:12.

Taking Ethics Seriously

How was the community to put the foundational teaching into practice? Several responses ensued during and after Muhammad's lifetime. What it meant to be a Muslim as expressed in the 'pillars of the faith' embodied key ethical duties. The most obvious was the rendering of alms or *zakat*, a form of organised charity for the common welfare. Generosity in giving was likened to planting in fertile soil, where the harvest was greater than the sowing – and a counter to avarice and usury. But there was also a deeper basis, of purifying one's wealth in atonement and gratitude. As such, *zakat* is obligatory for the believer; the poorest too could make a gesture of giving with the proper intention. *Zakat* was to evolve into a voluntary 'tax' for the public good, with formal rules for its calculation. A variant of this kind of giving was the *waqf* or endowment to establish institutions like hospitals, schools and mosques, with trustees to ensure continuity.

Other pillars of faith, like fasting during the month of Ramadan, also involved ethical commitments. Abstaining from food was a mark of solidarity with the hungry as well as an act of self-discipline or *adab al-nafs*. The annual pilgrimage or hajj marked the equality of all believers and needed high discipline in the journey and the rites. What were the proprieties on how to conduct them? On matters like marriage, divorce, contracts, inheritance, the limits of warfare, and the observance of the fast and of prayers, the Quran has a fair amount of 'technical' detail. It is also direct on behaviour such as wanton killing and infanticide, abuse of trusteeship (especially over orphans), adultery, theft, wasting natural resources and intoxication. Again, women are given formal legal capacity, rights to inherit and to fair treatment in marriage; hence they enjoy full moral equality with men, as well as exclusive rights over property brought into and acquired during marriage, against any claim by the husband. The radical shift from pre-Islamic ways is obvious.

But on these and other matters, there was room for interpretation on the details. Muhammad's daily encounters became the source of the hadith or traditions that helped to map out the ethos, with the endorsement of scripture (59:7, 33:21). His companions, four of whom ascended to the governance of the community from 632 to 661, also played a vital role. For the rest, it was left to a new class of theologians and jurists to develop the foundations as they applied to the warp and woof of daily living. Thus was born the sharia, literally 'the way'. The particulars of the way were the result of human endeavour, though the quest was felt to be guided by a superior Intellect:

> That 'God does not know particulars', as the Hellenized philosophers claimed, was for Muslim jurists and thinkers not only unthinkable but also a form of complex ignorance, for such a scenario would have left man to his own devices, where no law or deterrence, moral or otherwise, may be possible . . . The bottom line here is that no man, however wise, rational or otherwise 'philosophically predisposed', can rule the lives of his fellow men or dictate to them the terms of a good life . . . [W]hat is it that makes our ways of living good or bad, sound or unsound, destructive or healthy? To know all this is to listen to a higher voice, but to listen and understand is to interpret, and to interpret is to be engaged with God and his Speech.[8]

Within this moral universe, human acts are either about social affairs and relationships (*muamalat*) or about how we relate to the divine (*ibadat*). Both kinds of acts came to be classified in the sharia under one of five categories: obligatory, recommended, neutral, discouraged or prohibited. 'Obligatory' acts include *zakat*, fasting and prescribed prayers, while adultery, theft and intoxication are 'prohibited'; freeing slaves is 'recommended', while wasting scarce resources like water is 'discouraged'. There is fluidity to this schema which is moral/theological in the first place, and from which legal inferences are drawn. What is unlawful is sinful. Guilt and punishment are tied to intent and remorse, with plenty of scope to mitigate the seriousness of an offence. Only the gravest

---

[8] Wael B. Hallaq, *Sharia: Theory, Practice, Transformations* (Cambridge, 2009), p.83.

of acts may incur harsh penalties (*hadd*) appropriate to the time, such as flogging or the amputation of a hand, where the standard of evidence was rigorous from the outset.

By making the newly developing body of law accountable to ethical criteria, the risk of purely arbitrary measures of convenience or propriety was reduced. So was the prospect of an unfiltered borrowing of rules from the many prior codes, secular and religious, in the domain of *muamalat*. In some cases, such borrowings might be entirely sensible, as in matters of commerce and administration. But the radical reform of family law as well as aspects of public law could hardly be sustained without tying it to the new ethos. The risk of 'default' borrowing from assorted quarters only grew with the rapid expansion of the nascent Muslim community outside its heartland in Mecca and Medina. The outlying regions of Persia, Syria and Egypt, among others, had far more elaborate legal codes with legacies dating back to Justinian and Hammurabi. Their incorporation in the Arab empire put a premium on the rule of law – which meant quickly developing the sharia for such settings. Indigenous rules were retained where they did not offend the basics of sharia ethics; non-Muslim communities could keep most of their personal law.

All in all, the legal rules of the *fiqh* were gaining priority. The *fiqh* laid claim to legitimacy on the basis of scriptural foundations as well as ethical teaching. But the 'schools of law' that now emerged were writing manuals with rules that reached into life's every nook and cranny. While 'the paramount valuation of human conduct was moral, not legal', notes Fazlur Rahman, '*fiqh* and sharia became generally equated with specific rules'.[9] Everyday practicality was winning out over the theology, though tribunals could resort to informal principles of equity in settling some types of grievances (*mazalim*).

At the same time, other articulations on taking ethics seriously had emerged. Notably, there was the letter of instruction on civil justice by Ali b. Abi Talib as caliph, addressed to his

---

[9] 'Law and Ethics in Islam', p.5.

appointee in 658 as governor of Egypt, Malik al-Ashtar.[10] It spells out the nature of a 'social contract' on the basis of a commitment to justice as an overriding virtue – building on the spirit of the Medina constitution that Muhammad had negotiated in 623. Governance in the new empire was marked by episodes of arbitrary power, nepotism, unreasonable tax burdens on farmers and misuse of public funds. The caliph set out in specific terms to reaffirm key values: the governor must recognise the poor as 'most in need of justice', his relatives should receive no favours, he must appoint judges and administrators solely on merit, avoid unfair taxation and account fully for state revenues. He was to consult widely, rule 'with the agreement of the people' and resist the claim that 'I have been given authority, I order and am obeyed'. Lapses on the part of others deserved compassion. Ultimately, the practice and precept of justice were guided by *taqwa*, which is neither about fear nor desire for reward but the 'worship of the free'.

We have, then, an articulation of civil ethics in which accountability, integrity and fair play are also measures of religiosity. It should come as no surprise that the modernist Egyptian jurist and chief mufti, Muhammad Abduh (1849–1905), published a commentary lauding Ali's letter as instructive for our own time. The letter also reinforced the idea that for the ruler and the ruled alike, a commitment to practical ethics is less about compliance with a code than the cultivation of character, *akhlaq*. This was a more reliable guide to choices about right and wrong. Further, in his insistence that *taqwa* as well as love underlies the ideal of justice as a pervasive secular and spiritual value, Ali influenced the Sufi traditions in Islam. Stressing inward aspects of character as the key to sound choices, Sufi discourses took especially seriously the virtues of *hilm* and *ihsan* in grasping the deeper truths of an ethical life.

In the teaching of Harith al-Muhasibi (781–857) in Baghdad,

---

[10] Letter 33, *Nahj al-balagha*, tr. Sayid Ali Reza as *Peak of Eloquence* (New York, 1996), pp.534–49; analysis in Reza Shah-Kazemi, *Justice and Remembrance* (London, 2006).

where he was to mentor theologians and mystics alike, the linkage of inward and practical virtue is fully evident in his *Treatise for the Seekers of Guidance*. The train of thought was earlier evident in Hasan al-Basri (643–728), one of the founding figures of a pietist rationalism that sought 'justice' in all its varied meanings. This led Abu Nasr al-Farabi (c. 870–950) to a strikingly imagined 'virtuous city' (*al-Madina al-fadila*) where civil and spiritual pursuits are in fine harmony. Al-Farabi was much inspired by Plato's *Republic*, but his ethics of character and leadership is also tied to a faith sensibility among rulers and ruled. This mix was to find elaboration in *The Criterion of Moral Action* of Abu Hamid al-Ghazali (1058–1111), who as we shall see leaned heavily on the pietist side. By contrast, Farid al-Din Attar gave the mix an enchanting form in his epic poem *The Conference of the Birds*, a journey into the far reaches of the self and beyond.

A distinctively Muslim ethics, then, emerged across frontiers. Scripture, prophetic traditions, pre-Islamic *adab* and Mediterranean systems of law and thought, all fed into a fresh synthesis of theology, jurisprudence, philosophy, spirituality and more. If taking ethics seriously meant attending to the sharia, its details were but a part of the picture. What the Quran had to say on the pursuit of the good could hardly be exhausted by a code that was the outcome of daily human struggles with moral problems. Yet scripture and hadith left much to fill in when it came to the answers. In taking up the challenge, Muslims had to respond to some fundamental issues:

How should legitimate authority and leadership be exercised after the Prophet?
What was the scope of human free will in relation to the divine?
Was human reason a reliable means to steer through moral complexity?

It is to the diverse responses to these questions that we turn next.

Branches

With the Prophet's passing in 632, fateful choices lay ahead. For purposes of governance, a hard compromise was reached among most Muslim communities that would see leading figures in Muhammad's life take the helm. Abu Bakr, Umar, Uthman and Ali served as the 'rightly-guided' caliphs until 661, with both religious and secular authority. A decree on rules of war by Abu Bakr, for example, sought to uphold the spirit of the Quran:

> Do not act treacherously . . . Do not mutilate; do not kill children or old men, or women; do not cut off the heads of the palm-trees or burn them; do not cut down the fruit trees; do not slaughter a sheep or a cow or a camel, except for food. You will pass by people who devote their lives in cloisters; leave them and their devotions alone. You will come upon people who bring you platters in which are various sorts of food; if you eat any of it, mention the name of God over it.[11]

At other times, the mix of pragmatism and piety yielded less worthy results. In the so-called Wars of Apostasy (*Rida*), Abu Bakr firmly cast all dissent as a revolt against God. This had a lasting impact on readings of Islamic law, with the idea that leaving the faith amounted to punishable apostasy; yet the Quran clearly taught, 'Let there be no compulsion in religion: truth stands out clear from error' (2:256). Or consider Uthman's decision to appoint his Meccan kinsmen to key administrative posts across the domains. This ran against the grain of the 'Islamic' ethos that Umar, his predecessor, had pursued over the old tribal one; the ensuing civil strife cost Uthman his life and spilled over into the caliphate of Ali.

It was one thing for worldly and religious authority to be coupled in the Prophet, who after all had the approval of scripture. Could such authority be based on the political compromises that allowed

---

[11] J. Alden Williams, ed. *Themes of Islamic Civilization* (Berkeley, CA, 1971), p.262.

the early caliphs to govern? The issue was more troubling as the challenges of ruling over a vastly expanded umma piled up. It became obvious that such power must be tempered by the authority of the sharia. By the time leadership passed to Islam's first 'dynasty' of Quraysh clansmen who came to be known as the Umayyads (661–750), legitimate authority in matters of faith could hardly be asserted by the caliph. As we have seen, the greater the need for particulars in the sharia, the stronger the sway of *fiqh* – binding as law with a sacred aura. What followed was a flourishing of schools of law or *madhhabs*, with a sophisticated science of jurisprudence (*usul al-fiqh*) coming to the fore by the late eighth century. The many and varied *madhhabs* eventually rallied around four major ones, each named after a leading jurist: Hanbali, Hanafi, Maliki and Shafii. Those who espoused this approach to building on the 'tradition of the Prophet' or *sunna* came to be identified as 'Sunni' Muslims.

For many others in the umma, Muhammad had not left the issue of authority open to political negotiation at all. Rather, on his very last pilgrimage and in the presence of numerous witnesses (including the Prophet's companions), he made clear his choice of Ali as the next leader.[12] The merits and legitimacy of that designation were a *moral* issue with implications for the nature of leadership. While the precise scope of the implications in theology, law and practice would unfold over time, this much was clear: the rightful leaders after the Prophet were imams who had more than mere political authority in continuing the original teaching. This was the perspective of the Shia or 'partisans of Ali'. A school of law named after the Imam Jafar al-Sadiq (c. 702–765) emerged as dominant in the Shia tradition; the Jafari *madhhab* recognises the central role of the imam of the time or, in his absence, those who represent him. There were other Muslim communities who also parted with the 'majoritarian' Sunni consensus, such as the Kharijites and some Sufi persuasions.

---

[12] L. Veccia Vaglieri, 'Ghadir Khumm' (site of Muhammad's pronouncement), *The Encyclopaedia of Islam*, ed. H.A.R. Gibb et al. (rev. ed., Leiden, 1965), vol. 2, pp.993–4.

Whether in the larger communities of interpretation, the many spiritual orders (*tariqas*) or the diverse *madhhabs*, 'Islam' was very much a pluralist idea and practice from the earliest days. It would be surprising if this were not reflected in the ways in which ethics was to develop, often but not necessarily along the lines of sectarian or legal affiliation. Regional and social factors were also to shape choices – in gender relations, health care, ecological sensitivity and social proprieties. For example, with regard to the ethics of figural depiction in public places, including art, there was much latitude allowed in the near eastern and Asian milieus of Shia Safavids as well as Sunni Ottomans and Mughals. A less generous view prevailed in the more conservative societies of Arabia and the Maghreb for a variety of reasons, as shown in Fahmida Suleman's chapter in this volume.

But in the approach to core issues of moral responsibility, the paths taken were much affected by theology and law. These differences were to gain weight with the absorption of Hellenic writing. As fine translations in Baghdad of Aristotle's ethics and other works became available in the ninth century, a fresh intellectual current was unleashed. Ibn Miskawayh (c. 932–1030) wrote his landmark *The Cultivation of Morals*, al-Kindi (c. 801–873), al-Farabi and Ibn Sina (c. 980–1037) offered new scientific and philosophical ideas, while Abd al-Jabbar (c. 935–1025) championed a rationalist theology that al-Ghazali sought to counter – and thus inspired a famous retort from Ibn Rushd (c. 1126–1189). At the heart of these works were debates about moral agency as against predestination, and about reason and tradition as sources of our values. The outcomes would shape how the Quran, sharia and *fiqh* were understood both by scholars and ordinary Muslims, and hence mould the practice of ethics.

Human Capacity and Revelation

How do we know right from wrong? What is it that makes something 'good' or 'evil'? The answers for one of Islam's founding jurists, al-Shafii (c. 767–820), were ultimately quite plain. Revelation and its favoured interpreters, the prophets, were the source of moral values; they gave us the guidance we required. It was the task of law only to infer the details which filled the sharia and *fiqh*; too much speculation on these matters was a distraction from good practice. Shafii was committed enough to the quest for truth to insist that a jurist must change his ruling (*fatwa*) in the face of facts, but this did not allow one to look far beyond them. If I buy a dagger from a man whom I witnessed using it as a murder weapon, the contract of sale is perfectly valid. What counts is the form of the transaction; the inner workings are for God.

Some *madhhab*s were more willing to go beyond the form of the law and allow conjecture on what was in the public interest (*maslaha*) to influence a ruling. The Maliki jurist al-Shatibi was to draw out the terms under which public interest could over-rule the strict rules of *fiqh*, as long as the sharia's 'higher objectives' (*maqasid*) were intact. Still, even in the eclectic social milieu of Andalusia in the 14th century, al-Shatibi held to the view that Revelation and prophetic tradition were the sole source of truth:

> If reason is permitted to transcend the source of revelation, it would then be permissible to invalidate Sharia by means of reason – an inconceivable possibility. The very meaning of Sharia is to ordain for the subjects certain limits pertaining to their acts, pronounce-ments and beliefs . . . If reason is permitted to overstep one of these limits, then it can overstep all others, for what is good for one thing is good for that which is analogous to it.[13]

The tension between the truth of tradition and the claims of reason had earlier troubled al-Ghazali, and led him also to ponder the sharia's deeper purposes. He tells us, for example, of hearing that a disciple of the jurist Abu Hanifa evaded the payment of *zakat* by transferring to his wife the property on which it would have been due, and that she then did likewise; when this was reported to Abu Hanifa, he dismissed the matter on the grounds

[13] Hallaq, *Sharia*, p.512.

that the disciple was only exercising his rights. Al-Ghazali agreed with Abu Hanifa, who like Shafii is said to have turned down the caliph's offer of an appointment to a senior post on grounds of conscience. Whatever it was these jurists were upholding in the name of divine truth, it could hardly be the legal *fiqh*. We are back with sharia as a body of ethical tenets, beyond law as commonly understood. Yet if the sources were to be interpreted, how certain could we be (beyond the most direct commands) of getting this right? How much freedom did we have here? Could it be the divine will playing itself out through what we imagine is our action? Debates on these ideas were intense when Shafii and his fellow jurists founded their schools of law.

Two sharply varied perspectives were at stake. For one group, the Mutazilites, moral action meant human capacity and responsibility in the shadow of Revelation; the Asharites, on the other hand, saw divine command as the only legitimate basis for both truth and action. Ideas such as 'good', 'evil', 'justice' and 'obligation' had moral content for the Mutazilites outside of scripture, and the content could be grasped by reason. Indeed, this was why scripture could effectively use those terms, and appeal to our reason to grasp the plentiful 'signs' of divine presence. As Abd al-Jabbar put it:

> [W]e say that revelation does not necessitate the evilness or goodness of anything, it only uncovers the character of the act by way of indication, just as reason does, and distinguishes between the command of the Exalted and that of another being by His wisdom, Who never commands what it is evil to command.[14]

This 'objective' view of ethics was wedded to the premise that divine command was not arbitrary but rational and good. Since humans had the capacity for both reason and virtue, they were fully accountable for drawing on them as well as on Revelation.

For the Asharites, all this was heresy in giving no more value to Revelation than to human reason. All earthly action was possible

---

[14] Hourani, *Reason and Tradition*, p.104.

only by divine grace and God was not subject to our categories of value; on the contrary, ideas of 'good' and 'evil' are the result purely of divine will. In this 'theistic subjective' view of ethics, it falls to us simply to acknowledge what is divinely ordained. Yet if our actions are predetermined, can we be held accountable for them? Ashari (c. 873–935) replied that God actually creates all possible acts, but humans 'acquire' specific ones by choosing them (*kasb*); this is what makes us morally responsible. What the Asharites – who included Shafii – did was to buttress the claim of the *madhhabs* that the sharia and *fiqh* they were developing was a proper extension of the sunna and Revelation. This human endeavour would be less decisive in fixing the right practice if the Mutazilites were right.

By the time al-Ghazali threw his weight behind the Asharites, the balance in the Sunni world had tilted in their favour. We noted his concern about mixing the authority of mere legal rules with ethical principles; he would fill practical gaps in the Tradition by invoking the higher aims of the sharia to protect the faith, intellect, soul, progeny and property. While al-Shatibi was to take this further in his account of public interest, al-Ghazali's stance was innovative for its time. Yet he was conservative on the role of reason in theology and the law. Human intelligence served (with the aid of divine grace) to take us to Revelation, after which we must cultivate submission. General considerations of public welfare or doing good were not valid grounds for sharia rulings. At the same time, al-Ghazali stressed a strong personal ethics of wisdom and character, a '*fiqh* of the heart'. In the end, his was a synthesis of tradition, rationalism and spirituality that was larger than what his fellow Asharites allowed, but far short of what other thinkers found persuasive if human reason is taken as an active gift of the divine.

A rationalist drive had earlier fed the use of independent reasoning or *ijtihad* among the *madhhabs*; it was shrinking in scope by the 10th century in favour of emulation or *taqlid*, as the empire went through major political and social change. Al-Ghazali added to this conservatism – but it was not shared by the Shia, who were sympathetic to Mutazilite views. They held that reason and Revelation were fellow travellers, subject to the overarching guidance of the imam. This is clear in works such as *The Comfort of Reason* by Hamid al-Din al-Kirmani (c. 996–1021) and the *Ethics* of Nasir al-Din al-Tusi (c. 1201–1274), which built on the writings of the Greek philosophers. Disciplines of character are vital, but Shia thinkers also grappled with the *inherent* nature of acts as 'good' or 'obligatory', beyond self-interest or the consequences of an act. This was a firm rejection of the Asharite view that reason could not grasp such meanings.

Ijtihad was a constant aspect of guidance by the imam and his emissaries, and encouraged on the part of the community. With the establishment of the Jafari *madhhab* in the eighth century, and the vast compilation of hadith by Abu Jafar al-Kulayni (c. 864–941), an Imami Shia pietist rationalism began to thrive. Al-Kirmani and Shaykh al-Mufid (c. 948–1022), who was especially at home among Mutazilite thinkers, are illustrative figures. A practical turn came in the fusion of ethics and law when Qadi al-Numan (c. 903–974) devised the legal code for the governance of the Fatimids in Egypt (969–1171). His work remains to this day an influential guide to conduct within many Ismaili communities. The context in which it emerged was a vibrant culture of learning and cosmopolitanism based in Cairo, much like that of Baghdad under the Abbasids.

A similar setting was to nurture a blistering reply to al-Ghazali's traditionalism: that of Andalusia, where a *convivencia* of Muslims, Jews and Christians came out of successive regimes whose eighth-century origins went back to the Umayyads of Damascus. The retort came from Ibn Rushd of Cordoba in his 1184 opus, *Incoherence of the Incoherence*, which took direct aim at al-Ghazali's *Incoherence of the Philosophers*. Not only was it a critique of a traditionalism that Ibn Rushd saw as irrational, but it was also part of a vision that found harmony in philosophical reason and faith. This turned out to be as troubling for Christian thinkers like Thomas Aquinas (1225–74) as it was for the Asharite ethos that now dominated the Muslim world; yet it was to have a decisive impact on the Enlightenment and its rationalist ethics.

Convergences

That Ibn Rushd was neither a Mutazilite nor a Shia, but a Sunni who saw himself as fully in the Islamic fold, is a reminder of the diversity of ethical teaching. Yet this diversity had vital convergences. Sufi ideas on the nurturing of inner disciplines of mind and character spanned the work of al-Ghazali, al-Tusi, Ibn Sina and Ibn Rushd. Asharites and Mutazilites, Shia and Sunni, held that reason has limits in what it can ultimately discern of the larger meanings of scripture, which calls for personal openness to the wisdom of divine grace.[15] *Fiqh* as mainly the particulars of law was widely felt to be in tension with its moral underpinnings among jurists well versed in theology. And in *adab* as the pursuit of social and literary aptitudes, the overlap of diverse ethical ideas and practice was rich.

An example of the role of *adab* here comes from a tale spun by another 12th-century Andalusian, Ibn Tufayl, who like Ibn Rushd was a gifted polymath. *Hayy Ibn Yaqzan* is his colourful allegory on the 'awakening' of a child, Hayy, on an isolated tropical island where he is nurtured by a gazelle and learns survival skills from various animals. As he grows into a man, his astute mind turns to the meaning of life in all its complexity on this lush terrain, his place in it, and the implications for human beings. Alfred Ivry catches the spirit of inquiry thus:

> In a charmingly inventive way, Ibn Tufayl describes how Hayy, a propos of investigating the death of the doe that succoured and reared him, is led to think of the species of deer, then of other species, and finally of species, *per se*. Soon he is on to realizing the fundamental conceptual principle of sciences: primary and secondary substances, form and matter, prime matter and the

---

[15] See Abdulaziz Sachedina, 'Islamic Ethics: Differentiations', in W. Schweiker, ed., *The Blackwell Companion to Religious Ethics* (Oxford, 2005), pp.254–67; and Farhad Daftary, ed., *Intellectual Traditions in Islam* (London, 2000), notably chapters 4 and 9 on 'rationalism' and 'reason' in context.

elements, and causal efficacy. Working with these principles and using his innate skills of induction and deduction, combined with experiment and observation, Hayy proceeds from the natural sciences to astronomy and metaphysics. At an early stage of his deductions, Hayy is struck by a sense of the unity of being, a unity more significant than all apparent multiplicity and diversity.[16]

Ibn Tufayl artfully imports the ideas of Ibn Sina on the 'unity of being' as a way of approaching the nature of the divine, which Hayy finally grasps in terms drawn from the Quran as well as Sufi meditation. Intuition and reason are reconciled with Revelation, and lessons are offered on how we relate to animals and the environment. *Hayy Ibn Yaqzan* was to find its way beyond the Muslim world to an appreciative Enlightenment readership and, in all likelihood, inspired Daniel Defoe's novel, *Robinson Crusoe* (1719).

One finds a coming together of ethical stances also in social relations that span commerce and health. To take one example, with the founding of public hospitals in eighth-century Damascus and Baghdad (modelled on the *bimaristan* of Gundishapur in Persia), the first such institutions anywhere, a 'code' of propriety or *adab* was needed. Ishaq b. Ali Rahawi, Ali b. Abbas al-Majusi and Zakariya al-Razi were pioneers on this score, building on the Hippocratic oath but taking into account the new setting and the nature of actual encounters between patients and physicians. The rise of medical schools and psychiatric treatment added to the complexity, and the norms of propriety spread with the institutions themselves as far west as Cordoba. Perhaps the largest *bimaristan* was Cairo's al-Mansur, built in 1285 and visited by the historian al-Maqrizi (c. 1364–1442), who had this to say:

---

[16] A. Ivry, 'The Utilization of Allegory in Islamic Philosophy', in J. Whitman, ed., *Interpretation and Allegory: Antiquity to the Modern Period* (Leiden, 2000), p.167; see also L. Goodman, *Ibn Tufayl's Hayy Ibn Yaqzan: A Philosophical Tale* (Chicago, 1972).

I have found this institution for my equals and for those beneath me, it is intended for rulers and subjects, for soldiers and for the emir, for great and small, freemen and slaves, men and women . . . Every class of patient was accorded separate accommodation: the four halls of the hospital were set apart for those with fever and similar complaints; one part of the building was reserved for eye-patients, one for the wounded, one for those suffering from diarrhoea, one for women; a room for convalescents was divided into two parts, one for men and one for women. Water was laid on to all these departments . . . [E]ven those who were sick at home were supplied with every necessity.[17]

Endowments or *waqfs* came to sponsor the *bimaristan*, where physicians were trained not only in medicine but also in the humanities, often with great expertise in theology and Quranic exegesis. The idea of health as a 'rational' concern took wing as the natural sciences thrived in the Abbasid Near East, Fatimid Egypt and Umayyad Andalusia. Equal and free public access to the *bimaristan* was not merely an ideal but a practical reality. This institutional ethos was all but unheard of outside the Muslim world until well into the Middle Ages, when Ibn Sina's *Canon of Medicine* (1025) also found its way into Latin and Hebrew as the leading text on practice. The values that informed this ethos were the result not of a specific stance in theology or law, but of a broad thrust that crossed such boundaries and went back to the earliest days of Islam.

The crossing of boundaries was, of course, just as true in the encounter with the Byzantine, Hellenic, Indian and Persian traditions – but also with Chinese and sub-Saharan African ones. Their influence thrived in settings like the Silk Road and Timbuktu. Again, this is no less true of sharings with western traditions. On occasion, it is about how ethical problems draw out similar responses across frontiers, such as in the emphasis

---

[17] William Osler, *The Evolution Of Modern Medicine* (Whitefish, MT, 2004), pp.73–4; see also Michael H. Morgan, 'Healers and Hospitals', in *Lost History* (Washington, DC, 2007), pp.179–218.

on intention in the work of al-Tusi and later in that of Immanuel
Kant (1724–1802). In this vein, dialogue ensues in sorting through
the overlapping ways of seeing the human condition.

This Companion

Like the allegory of *Hayy Ibn Yaqzan*, the classical 'health code'
was both universal in its leanings and distinctive in its moral wellsprings. Much the same is true of values that emerged directly
from the debates surveyed above. Charitable giving, for example,
was shared with the Judeo-Christian ethos but took an Islamic
turn in being reconceived as part of an ethic of care. How did
such 'roots and branches' carry Muslim ethics into the modern
period – and what are the specific ideas and actions that still
matter the most? Where has practice fallen short of ideals and
what should we do about such deficits?

The ten chapters that follow take up these queries from a variety
of stances. They share the conviction that there is far more to the
picture than 'following rules', and that Muslims have long striven
to sort through what the 'good' actually means. Back in the 14th
century Ibn Khaldun felt that 'social organisation' was less about
law and order than the moral vision of how a society is to be
governed. Ethics had made the leap from the virtues of the individual and community to those of the state. It began four centuries
earlier with al-Farabi's 'virtuous city', whose mix of 'statecraft with
soul craft' is, for Charles Butterworth in this volume, the trunk
linking the roots and branches. Sacred and secular, *din* and *duniya*,
were to find unity in a train of thought which ripened in the
rationalism of Ibn Rushd. Butterworth sees the retrieval of this
teaching as vital today not only for Muslims but also for a 'Western
rationalism' alienated from faith.

Such alienation, for Seyyed Hossein Nasr, covers the larger
interplay of tradition and modernity. The price is paid in a domain
of ethics which grips our attention today: the environment. Nasr's
chapter shows that a 'theology of nature' in which humans are an
integral part of their environment is central to Islamic thought,
building on rich Quranic and hadith evocations of nature as sacred.

The sharia upholds the vision in numerous principles on water, soil and forests, favouring a lifestyle that leaves a 'light footprint'. Medicine, astronomy and physics in the classical age held a world-view that was at the opposite end of the 'conquest of nature' stance which ushered in western modernity. Towns and cities that cherished green spaces, waterways and sensitive animal husbandry gave way to an urban modernity more disturbing in much of the Muslim world than the West. Nasr calls on activists, scholars and *ulama* to spur an ecological sensitivity that isn't simply about 'outward effects, but also its spiritual and religious dimensions'.

The appeal to 'tradition' here is not only about scripture, sharia and philosophy. Nasr and Eric Ormsby take up the dense webs of literary *adab* from poetry to storytelling that offer ethical lessons in unique ways, with themes ranging from the treatment of animals and fellow humans to the nature of just governance. Ormsby marvels at how effective Muslims were in retelling Indian, Greek and Persian tales and making them utterly their own. *The 1001 Nights, Kalila wa Dimna* and the *Epistles of the Brethren of Purity* are among the best known in a vast repertory where entertainment and ethics are interwoven. In the hands of a wandering scholar like Nasir-i Khusraw, a tale overtly directed at the narrator himself is a potent tool of advice to people high and low. His lessons about an awakened intellect speak of how he strove to 'change the state of things', taking full responsibility for his acts in giving the advice: 'You are the author of your own disastrous star; don't look up to heaven for some luckier star.'

Often, like Shahrazade in *The 1001 Nights*, the narrator was female; in earlier days, the authenticity of hadith reports was attested by Aisha, the Prophet's wife, while Zaynab defiantly kept alive the record of her brother Hussein's martyrdom in Shia tradition. But women generally were to become less valued as public actors, and Zayn Kassam recounts the cost of this erosion in matters of law and social ethics. Perhaps more than in any other encounter between culture and faith, the ethics of gender exemplifies how much the reading of scripture – and thence the making of law and tradition – is framed by context. Kassam singles out two sets of practices that bring to the fore the tyranny of patriarchy: 'honour' crimes and female genital mutilation (FGM). Like other forms of gender violence, they are accounted for by social factors which distort the values they claim to uphold. Kassam shows how Muslim women activists, religious and secular, have used 'ethical resources that range from scriptural texts to networks of solidarity' in garnering legitimacy to face down the offenders.[18]

An underlying issue that pervades many other themes explored in this volume is the separation of public and private. This affects, for example, how honour and sexuality are cast in relation to women in the practices discussed by Kassam (and not just among Muslims). Many aspects of the sharia reflect a concern with 'public-ness', from modesty in attire and display to monitoring of conduct in the marketplace. Fahmida Suleman's chapter offers a vivid illus-tration of this: religious spaces came to be subjected to strict rules of display in which figural art was improper and calligraphy triumphed. This extended to other expressions of public art, including painting and sculpture – but as noted earlier, not in all Muslim societies and historical periods. As in attitudes toward women, cultural context was vital in how propriety was under-stood.

Appreciating the role of culture is also critical in other fields. Mediation of disputes about property and matrimonial relations – the subject of Mohamed Keshavjee's chapter – requires skill in parsing perception and reality on what 'Islam' prefers. *Sulh* or the amicable resolution of disputes outside the formal bounds of law enjoys high esteem in the Quran, both in private and public matters (4:35, 4:58). Ethical values are tested as material interests clash with the enjoining of equity and generosity. As globalisation brings diverse Muslim and non-Muslim cultures into daily contact, Keshavjee finds that a 'pluralist ethics' sensitive to difference may well provide solutions that more rigid laws cannot. This view is shared in Rodney Wilson's discussion of economic ethics, from

---

[18] An outstanding example is the Yemen Women's Union, founded in 1974, with a record of providing an ethical critique of public policy in areas from FGM and child marriage to female literacy and poverty reduction: http://www.yemeniwomenunion.org/en/index.htm

'sharia finance' to strategies of development. Public welfare is a
key facet of the sharia's view of social relations or *muamalat*: with
zakat and *waqfs* there are arrangements for lending and entre-
preneurship that seek to be non-exploitative. Traditionally, *fiqh*
has been guided by these tenets. The recent global crisis in public
finance, notes Wilson, has energised for Muslims an already 'strong
interest in altruism in economic behaviour, in the wider context
of proper motivation for economic choices'.

Public–private considerations play a lively role in health care
too. We saw earlier that a shared duty of care for the health of
the community has had a critical place in Islam, from the rise of
public medicine to the evolution of the *bimaristan* and the role
here of *waqfs*. What this means in practice, as Abdallah Daar and
Ahmed al-Khitamy show in their chapter, is that public health
care must take into account expectations of propriety that might
elsewhere be deemed private. For example, dietary rules and rituals
of cleanliness and prayer run across the public–private divide in
what Muslim patients may expect of themselves and their care-
givers. Then there are choices, in areas such as abortion and
euthanasia, where teachings can vary among Muslims despite a
shared reverence for life and wellbeing. In all these matters, individual wellbeing and autonomy need to be balanced against wider
considerations of the public good. Daar and al-Khitamy call attention to the 2005 Universal Declaration on Bioethics and Human
Rights, which urges 'moral sensitivity and ethical reflection' in
aiming at 'pluralistic dialogue about bioethical issues between all
stakeholders'. Muslim states were full participants in the making
of the Declaration, and their stake in the emerging guidelines is
obvious.[19]

In public health, as in economics and conflict resolution, secular
and religious ethics are closely tied; professional codes of practice
often have roots in religious tenets. Yet a secular basis is commonly
felt to be the 'modern' way to an inclusive approach, especially in

---

[19] See Henk Have and Michèle Jean, eds., *The UNESCO Universal Declaration
on Bioethics and Human Rights: Background, Principles and Application* (Paris,
2009).

pluralist settings. Modernity itself is generally felt to be a journey away from limiting traditions. Reza Shah-Kazemi's chapter on tolerance tests the integrity of that view. The cherished basis of modern tolerance in 17th-century European liberalism has deep links to an Ottoman ethos, which in turn has Andalusian, Fatimid and other antecedents. The idea that minority rights were first enshrined in European codes ignores a long record of legal protection in the Muslim world (and other civilisations). Further, notes Shah-Kazemi, frameworks that favour 'putting up' with diversity leave out any real empathy or engagement with the Other. Yet this is what marks the 'expansive vision' that is found in the Quran, one which Muslims have struggled to lived up to. Shah-Kazemi, like Ramin Jahanbegloo in his chapter on nonviolence, is well aware that contemporary Muslim societies have fallen far short of these teachings. But, they both argue, it is in the teachings rather than just secular codes that pluralist engagement is best grounded.

In the wake of 11 September 2001, Muslim exemplars of an ethics of nonviolence – such as Abdurrahman Wahid, Mahmoud Taha, Khan Ghaffar Khan and Fethullah Gülen – recall the vitality of progressive traditions. 'It is important to resist the claim', argues Jahanbegloo, 'that civil and political modernity depend on the primacy of secular reason over Muslim narratives.' That would mean stripping away ethical attachments and solidarities which give meaning to identity; without them, humans seem to do a poor job of steering through modernity. The attachments and solidarities are what this *Companion* aims to address. They are essential to our encounter with issues of ecology and climate change, genetic therapies and care of the aged, extreme inequality and responsible governance, gender equity and political violence, access to quality education and information technology. We invest in the 'rule of law' our aspirations on how key public and private values are protected, and understandably so. But an account of the good must reach beyond utilitarian codes and arrangements. A globalised world calls for an 'ethical sensibility that can be shared across denominational lines and foster a universal moral outlook'.[20] For Muslims, this is about ends and means, intention and results, with accountability to and beyond the here and now.

Further Reading

Ernst, Carl, 'Ethics and Life in the World', in C. Ernst, *Following Muhammad: Rethinking Islam in the Contemporary World*. Chapel Hill and London, 2005, pp.107–162.

Fakhry, Majid. *Ethical Theories in Islam*. Leiden, 1994.

Kamali, Mohamed Hashim, 'Law and Society', in J.L. Esposito, ed., *The Oxford History of Islam*. Oxford, 1999, pp.107–53.

Nanji, Azim, 'The Ethical Tradition in Islam', in A. Nanji, ed., *The Muslim Almanac*. New York, 1996, pp.205–11.

Ramadan, Tariq. *Radical Reform: Islamic Ethics and Liberation*. Oxford, 2009.

Sajoo, Amyn B. *Muslim Ethics: Emerging Vistas*. London, 2009.

Schweiker, William, ed. *The Blackwell Companion to Religious Ethics*. Oxford, 2005.

Shahrur, Muhammad. *The Qur'an, Morality and Critical Reason*, tr. Andreas Christmann. Leiden, 2009.

Singer, Amy. *Charity in Islamic Societies*. Cambridge, 2009.

Soroush, Abdolkarim. *Reason, Freedom and Democracy in Islam*, ed. and tr. M. Sadri and A. Sadri. Oxford, 2000.

---

[20] His Highness the Aga Khan, Remarks at Symposium on Cosmopolitan Society, Evora University, Portugal, 12 February 2006, in his *Where Hope Takes Root* (Berkeley and Toronto, 2008), pp.101–11.

2

Early Thought

Charles Butterworth

In classical Islam, human beings are seen as political by nature. The great historian Ibn Khaldun (c. 1332–1406) affirms in his *Muqaddima* the adage that 'human social organisation is necessary', and shows how the idea of a 'regime' or *siyasa* is understood by the philosophers to include the ethical (what concerns the 'soul and moral habits'):

> They call the social organisation that obtains what is required 'the virtuous city' and the rules observed with respect to that 'the political regime'. They are not intent upon the regime that the inhabitants of the community set down through statutes for the common interests, for this is something else. This virtuous city is rare according to them and unlikely to occur. They speak about it only as a postulate and an assumption.[1]

Ibn Khaldun likely refers here to al-Farabi (c. 870–950), for two reasons. First, al-Farabi is cited more frequently than any other thinker in the *Muqaddima*. Second, he was well-known as the author of the *Book of the Political Regime* (*Kitab al-siyasa al-madaniyya*). Linking ethical training or soul-craft with the political

---

[1] Ibn Khaldun, *Muqaddimat Ibn Khaldûn, Prolégomènes d'Ebn-Khaldoun, texte Arabe, publié, d'après les manuscrits de la Bibliothèque Impériale*, ed., M. Quatremère (Paris, 1858; repr. Beirut, 1970), vol. 2.127, pp.6–14. The translation here is mine.

or statecraft is the hallmark of al-Farabi's thought. His skill in directing attention to the political, in making it central to every investigation, so dominates his writing that he has long been seen as the founder of political philosophy in medieval Islam.

Setting the political above all else seems so crucial to al-Farabi and those who follow his lead that it gives us a measure by which to categorise the many thinkers in the medieval Arabic/Islamic philosophical tradition who have written on ethics. Al-Farabi's two best-known predecessors, al-Kindi (c. 805–873) and al-Razi (c. 854–925), present an ethical teaching without reflection on the political. Yet his successors, especially Ibn Sina (c. 980–1037) and Ibn Rushd (c. 1126–1198), join al-Farabi in tying together ethics and politics. I will examine in this chapter the ethical teaching of these first two philosophers and what keeps it from being linked to political thought until the coming of al-Farabi, before looking at how he so convincingly manages to bring these two pursuits together. Finally, I will consider how Ibn Sina and Ibn Rushd preserve that bond.

Al-Farabi's Predecessors

Al-Kindi

Abu Yusuf b. Ishaq al-Kindi was widely acclaimed as 'the philosopher of the Arabs'. He was at home in Greek, Indian and Persian thought, and regarded as an especially skilled editor of Greek philosophical works. His work spanned astronomy, logic, mathematics, medicine and philosophy – and he served as a tutor and astrologer in the courts of two caliphs. Al-Kindi was a highly prolific author, but only a few of his works relate to ethics, and the teaching he sets forth in them is quite limited.

In his *Epistle on the Number of Aristotle's Books and What is Needed to Attain Philosophy*, al-Kindi speaks in passing of ethics and even of Aristotle's writings on ethics. But he only goes into the ethical teaching set forth by Aristotle or ethics in general as a by product of abstract philosophy. Again, al-Kindi's *On the Utterances of Socrates* consists mainly of anecdotes about the kind of ascetic moral virtue so often attributed to Socrates[2]. It is only in the *Epistle on the Device for Driving Away Sorrows* that he reflects at any length on ethics or moral virtue.

In his *Epistle on the Number of Aristotle's Books*, al-Kindi argues that Aristotle's philosophy offers insufficient guidance for the attainment of man's goal: virtue. He presents Aristotle's practical teaching as depending upon a knowledge of metaphysics, yet doubts as to whether such knowledge is accessible to human beings. At the same time, he characterises the only other science that can claim to offer such knowledge, divine science, as being beyond the reach of most human beings and without practical content. Clearly, another science is needed, perhaps a human one that presupposes neither metaphysical knowledge nor divine inspiration – but rather favours the practical reasoning in the *Epistle on the Device for Driving Away Sorrows*.[3]

The book is very limited in scope, and the devices presented in it for driving away sorrow are quite simple. Al-Kindi reasons about a human phenomenon from the perspective of things we all know and have observed or even experienced. He calls upon that experience to set forth his teaching about the nature of sorrow. Even when he urges the reader to consider the activity of the Creator or to entertain the notion that there is a homeland beyond earthly existence, he does so on the basis of common opinion rather than on the basis of any divinely revealed texts. The asceticism he eventually urges is grounded upon common sense arguments about true human needs, not upon an appeal to otherworldly goals.

From the very outset, al-Kindi assigns firm limits to this treatise and, in closing, restates them. He understands his task as that of offering arguments that will combat sorrow, reveal its flaws and arm against its pain. Noting that anyone with a virtuous soul and

---

[2] For anecdotes and sayings that involve Socrates in Arabic, see I. Ilon, *Socrates in Mediaeval Arabic Literature* (Leiden, 1991).

[3] For an English translation, see G. Jayyusi-Lehn, 'The Epistle of Yaqub ibn Ishaq al-Kindi on the Device for Dispelling Sorrows', *British Journal of Middle Eastern Studies*, 29 (2002), pp.121–35.

just moral habits would reject being overcome by vices and seek protection against their pain and unjust dominion – which implies that sorrow counts among the vices – al-Kindi says simply that what he has presented here is 'sufficient'. He admits at the end of the book that he has been somewhat wordy, but excuses himself on the grounds that the paths to the goal sought here are almost unlimited, and insists that reaching it provides what is sufficient. What is the goal for al-Kindi? It is to offer the admonitions that are to be placed firmly in the soul as a model. For this will grant security from the calamities of sorrow and arrive at 'the best homeland', 'the lasting abode and the resting place of the pious'. In essence, the reader is urged to pay less attention to the things prized by fellow human beings, and to concentrate on what is most important for a human life directed to something beyond sensual pleasure.

For al-Kindi, one cannot cure a sickness or ease a pain without knowing its cause, so one must begin by understanding the nature of sorrow. 'Sorrow is a pain of the soul occurring from the loss of things loved or from having things sought for elude us.' Since it is clear that no one can acquire all the things he seeks nor avoid losing any of the things he loves, the only way to escape sorrow is to be free from these attachments. Dependent as we are upon our habits to attain happiness or avoid misery, we must school ourselves to develop the right kind of habits – ones that lead us to delight in the things we have and to be consoled about those that elude us. Thus, the cure of the soul consists in slowly ascending in the acquisition of praiseworthy habits from the minor and easily acquired to the harder and more significant, while building patience in the soul for things that elude it and consoling it for things lost.

Yet the argument up to this point is more theoretical than it is practical. Al-Kindi has explained why people become sad and how they can avoid sorrow by changing their habits and their perspective on the world. In short, he has set forth no practical device yet for driving away sorrow once it arises. He has not done so because these changes are simply too radical; they demand too much of human beings. Moreover, it is far from clear that we can avoid sorrow while living as normal human beings. This, it would seem, is the point of the exhortation that closes the theoretical part of the book, that 'we ought to strive for a mitigating device to shorten the term of sorrow'. The devices to follow will keep us from misery; they may even allow us happiness insofar as they help us overcome the effects of sorrow, but they will not help us escape the losses that cause it.

Al-Kindi then lists ten devices – but digresses at one point to relate anecdotes and a parable as well as to reflect on the way the Creator provides for the wellbeing of all creatures. The digression, and especially the allegory of the ship voyage discussed below, moves the discussion to a higher level by indicating that our sorrows come from possessions. All of them, not merely the superfluous ones, threaten to harm us. Our passage through this world of destruction, says al-Kindi, is like that of people embarked upon a ship 'to a goal, their own resting-place, that they are intent upon'.

When the ship stops so that the passengers may attend to their needs, some do so quickly and return to wide, commodious seats. Others – who also tend quickly to their needs, but pause to gaze upon the beautiful surrounding sights and enjoy the delightful aromas – return to narrower, less comfortable seats. Yet others – who tend to their needs, but collect various objects along the way – find only cramped seating and are greatly troubled by the objects they have gathered. Finally, others wander far off from the ship, so immersed in the surrounding natural beauty and the objects to be collected that they forget their present need and even the purpose of the voyage. Of these, those who hear the ship's captain call and return before it sails, find terribly uncomfortable quarters. Others wander so far away that they never hear the captain's call and, left behind, perish in horrible ways. Those who return to the ship burdened with objects suffer so that, due to their tight quarters, the stench of their decaying possessions and the effort they expend in caring for them, most become sick and some die. Only the first two groups arrive safely, though those in the second group are somewhat ill at ease due to their more narrow seats. Noting at the end of the allegory as at the beginning that the voyage resembles our passage through this world, al-Kindi likens the passengers who endanger themselves and others by their quest for possessions to the unjust we encounter along the way. At issue is the trouble undue attachment to possessions brings upon ourselves and others.

Conversely, the just are those who attend to their needs or business quickly and do not permit themselves to become burdened with acquisitions or even to be sidetracked into momentary pleasures. All the passengers are bound for their homeland, but it is not clear where that is. At one point, al-Kindi says that we are going to 'the true world', and at another that the ship is to bring us to 'our true homelands'. There is no doubt that whether the destination be one or many, it can be reached only by acquiring the habits that eschew material possessions. Beyond that, al-Kindi says nothing, nor does the rest of the epistle shed light on this issue.

The allegory emphasises the voyage and the conduct of the passengers. As one who calls to the passengers, the captain may be compared to a prophet. Like a prophet, he calls only once. Those who do not heed the call are left to their misery, even to their perdition. Yet the content of the call is only to warn about the imminent departure of the ship. The captain offers no guidance about what to bring or leave; he merely calls. Perhaps more precision is not needed. The allegory is presented merely as a likeness of our earthly voyage.

The goal pursued in this treatise is less that of learning about our end than learning how to make our way here comfortably. Al-Kindi has already spoken about the habits we need to acquire to accomplish this goal, but thus far his advice has seemed highly ascetic. The allegory shows that we have nearly complete freedom over the way we conduct ourselves on our voyage. How we use it determines whether we reach our goal comfortably or suffer throughout the voyage and perhaps perish. To voyage without troubling ourselves or others, we must be almost insensitive to our surroundings.

In this sense, the *Epistle on the Device for Driving Away Sorrow* confirms al-Kindi's teaching about human virtue in the *Epistle on the Number of Aristotle's Books*. As long as we know of no purpose for human existence, our goal must be virtue – above all, moral virtue. In other words, pleasure, wealth and power are insufficient goals because they are for the sake of something else, yet in the absence of certainty about why the world exists or what is our place in it, good conduct is the only reasonable pursuit. The virtue praised here comes closest to moderation, but is also similar to courage. And in pointing to the way others commit injustice by amassing possessions, al-Kindi alerts us to the requisites of justice.

The primary lesson is that these kinds of virtuous habits provide comfort during our earthly voyage and preserve us so that we may eventually arrive at the true world and our homeland, wherever it may be. Apart from pointing to our lack of wisdom as a problem, the epistle tells us nothing about that most important virtue. Nor does al-Kindi make any attempt here to tell us how we can act to improve our condition and that of those around us. His teaching provides strategies for coping, especially with personal loss, and accepts the milieu in which we live as a fixed variable – that is, as something not worth trying to alter. We learn to put up with it, even to come to terms with it in such a way that we improve our own lives. At best, al-Kindi offers here a call of sorts for citizen education – teaching the importance of making one's possessions fewer – but he sets forth no broader political teaching.

Al-Razi

Muhammad b. Zakariyya al-Razi was mainly a physician and teacher of medicine, while often serving as an advisor to various rulers. His writings include over 200 books, treatises and pamphlets. Though his writing apparently led to a paralysis of the hand and impaired eyesight, he nonetheless continued writing with the help of secretaries and scribes.[4] It is difficult to form an appreciation of al-Razi's ethical teaching because so few of his writings have come down to us and because the major source for our knowledge

---

[4] For al-Razi's works, see *Rasail falsafiyya*, ed. P. Kraus (Cairo, 1939; repr. Beirut, 1973); and C.E. Butterworth, 'The Origins of al-Razi's Political Philosophy', in *Interpretation*, 20 (1993), pp.237–57.

of what he believed is an account by his arch critic, the Ismaili *da'i* Abu Hatim al-Razi.

We do have an important work al-Razi wrote in his later years, the *Book of the Philosophic Life*. There he seeks to justify his conduct against what he sees as contradictory criticisms levelled by unnamed individuals whom he describes as 'people of speculation, discernment and attainment', and reflects on the value of devoting oneself to philosophy and taking Socrates as a model for this way of life. His critics accuse al-Razi of turning away from the life of philosophy because he socialises with others and busies himself with acquiring money – activities shunned by the Socrates known to them – but they also blame the ascetic life of Socrates for its evil practical consequences. In other words, al-Razi is as wrong in turning away from Socrates as he is to have followed him in the first place.

Al-Razi replies to these charges and offers insight into his fuller teaching without ever exploring why Socrates made his famous conversion, that is, changed from a youthful asceticism to a mature involvement in all-too-human activities. Even though he could present the turn as evidence that Socrates also deemed it wrong, al-Razi treats Socrates' asceticism as merely a zealous excess of youth. Since Socrates abandoned it early on, he sees no need to consider whether a life so devoted to the pursuit of wisdom that it ignores all other concerns is praiseworthy, or whether the good life is the balanced one he describes as his own at the end of the book. Al-Razi refrains from blaming Socrates for his ascetic practices, because they led to no dire consequences.

Still, the issue cannot be ignored, for it points to the broader question of whether the pursuit of philosophy must be so single-minded that it takes no account of the needs of men or, differently stated, whether the proper focus of philosophy is nature and the universe or human and political things. Al-Razi does not immediately distinguish between the two: he identifies practising justice, controlling the passions and seeking knowledge as characteristic of the pursuit of philosophy and praiseworthy in the life of Socrates. By stressing that Socrates abandoned asceticism so as to participate in activities conducive to human wellbeing, al-Razi avoids asking whether it is wrong as such or against nature. He judges it instead in terms of its results and deems it wrong only when following it threatens the wellbeing of the ascetic or of the human race. Such a tactic also allows al-Razi to avoid having his critics impugn him for being sated with desires just because he does not imitate the earlier asceticism of Socrates.

The point is eminently sensible, but al-Razi weakens it by arguing that however much he may fall short of Socrates' early asceticism (a position he has made defensible), he is still philosophical if compared to non-philosophic people. He would have been on more solid ground if he had admitted that asceticism is always a threat to the world we live in, then praised the healthy results of the life of the reformed Socrates. Instead, he fails to give an adequate account of the balanced life – which he could have done by showing that Socrates' earlier asceticism kept him from fully pursuing philosophy, in that it prevented him from giving due attention to questions about human conduct. Al-Razi refrains from this because it would take him away from his major goal: setting forth the argument that completes his depiction of the philosophic life. This in turn depends upon his full teaching, and he offers a summary of it by listing six principles (taken from other works), of which he develops two. One, phrased almost as an imperative, asserts that pleasure is to be pursued only in a manner that does not bring on greater pain; the other is about the way the divinity has provided for all creatures.

This latter principle obliges humans not to harm other creatures. In his elaboration of this principle, al-Razi leads the reader to issues of political importance: the natural hierarchy between the different parts of the body and between the various species, then a presumed hierarchy among individuals within the human species. Such distinctions allow him to formulate a provisional definition of morality, something he calls the upper and lower limits. Briefly, accepting differences in birth and habit as fixed and as necessarily leading to different pursuits of pleasure, al-Razi urges that one not go against justice or intellect (understood naturally and according to revelation), nor come to personal harm or excessive indulgence in pleasure. The point is that since some people can afford more ease than others, the rule must be flexible. Although he urges that less is generally better, the disparities caused by differences in fortune do not provoke him to suggestions about the need to strive for a more equal distribution of wealth, or to regulate the way it is passed on. Completely avoiding such excursions into politics and political economy, al-Razi notes merely that the less wealthy may have an easier time of abiding by the lower limit, and that it is preferable to lean more towards that limit.

All of this is captured in what al-Razi calls the sum of the philosophic life, which is 'making oneself similar to God ... to the extent possible for a human being'. This summary statement is extraordinarily subtle and inventive. It consists of four basic parts. Al-Razi begins by asserting certain qualities of the Creator. He then seeks a rule of conduct based on an analogy between the way servants seek to please their sovereigns or masters and the way we should please our Sovereign Master. Next he draws a conclusion from that analogy about the character of philosophy. And he ends with the declaration that the fuller explanation of this summary statement is to be found in his *Book of Spiritual Medicine*.

The interested reader must turn to this book, al-Razi says, because it sets forth (a) how we can rid ourselves of bad moral habits, and (b) the extent to which someone aspiring to be philosophic may be concerned with gaining a livelihood, acquisition, expenditure and seeking to rule. Hence the picture of the philosophic life here raises questions that al-Razi identifies as relating to moral virtue, especially moral purification and human affairs – economics as well as political rule. Insofar as philosophy may be defined as seeking knowledge, struggling to act justly and being compassionate as well as kindly, it does encompass matters falling under moral virtue or ethics, household management or economics, and political rule. This allusion to the *Book of Spiritual Medicine* only underlines what has already been made clear by introducing the two principles from his larger teaching. He notes almost in passing, confident that the reader discerns how divine providence for all creatures warrants some serving others, that it is perfectly justifiable to distinguish between human beings in terms of how essential they are to the well-being of the community.

In the concluding words of this treatise, then, as part of his final self-justification, al-Razi asserts that philosophy consists of two parts, knowledge and practice. Anyone who fails to achieve both cannot be called a philosopher. His own role as a philosopher is made evident: his writings testify to his knowledge, and his adherence to the upper and lower limits proves his practice. Yet he clearly prizes knowledge more. Practice, and especially political practice, is subordinated to knowledge in all of al-Razi's ethical writings.

Al-Farabi's Moral and Political Teaching

Celebrated as 'the second teacher' after Aristotle, Abu Nasr al-Farabi is renowned for his teachers as well as his teaching. He studied logic with Yuhanna b. Haylan, Arabic with Ibn al-Sarraj and philosophy with Abu Bishr Matta b. Yunus. He is notable too for his travels. Al-Farabi sojourned in Bukhara, Marv, Baghdad, Damascus and Cairo; he may also have spent time in Byzantium. His writings, extraordinary in their breadth and deep learning, extend through all of the sciences and embrace every part of philosophy. He wrote numerous commentaries on Aristotle's logical treatises, was knowledgeable about his physical writings, and is credited with an extensive commentary on the *Nicomachean Ethics*. In addition to writing about Plato's and Aristotle's general philosophy – prefaced by his own adaptation of it to the challenges posed by Islam – in the *Philosophy of Plato and Aristotle*, he also wrote a commentary on Plato's *Laws*.

Of the many works that illuminate al-Farabi's ethical and political teaching, *Selected Aphorisms* (*Fusul muntazaa*) reveals most clearly how he looks to Plato and Aristotle for guidance in practical and theoretical matters. Indeed, in the subtitle he declares his reliance upon them and goes on to weave together in a most novel manner key themes from Plato's *Republic* and Aristotle's *Nicomachean Ethics*. The goal of the work, as indicated in the subtitle, is to set forth: 'Selected aphorisms that comprise the roots of many of the sayings of the ancients concerning that by which cities ought to be governed and made prosperous, the ways of life of their inhabitants improved, and they be led toward happiness.'[5]

The book contains 96 maxims that encompass the foundations, principles or grounds of several – not all – of the sayings of the ancients, or Plato and Aristotle. Al-Farabi begins with and develops a comparison between the health of the soul and that of the body. Quite abruptly, he starts by defining the health of each and then explains how the health of the more important of the two – that of the soul – may be obtained and its sickness repulsed. The first word of the *Selected Aphorisms* is simply 'soul', while the last is 'virtue'.

As he moves from 'soul' to 'virtue', al-Farabi first enters upon a detailed examination of the soul, and then gives an account and justification of the well-ordered political regime it needs to attain perfection. At no point does he speak of prophecy or of the prophet or legislator. He is equally silent about the philosopher and mentions 'philosophy' only twice. On the other hand, al-Farabi speaks constantly of the statesman (*madani*) and of the king.

Al-Farabi calls upon the ancients to identify the political order that will achieve human happiness. The individual who succeeds in understanding how a political community can be well ordered – whether a statesman or king – will do for the citizens what the physician does for individual sick persons. He will accomplish for the citizens who follow his rules what the prophet accomplishes for those who follow his. Yet to attain such an understanding, one must first be fully acquainted with the soul as well as with political life. More precisely, the virtuous political regime is the one in which the souls of all the inhabitants are as healthy as possible: 'the one who cures souls is the statesman, and he is also called the king'.

This is why such an obviously political work contains two long discussions of the soul. One, very similar to the *Nicomachean Ethics*, explains all the faculties of the soul except for the theoretical

---

[5] Abu Nasr al-Farabi, *Fusul muntazaa*, ed. F.M. Najjar (Beirut, 1971), on which I base the discussion here. For an English translation, see al-Farabi, *The Political Writings*, tr. Charles Butterworth (Ithaca, NY, 2001), pp.1–67.

part of the rational faculty. The other analyses this theoretical part and its companion, the practical part, by discussing the intellectual virtues; it also investigates the sensible and erroneous opinions on the principles of being and of happiness.

Al-Farabi proceeds in this work without formal divisions: each moral discussion is preceded and followed by other groups of maxims that go more deeply into its political teaching. Thus, the discussion of the soul in general is preceded by a series of analogies between the soul and the body, as well as between the soul and the body politic, and then followed by a discussion on domestic political economy, and an inquiry into the 'king in truth' (the person who is truly a king). Thereafter, the second discussion of the soul is followed by an inquiry into the virtuous city. Then he investigates sensible and erroneous opinions, before giving an account of the virtuous regime. After each moral discussion, the tone seems to become more elevated, as though the political teaching were driven or given direction by the moral teaching.

In the analogies that open this book, al-Farabi compares the body to the soul as though it were better known than the body, and boldly defines what constitutes the health and sickness of each. The health of the soul consists in its traits being such that it can always do what is good and carry out noble actions, whereas its sickness is for its traits to be such that it always does what is evil and carries out base actions. With one important difference, the description of the health and sickness of the body is nearly identical to that of the soul: the body is presented as doing nothing without first having been activated by the soul. After the good traits of the soul have been denoted as virtues and the bad traits as vices, al-Farabi ends this analogy.

His comparison of the physician with the statesman or king – in that the first cures bodies and the second cures souls – takes al-Farabi beyond the individual level. He sees the health of the body (the 'equilibrium of its temperament') as distinct from the health of the city (the 'equilibrium of the moral habits of its people'). Whereas the focus of bodily health is always the individual body, so that the physician is concerned with individuals as such, the statesman aims at the equilibrium of the city and is concerned with the totality or at least the plurality of its inhabitants, not with each one as an individual. If the statesman can arrive at his ends only by establishing equilibrium in the moral habits of all the inhabitants, so much the better for them; but al-Farabi no longer speaks explicitly of individuals.

Rather, he now speaks more readily of the community – of the city – and rarely evokes the image of the individual soul. He emphasises the moral habits of the people of the city as compared to the temperament of the individual body. The effect is to underline the importance of the art of statesmanship as greater than that of the physician. After all, it is the statesman who determines how the healthy body will be employed in the city. It falls not to the physician but to the king to prescribe what actions the healthy citizen, sound of body as well as of soul, ought to carry out.

Put another way, moral purpose distinguishes the task of the statesman/king from that of the physician. The physician's task is merely to heal, without asking how restored strength or improved sight will be used, whereas his counterpart must reflect on how the benefits of the civic or kingly art will affect the persons to whom it is applied – how their souls may be healed so that they carry out actions of service to the city. In this sense, the relationship between 'the art of kingship and of the city with respect to the rest of the arts in cities is that of the master builder with respect to the builders', and 'the rest of the arts in cities are carried out and practised only so as to complete by means of them the purpose of the political art and the art of kingship'. Since the greater complexity of this art confirms its superior importance, al-Farabi insists that such an individual needs to be aware of 'the traits of the soul by which a human does good things and how many they are', as well as of 'the devices to settle these traits in the souls of the citizens and of the way of governing so as to preserve these traits among them so that they do not cease'. Once again, this manner of going about his discussion of 'the science of morals' allows al-Farabi not only to associate it with politics, but also to subordinate the moral part of the soul to the intellectual part. In effect, the statesman/king figures out how to legislate for the city by means of the intellectual part – and then to establish a hierarchy among the moral habits themselves. The latter belong to the part of the soul concerned with moderation, courage, liberality and justice.

By the end of his first extensive discussion of the soul, all of the moral virtues except for justice have been discussed in some detail. Al-Farabi has explained what these habits are as balanced traits of the soul, and indicated how to bring them about. He specifies how the statesman/king must seek the health of each part of the city with an eye to the way its health or sickness affects the whole city, just as the physician must look to the health of the whole body when treating a particular limb or organ. As this section closes, al-Farabi seems to restate the parallel between the physician and the statesman/king, but does so by introducing a new term: instead of talking about the statesman (*al-madani*), he now speaks of the 'governor of cities' (*mudabbir al-mudun*). The change in terminology is minor, but it allows for a new inquiry, which explains the groupings formed by human beings. He explains that the ways people live – ephemeral as such matters are – influence their characters. More important still is what cities aim at, the common goal pursued by their citizens.

This leads al-Farabi to make distinctions that raise the tone of the discussion and, above all, to introduce happiness – even ultimate happiness – into the discussion for the first time. Now we need to distinguish between different kinds of rulers; we need to know who truly deserves to be called a king. When we learn what characterises this individual, it becomes evident that we need to understand better how he has come to discern human happiness. Differently stated, we need to learn about the intellectual virtues: wisdom and prudence.

It is not possible here to follow al-Farabi step by step through the rest of the work. But it should now be clear how he successfully fuses statecraft with soul-craft. Drawing on Plato and Aristotle, his ethical teaching leads necessarily to his political teaching.

Al-Farabi's Successors

Of al-Farabi's many successors, we focus here upon Ibn Sina and Ibn Rushd. Other key figures include Ibn Bajjah (c. 1095–1138), Ibn Tufayl (c. 1110–1185), Yahya b. Adi (c. 893–974), a student of al-Farabi, and Ibn Miskawayh (c. 940–1030).[6] All attest to the legacy of al-Farabi in regard to the intertwining of ethics and politics in this formative phase of Islamic thought.

Ibn Sina

Of all the thinkers in the medieval Muslim world, we are best acquainted with the life of Abu Ali al-Husayn Ibn Sina or Avicenna, thanks to the efforts of his devoted pupil and long-time companion, al-Juzjani. He preserved what resembles an autobiography of Ibn Sina, with his own biographical appendix. From it we learn that Ibn Sina was a tireless learner from the days of his youth to his death. Nowhere is this dedication more evident than in his massive encyclopedic work, *The Healing (al-Shifa)*.

This work spans the fields of logic, natural science, mathematics and metaphysics. One might think that Ibn Sina's *Healing* was devoted solely to theoretical philosophy or science, with little to say about practical matters. Indeed, not until the very end of his discussion of metaphysics does he speak of the practical sciences or arts of ethics and politics. As he puts it, this 'summary of the science of ethics and of politics' is placed there 'until I compose a separate, comprehensive book about them'.[7]

Ibn Sina's fuller teaching reveals, however, that ethical and political science belong after divine science. Indeed, they are the

---

[6] On their works, see *Rasail Ibn Bajjah al-Ilahiyya*, ed. Majid Fakhry (Beirut, 1968); *Ibn Tufayl's Hayy Ibn Yaqzan*, tr. Len Goodman (New York, 1972); Yahya b. Adi, *The Reformation of Morals*, tr. Sidney Griffith (Provo, UT, 2003); and Ibn Miskawayh, *The Refinement of Character*, tr. Constantine Zurayk (Beirut, 1968).
[7] Avicenna, *Kitab al-shifa, al-mantiq, al-madkhal*, ed. G. Anawati, M. El-Khodeiri and F. El-Ahwani (Cairo, 1952), vol. 11, p.1213.

human manifestation of divine science – its practical proof. They testify to divine providence for humankind and thus to the truth of revelation more clearly than any of the other sciences investigated in the *Healing*. Yet because the correctness of what they teach can also be verified by Aristotelian or pagan reasoning processes, Ibn Sina must elucidate the relationship he discerns between pagan philosophy and the revelation accorded the Prophet Muhammad.

Ibn Sina's description of Plato's *Laws* as a treatise on prophecy provides a clue to how much he deems philosophy and revelation to be interrelated. Similarly, the attention he gives to the political aspects of prophecy and divine law in the *Healing* leads to reflection upon the most fundamental political questions: the nature of law, the purpose of political community, the need for sound moral life among the citizens, the importance of providing for divorce as well as for marriage, the conditions for just war, the considerations that lay behind penal laws, and the end of human life. Ibn Sina's political teaching here provides an introduction to the fundamentals of political science and alerts readers to the need to think carefully about the strong affinity between the vision of political life set forth by the pagan Greek philosophers and that exceptional individual who surpasses philosophic virtue by acquiring prophetic qualities.

In other words, Ibn Sina shows in his statement on politics precisely what a law-giver needs to provide for when seeking to form a political community. His willingness to find common purpose between philosophy, even pagan Greek philosophy, and prophecy forces the thoughtful reader to inquire about the way in which awareness of the principles of political wellbeing is acquired.

Ibn Rushd

Abu al-Walid b. Rushd or Averroes was a practising judge and jurist, physician, princely advisor, an accomplished commentator on Plato and Aristotle, and much concerned with theoretical and practical problems of his day. His far-reaching achievements in jurisprudence, medicine, poetry, philosophy, natural science and theology were recognised by fellow Muslims as well as by the Christians and Jews who first translated his writings into Hebrew and Latin. But he was known above all for his commentaries on Aristotle – commentaries that range across the whole of Aristotle's works. He also wrote a commentary on Plato's *Republic*, this ostensibly because Aristotle's *Politics* was unknown to the Arabs. Moreover, he wrote in 1179–80 on topics of more immediate concern to fellow Muslims: the *Decisive Treatise* on the relationship between philosophy and divine law as well as the *Incoherence of the Incoherence*, an extensive reply to al-Ghazali's attacks on al-Farabi and Ibn Sina.

In these works, Ibn Rushd forcefully pleads that philosophy serves both religious and political wellbeing. It is ever the friend of religion, seeking to discover the same truth as religion and to bring the learned to respect divine revelation. Though convinced that science, and with it, philosophy had been completed by Aristotle, Ibn Rushd thought philosophy still needed to be recovered and protected in each age. To these goals he addresses himself in all of his works. The commentaries on Aristotle and Plato are intended to recover or rediscover the ancient teaching and explain it to those who can profit from it, while the public writings on issues of the day seek to preserve the possibility of philosophical pursuits in an increasingly hostile religious environment. From Ibn Rushd's *Commentary on Plato's Republic* we learn above all that the best regime is one in which the natural order among the virtues and practical arts is respected.[8] The practical arts and the moral virtues exist for the sake of the deliberative virtues, and – whatever the hierarchical relationship between the practical arts and the moral virtues – all of these exist for the sake of the 'intellectual virtues' (relating to applied wisdom and skills). Only when this natural order is reflected in how a society is organised and governed can there be any assurance that all of the virtues and practical arts will function as they ought. In order to have sound practice, then, it is necessary to understand the principles on which such practice

---

[8] See Ralph Lerner, *Averroes on Plato's 'Republic'* (Ithaca, NY, 1974).

depends: the order and the interrelationship among the parts of the human soul. He reaches the same conclusion, albeit much more rapidly, by identifying the best regime in his *Middle Commentary on the Rhetoric*, as the city whose opinions and actions are in accord with what the theoretical sciences prescribe.

These principles allow Ibn Rushd to identify the flaws in the regimes he sees around him more clearly. They are faulted either because they aim at the wrong kind of goal, or because they fail to respect any order among the human virtues. Thus he blames democracy for the emphasis it places on the private, and for its inability to order the desires of the citizens. In his *Commentary on Plato's Republic*, he first emphasises the need to foster greater concern for the public sphere and to diminish the appeal of the private; then he explains man's ultimate happiness in order to indicate how the desires should be properly ordered. A broad vision of the variety within the human soul and of what is needed for sound political life leads Ibn Rushd to endorse the tactics and in some respects the principles of Plato's politics.

Conclusion

The distinctions which scholars habitually draw between Plato and Aristotle are precisely the ones al-Farabi seems to delight in collapsing, fudging or ignoring. Pursuing common goals and teachings, his Plato and Aristotle differ only in the paths they take toward them. Above all, they perceive ethical teaching to be first and foremost a political undertaking. From them, al-Farabi learns that citizen virtue must be the primary concern of the law-giver. Forming the character of citizens and helping them achieve the highest of human goods – ultimate perfection – is the end at which he must aim. So character formation takes precedence over institutions and even the kinds of rule. Determining who rules is less important than ensuring that the ruler has the qualities – moral and intellectual – for leadership. And should a single person having the required qualities not be found, leadership passes to two or more, assuming that they come to have those qualities. This sums up what we learn from al-Farabi and from those who, like Ibn Rushd as well as (to a certain extent) Ibn Sina, follow in his footsteps.

Yet if this is the right conclusion from what al-Farabi has to say here, does it not clash with what Socrates has to say about the importance of a philosopher having some notion of the good if he is to rule well, and with Aristotle's emphasis on contemplation immediately before calling attention to the need for laws as a means of making good citizens? Put another way, is not sound theory the basis for sound practice? The answer to this question separates al-Farabi and Ibn Rushd (and, again, Ibn Sina to some extent) from al-Kindi and al-Razi. Insofar as the latter two subordinate the practical to the theoretical, their ethical teaching is limited to the individual. Even though it is uncertain whether al-Farabi and his companions succeed in finding an independent ground for practice, they oblige the thoughtful reader to travel that road. In doing so, the reader becomes as tantalised with the challenge of law-giving as were Adeimantus and Glaucon under the spell of Socrates. That, in the end, is the significance of linking an ethical teaching with a political one.

Ibn Khaldun understood this and did his utmost to pass on the teaching in his massive philosophy of history. Indeed, it deserved to be protected and passed on given how it provides for the interface of reason and faith. But such was not to be. Voices clamouring for more literal interpretations of scripture, pursuit of mystical rapture and slavish acceptance of wilful rule gained greater attention. Thus the political and ethical work of al-Farabi, Ibn Rushd and Ibn Sina passed into oblivion until sometime in the mid-19th century, when it came to light as foreign scholars indulged their curiosity about those relics of a past age. Their political and ethical thought had not been passed on to the West by the Christian Scholastic movement of Thomas Aquinas and Peter Abelard. If that had happened, how might the course of Western rationalism – especially its antagonism toward religion and religious figures such as prophets – have been altered?

Recovering and understanding this older body of reflection is a task that falls to those who discern its value. Will they now dare to revive those ever-present questions about the best kind of human life, along with the pressing matter of how reason relates to revelation? This is not, of course, a task only for Muslims. Ultimately, it is about becoming fully engaged in the search for wisdom about the way human beings are to live with one another.

Further Reading

Adamson, Peter and Richard C. Taylor, eds. *The Cambridge Companion to Arabic Philosophy*. Cambridge, 2005.

Butterworth, Charles E., ed. *The Political Aspects of Islamic Philosophy*. Cambridge, MA, 1992.

Cook, Michael. *Commanding Right and Forbidding Wrong in Islamic Thought*. Cambridge, 2001.

Fakhry, Majid. *Ethical Theories in Islam*. Leiden, 1994.

Hourani, George F. *Reason and Tradition in Islamic Ethics*. Cambridge, 1985.

Hovannisian, Richard G., ed. *Ethics in Islam*. Malibu, CA, 1985.

Mahdi, Muhsin S. *Alfarabi and the Foundation of Islamic Political Philosophy: Essays in Interpretation*. Chicago, 2001.

coughcoughcoughcoughcough# 3

Literature

Eric Ormsby

Introduction: The King and His Three Sons

Once upon a time, there was a king who was not only wise and just but had everything a king could desire. He was rich and powerful; his kingdom was at peace. But for all his success, his rule was troubled. For the king had three sons, and when he looked at them, he knew in his heart that not one of them was fit to succeed him on the throne. His sons were complete ignoramuses. Even if they weren't truly stupid, they lacked good judgement or the least trace of useful knowledge. Maybe their minds were asleep, he thought. But if so, how to wake them? How could any one of them rule a mighty kingdom? The king was baffled. He did what parents have always done: he turned to the experts. He called his court into session and quizzed his ministers, his courtiers, his wise men. They muttered, they scratched their beards, and finally one of them remarked that the study of grammar alone took twelve years, and that was merely the beginning of a proper education. So much for the experts. Such advice was no help at all. As a Moroccan proverb puts it, 'Among the walnuts only the empty one speaks.'

Just when the king was despairing, one of his ministers recalled that he had heard of an exceptional teacher. Why not send the three princes to sit at the feet of this sage? The king summoned the sage for an interview and was so impressed by his learning that he promised him a huge reward if he would take the education

of his sons in hand. The sage was too wise to be tempted by money
but he did like a challenge. He promised to educate the three
dunces in record time. 'In six months', he declared, 'your sons will
possess unsurpassed knowledge of all branches of practical wisdom.'
And he concluded by exclaiming, 'Hear! This is my lion-roar.'

It is no coincidence that the sage compared his words to a lion's
roar. For he taught the three clueless princes by telling them
stories, stories which all have talking animals as their characters
– not only monkeys and bears, crows, turtles and elephants but,
especially, a clever pair of jackals named Karataka and Damanaka.
These are Sanskrit names, like the name of the sage himself, Visnu
Sharma. And the book of tales which Visnu Sharma put together
for the three princes has the Sanskrit title of *The Panchatantra*,
which means 'the five books of good sense' (*tantra*).

It may seem strange to begin a discussion of the popular literature of ethics in the Muslim world with a tale dating from some
three centuries before the coming of Islam. Yet from its very origins,
Muslim ethical literature drew on a wide range of sources – Greek,
Indian and Persian, among others. Furthermore, the book in which
this tale is told forms one of the first and most important examples
of Muslim ethical writing. *The Panchatantra* was translated into
Arabic in the eighth century and the jackals Karataka and
Damanaka had their Sanskrit names turned into Kalila and Dimna.
The collection of their fables, known forever after as *Kalila and
Dimna*, influenced later Arabic literature as well as the tradition
of Muslim practical ethics, as much because of its charming style
as for its content.

Kalila and Dimna is one of the earliest examples of a genre
known as 'the mirror for princes', the most famous Western example
of which is *The Prince* by the Florentine humanist Niccolo
Machiavelli (1469–1527). Such books form an essential part of
the larger tradition known as *adab*, an Arabic word which now
means simply 'literature' but in the Muslim middle ages stood for
culture and refinement. A person with *adab* knew how to write
well in prose and verse, had polished manners, and was skilled
not only in good behaviour in society but cultivated a strong ethical
awareness. *Kalila and Dimna*, like the many later 'mirrors for

princes' it inspired and influenced, was originally written for the benefit of rulers; it set out to teach them not only how to get power (hard enough) but how to hold on to it (even harder). Nevertheless, their broader aim was to educate kings and princes on proper royal conduct; they taught them statecraft but at the same time, they emphasised the importance of justice, integrity and prudence. And though intended for an elite audience, such works became widely popular; they weren't only guides to good behaviour, their moral lessons had universal appeal.[1]

In the Islamic world, as in the world of ancient India, stories served as a favourite means of conveying moral teachings. They were medicine coated in honey, as one Muslim author described them. It isn't really surprising that the ancient fables of *The Panchatantra* would make their way eventually into Muslim culture; they were irresistible to a civilisation with an equal passion for ethics and for the telling of tales. This is, ultimately, a global phenomenon. Stories and proverbs travel the world without the benefit of passports, a portable wisdom drawn from the common experience of humanity.

The kind of 'ethics' I will be discussing here is neither the high-minded, more speculative ethics of the Muslim philosophers, nor the ethical doctrines of the Sufi masters. Rather, it is the popular ethical literature of early Islam – and thus 'foundational' to its literary tradition – aimed at helping its readers become successful in life while at the same time improving their character; it is a literature which freely mixes entertainment and instruction, light-hearted diversion and stern moralising, and sometimes all at once. Most literature of this sort, whether the *Fables* of Aesop or *The Panchatantra* itself, has certain common characteristics, and the Islamic forms are no exception.

First, they are writings designed to be *memorable*. Whether they take the shape of proverbs or poetry or fables, they stick in the mind. To deliver a truth about how we ought to live, and to make sure that it becomes part and parcel of a reader's own way of life,

---

[1] See Louise Marlow, 'Advice and Advice Literature', in M. Gaboriau et al., eds., *The Encyclopaedia of Islam*, 3rd edn (Leiden, 2007), vol. 1, pp.1–32.

that truth must be presented in a manner that captures the attention. There is a reason for the short, snappy, jingle-like form of the proverb: it echoes in the memory. If we hear someone quote the proverb, 'Trust him but pray behind him', we may laugh or be mildly shocked, but we remember it. When we hear a poem recited, the music of its language – its rhythm or beat, its rhymes – lingers behind; such devices make the poem easier to learn by heart. The same is true of fables, parables and stories. They present characters and situations that may surprise us but which we recognise; they speak to our own experience of life. When proverb, poem and tale occur together, as they do in many classics of Islamic ethical literature such as the *Rose Garden* of Sadi (discussed below), they become especially powerful.

Stories also have a *universal* element. They travel unstoppably from one culture to another. They represent our shared experience in a way no other form can do as well. Proverbs have this quality too (unlike poetry, which is bound up in the language of its composition). Stories and proverbs contain a down-to-earth wisdom drawn from our long collective experience. They speak to women as well as men, young as well as old, across the frontiers of culture, geography and politics.

This doesn't mean that stories or proverbs or other forms of ethical literature are identical across frontiers, or that the message is always the same from one culture to another. Part of their enduring appeal lies in that special twist, that distinctive flourish, which one culture, one tradition, gives to an age-old truth. In the ethical literature of Islam, in all its forms, there are flashes of original brilliance rarely found anywhere else. Whatever Muslim ethical writers took from ancient Greece or India, or from other older cultures, they made it unmistakably their own. This was not only due to the wit and power of invention of these authors; it was a result of the powerful ethical message of Islam itself.

Even when the spirit of a tale or a poem seems quite 'secular', as in so many episodes of *The 1001 Nights*, the narrative is subtly infused with Islamic values. In the end, behind all the tales to be told, there stands what the Quran calls 'the most beautiful of stories', that of Yusuf in the 12th *sura*. It is a story that offers a vivid example of how we ought to live. So do the Traditions or hadiths of the Prophet Muhammad and of the imams, which take the form of stories. The *Sira* or biography of the Prophet provides yet another instance. Again, in later centuries, such collections as *The Tales of the Prophets* or the many collections drawn from the lives of the Sufi masters, use anecdote and parable for dramatic illustrations of good moral conduct. All of these ethical and spiritual writings use narrative to convey their message. As a result, storytelling has enjoyed privileged status in Muslim literature.

Hence it is not surprising that Muslim authors would turn to the fable or the tale when they wished to provide ethical guidance. Such forms had the prestige of sacred example behind them. Even so, the literature of ethics in Islam is much broader than this might suggest. From the beginning, Muslim writers sought to give their readers practical advice; this was 'worldly wisdom' and often it has a frank, even cynical tone. There was good reason for this. Such authors wished to guide people along paths that would lead not only to salvation but to a good life in this world. So they counselled on how to behave honourably in shady situations, how to spot pretence or trickery, how to avoid being duped, and they gave tips on how to prosper. Ibn al-Muqaffa, one of the earliest such writers, held the goal of ethics to be nothing less than the achievement of human happiness in this world and in the next.

The Quran and the Traditions put special emphasis on the hereafter; the truths that they reveal concern ultimate things. Still, the affairs of everyday life bring with them all sorts of dilemmas and perplexing questions – relations between parents and children, the bonds of friendship, the demands of the marketplace and, perhaps most importantly, the principles of good governance (where 'good' is both 'just' and 'successful'). What emerged out of such everyday perplexities was a literature of common sense, not so different in aim from the 'how-to' and 'self-help' books of today, but with a crucial exception. Unlike our present-day dispensers of self-improvement, Muslim authors put all the style, wit and learning they possessed into their books. The beauty and the elegance of their compositions stood as a testimony to the soundness of their advice.

Animal Fables

As it turned out, the teachings of Visnu Sarma worked. Within six months the king's three sons had become clever, well-informed and, if not wise, at least well on their way to wisdom. Each of the three was prepared to step into his father's royal shoes. How did the sage accomplish this? He instructed the three young dolts by telling them stories, and not just any stories but stories about animals – all collected in *The Panchatantra*, which very quickly became one of the most popular books ever compiled. Over the centuries it has been translated into almost every known language from Arabic and Persian to Hebrew, Latin, Turkish and Malay; there are versions in every European language as well. Its influence has been enormous.

One of the earliest translations came at the request of the Persian Sasanian ruler Anushirvan (531–59), who had heard reports of the marvellous book. He sent Burzoe, his court physician, to India to obtain a copy. The precious volume was kept under lock and key but after many adventures, and much bargaining, so the story goes, Burzoe managed to bring it home to Iran. He then translated the book from Sanskrit into Pahlavi, an older form of Persian. It was this translation which some two centuries later fell into the hands of one of the greatest of the classical Arabic writers, the brilliant and ill-fated Ibn al-Muqaffa (c. 720–756).

It is with Ibn al-Muqaffa that an Islamic literature of ethics begins. He was born in the province of Fars into a Zoroastrian family and given the name Rozbih. His father had served as a tax collector under the dreaded Umayyad governor of Iraq, al-Hajjaj b. Yusuf, and had been tortured and executed for embezzlement ('Ibn al-Muqaffa' literally means 'the son of the mutilated man', a reference to his father's ordeal). Though Persian-speaking, Ibn al-Muqaffa mastered Arabic and came to be considered one of the finest stylists in the language; his books are still held up as models of literary elegance. He converted to Islam and rose to become a secretary to one of the Umayyad governors; when the Umayyads were overthrown by the Abbasids, Ibn al-Muqaffa landed on his feet and continued to serve at court. This position led to his downfall; he became rich and like his father was accused of misusing royal funds. He was only 36 when he too was put to the torture and executed.

All of Ibn al-Muqaffa's surviving writings are books of advice in one form or another. Whether advising the caliph on affairs of state or laying out the principles of a happy and successful life to readers at large, he remains a shrewd and practical moralist. Ibn al-Muqaffa was steeped in both Greek philosophy and the lore of the ancient Persians (his son would later become one of the first translators of Aristotle's logical works into Arabic). He believed that the surest guide to the good life lay in the correct use of the intellect; and by 'the good life' he meant a life that combined the highest ethical conduct with a realistic understanding of human affairs, that led to happiness both in this world and the next. It was a life in which the intelligence which God gave to man played the key role. In his introduction to *Kalila and Dimna*, he wrote:

> The intellect is the means to every good, the key to all happiness. No one can afford to dispense with the intellect. It is acquired through experience and through cultivation. There is an instinct proper to the intellect which lies hidden in human beings; it is concealed like the fire in the flint-stone whose gleam is not shown or seen until someone kindles it. But when it is kindled, then its true nature appears.[2]

If the intellect is 'hidden in human beings' and only appears when it is 'kindled', this means that it is able to develop and grow. The training and cultivation of the intelligence is one of the aims of practical ethics. If philosophical reasoning is too abstract for

---

[2] *Kitab Kalila wa-Dimna* (Bombay, 1968), p.61. All translations from this text are my own.

most readers – and especially for children – the same lessons can be taught in fables and parables. All of them are calculated to sharpen the intelligence.

Still, intellect alone is not enough. In the same introduction Ibn al-Muqaffa wrote, 'When the reasonable person has understood this book and gained all the knowledge which is contained in it, he must act on the basis of what he has learned so that he derives benefit from it and he must make it a model from which he never swerves.' His guiding principle is that knowledge and action are one. 'Knowledge is perfected solely in action; it is like a tree and action is its fruit.'[3] Although Ibn al-Muqaffa spells these principles out in detail in his formal ethical treatises, in *Kalila and Dimna* he dramatises them. They are no longer abstract notions but living lessons. In fables, we see them played out in life as it is lived every day.

As one example, consider the fable of the Fox and the Drum, as told by the jackal Dimna:

> They maintain that a fox came to a forest in which a drum hung suspended from a tree. Whenever the wind blew against the branches of that tree, it set it in motion so that it struck the drum and a great voice was heard coming out of it. The fox drew near to catch the sound of that mighty voice but when he came close, he discovered that the drum was enormous. He was sure that there had to be an abundance of fat and meat inside the drum. He pawed at it until he split it open. When he saw that it was hollow and had nothing inside, he said, 'I don't really know; maybe the flimsiest things have the loudest voices while the mightiest are mute as the dead.'[4]

And Dimna notes, 'I've fashioned this example for you only so that you might know that that voice which so terrifies us is found to be, when we draw close to it, much slighter than that which is in ourselves.' The fable seems straightforward but it isn't. The fox

---

[3] *Kalila wa-Dimna*, p.62.
[4] *Kalila wa-Dimna*, pp.105–6.

is first frightened by the noise of the drum but then he grows curious. When he sees how big it is, greed gets the better of him; he convinces himself that the drum is actually a carcass rich in fat. When he discovers that it is hollow, he is more puzzled than disappointed. The drum was nothing but an empty booming and the moral would seem to be little more than the truism that appearances can be deceiving.

But Dimna's comment corrects that first impression. We may be terrified by appearances – here, the loud sound of the drum – only to realise that the 'voice' hidden within us is in fact more to be feared. It is the fox's greed which deceived him; that unheeded voice proved more treacherous than the hollow drum struck by the wind. There is thus a triple moral to the tale: appearances are deceiving; things which look or sound terrible may not be; it is the inner voice that we fail to heed which proves our undoing. If we compare Ibn al-Muqaffa's translation with the Sanskrit original, we notice right away that in his version the tale has become simpler and subtler. In *The Panchatantra* the moral is straightforward: we shouldn't give way to fear in the face of empty bluster.[5] In *Kalila and Dimna* the moral is rather that we are deceived by appearances because we deceive ourselves.

In his version, Ibn al-Muqaffa reduced the story to its essence but at the same time deepened it; it has become a fable of the failure of the intellect to see things as they are. This provides a good example of Ibn al-Muqaffa's method. He strips the story to its bones, omitting fancy turns of phrase and snippets of verse, and then gives it a small twist so that its hidden meanings can be seen. As a result, *Kalila and Dimna* becomes more than a plain translation; it becomes a new and original creation. It would be widely imitated by later writers, such as the great al-Jahiz in the ninth century, who would expand the genre to include sharp character sketches of human types – especially all varieties of miser and skinflint alongside his fabulous animals (Pl. 1–3). Finally, it is not surprising that it was Ibn al-Muqaffa's Arabic translation,

---

[5] See Visnu Sarma, *The Panchatantra*, tr. Chandra Rajan (London, 2006), pp.31–2.

rather than *The Panchatantra* itself, which served as the text on which most later translations, into dozens of languages, were based.

The Poetry of Advice

From the earliest times, poetry has been seen as a source of wisdom. That is partly because poetry seemed to have a supernatural origin, coming to the poet from outside him or herself. The very word 'inspiration' means a process of being 'breathed into' by a spiritual influence. In Muslim tradition, such inspiration was often suspect. Poets were more likely to be inspired by an evil spirit – a *jinn* or even Iblis himself – than by a good one; and this is why certain poets were described as *majnun*, a word which has come to mean 'crazy' but which originally meant 'inspired by a *jinn*'. This is one of the reasons why the Quran emphasises in several passages that the Prophet Muhammad is not a poet; for poets, the Quran tells us, 'are liars' who 'say what they do not do' (26:223–6).

This may well have served to make Muslim poets more honest in their verse. In any case, poetry became one of the chief ways in which Muslim writers have offered ethical guidance over the centuries. As mentioned earlier, the use of rhyme and rhythm helped to drive advice home but there was another reason as well: poetry can pack a lot of meaning into a very few words. Unlike a sermon or a long drawn-out treatise, it delivers its message quickly. This is, of course, why advertising so often uses rhyming slogans and catchy jingles; the message sticks in the mind.

Wisdom poetry, or the poetry of advice, isn't popular nowadays. We don't expect or want moral guidance from most of our poets, and usually with good reason. Poets today may latch onto fashionable causes but they shy away from offering their readers broad advice on how to live; most poets would consider that 'preachy' or 'condescending'. This contemporary attitude makes it hard for us to appreciate much of the poetry of the past, and especially traditional Muslim poetry. Words in this tradition aren't just the raw material of a poem; they share in the sacred. It was through words, after all, that God chose to reveal Himself in the

Quran. If a poet was gifted enough to use words well, he or she enjoyed special prestige; a good poet was expected to demonstrate not only wit and skill but moral and spiritual insight.

It would be hard to find any poet in the classical tradition, whether in Arabic, Persian, Turkish or any other language spoken by Muslims, who does not include moral advice in his verse. For such advice was deemed as 'poetical' as the nightingale or the rose. There are two, however, who have pride of place in this tradition. They are Nasir-i Khusraw, the great Ismaili *daʿi* (missionary), philosopher, traveller and poet, and Sadi of Shiraz, usually known simply as 'Shaykh Sadi'. Both wrote in Persian and are considered among the four or five greatest of Persian poets. Their works are lyrical and ethical in almost equal measure.

Nasir-i Khusraw

As a Fatimid *dai* and later *hujja* (representative of the Ismaili *dawa*) for the entire territory of Khurasan, Nasir-i Khusraw (c. 1004–77) had a duty to instruct and yet it is obvious that he writes not from obligation but out of passion and conviction. There is a good reason for this, as we will see. His works in prose deal with complex theological and philosophical matters or, as in his famous *Safarnama* (*Book of Travels*), provide a detailed factual record of the seven years he spent journeying; but his poetry speaks of trials and tribulations, as well as of burning convictions. Remarkably enough, his literary career began only in middle age; all his works, whether in prose or verse, were written after his fiftieth year. They were the products of a radical change in his life.

In the course of his travels, he arrived in Fatimid Cairo on 3 August 1047. There, inspired by none other than the Imam-caliph al-Mustansir and the chief *dai* al-Muʾayyad fiʾl-Din al-Shirazi (himself a fine poet), Nasir came to embrace the Ismaili way of Islam. But this process of conversion had begun long before. As he tells us in the preface to his *Book of Travels*, he set out on his journey in 1045 as a way of reforming and purifying his character. He had spent most of his working life as a government official under the Ghaznavids (c. 962–1186) and Seljuqs

(c. 1037–1194); his private life was given over to drinking and idle amusements. He was like a man who suddenly woke up one day from a long sleep to find himself grown old but without having become either wiser or more virtuous.

His awareness that he must change his own life is one of the elements which give Nasir-i Khusraw's 'poetry of advice' much of its power. 'I reflected that until I changed all my ways I would never find happiness', he tells us at the very beginning of his *Book of Travels*.[6] His advice is always directed to himself as well as to others. He does not preach from a comfortable distance; he knows how hard it is to change one's life and this knowledge lends urgency to his verse. He begins one long ode, or *qasida*, with the line, 'Now it is fitting that I change the state of things and strive to attain that which is best.'[7] But how is it possible to make such a change? This is the difficult question that all Nasir-i Khusraw's works set out to answer. As he makes clear in prose and poetry, there is only one way, one answer, and that is through knowledge. But knowledge doesn't simply mean gathering information; knowledge demands to be acted upon. This is, as we have seen, one of the ethical messages which Ibn al-Muqaffa had delivered three centuries earlier; it is one of the strongest and most consistent ethical principles in the Islamic tradition. In one of his prose works Nasir-i Khusraw wrote, 'Know, O brother, that human liberation lies in knowledge. Man has two things by which he can receive knowledge: one of them is the heart by which he knows, and the other is the body with which he puts that knowledge into practice.'[8]

How do we gain such knowledge? We gain it, Nasir tells us, through the intellect. But the intellect needs awakening. We are all like the king's three sons whose minds seemed asleep. Our native intelligence needs a good wake-up call. 'Why do you think

[6] Alice Hunsberger, *Nasir Khusraw: The Ruby of Badakhshan* (London, 2003), p.49.

[7] Translated by Julie Meisami, in *An Anthology of Ismaili Literature: A Shi'i Vision of Islam*, ed. H. Landolt et al. (London, 2008), pp.271–5.

[8] Nasir Khusraw, *Knowledge and Liberation: A Treatise on Philosophical Theology*, ed. and tr. F.M. Hunzai (London, 1998), p.101.

God gave you a mind? To eat and sleep like a donkey?' In all his work, Nasir struggles against what he calls 'a religion of donkeys', a faith that is plodding and thoughtless. Knowledge depends on the constant development of understanding, for only thus can we hope to become not only enlightened believers but better human beings. The knowledge he praises throughout his poetry is a total knowledge; it involves the mind and the body. In another ode he states:

> Know that God has never commanded anything but truth:
> Speak the truth, think the truth, begin the truth, and
> produce the truth.[9]

This emphasis on knowledge and the intellect in the service of truth is crucial to Nasir-i Khusraw's ethical teaching. It is important to keep in mind that the word for 'truth' is *haqq*, which in both Arabic and Persian means 'God' as well as 'truth'. Nevertheless, truth is not just given to us; we have to work for it. Nasir believes strongly in human free will; belief and unbelief, happiness and misery are not predetermined by God but lie within our grasp:

> Although God creates the mother and the breast and the milk,
> The children must draw the mother's milk for themselves.

In other lines which have become proverbial, he wrote in the same vein:

> You are the author of your own disastrous star;
> Don't look up to heaven for some luckier star.

These two principles alone – the supremacy of knowledge and the reality of human free will – demonstrate how wrong critics of Nasir-i Khusraw's position (and of Ismaili doctrine in general) have been. Scarcely a generation later, the theologian Abu Hamid

---

[9] Excerpts from poems quoted here are in my own translation, unless noted otherwise.

al-Ghazali (c. 1058–1111) would attack Ismaili teaching for promoting blind and unthinking allegiance to the imam. The truth is quite the opposite. No tradition places greater significance on the use of the intellect and on reasoned discourse. And no medieval thinker does so more than Nasir-i Khusraw, for whom it is the guiding concept of both ethics and his metaphysics. But of course, this raises the difficult question of what he means by 'knowledge' or by 'truth'. Throughout his work, the truth is shown to be not only subtle but virtually limitless. As a master of *ta'wil* or symbolic interpretation (of scripture and of the world itself), Nasir-i Khusraw knows that there is a natural limit to the ordinary human intellect. The deep inner truth (*batin*) cannot always be discovered beneath the outer surface meaning (*zahir*) of things by the intellect alone; for the farther limits of truth, even the most intelligent human beings require the guidance of an illumination which only the imam can provide. In Nasir's work, the truth appears on differing levels. Hence when he speaks of 'devils' in his poetry, he means this term not literally (with reference to the Seljuq Turks) but in a deeper ethical sense; as he explains elsewhere, a 'devil' is one who is a slave to bodily appetites, that is, a person who has not used his intellect to curb his passions. So too a 'beast' is one who prefers the laziness of habit in his thinking to the cultivation of his intelligence. Poets often use such figurative language, yet here it is rarely mere rhetoric but almost always has deeper levels of meaning.

It would be misleading to leave the impression that Nasir-i Khusraw's poetry consists of nothing but wise maxims and ethical precepts. In fact, he was one of the first to take the old form of the *qasida* and reinvent it in Persian. For poets writing in Arabic, the *qasida* had always been the most admired and respected form, sometimes stretching to over a hundred lines with the same rhyme and meter throughout. It had been used mainly for elaborate descriptions of desert landscapes, for laments over lost loves, or for stoical reflections on human destiny. In Nasir-i Khusraw's hands it became subtler, more personal, capable of moving from grand statements of metaphysical truth ('God in His oneness, most ancient of all . . .') to pithy punchlines ('This world of yours is a cat that eats her kittens . . .'). For him, writing itself serves as a symbol for the practice of virtue:

> Your soul is a book, your deeds are like writing:
> Do not write anything but a beautiful script on your soul!
> Write nothing but what is entirely good in the book!
> For in your own hand, O brother, you hold the pen.

Sadi of Shiraz

Sadi (c. 1184–1291) stands in almost complete contrast to Nasir-i Khusraw. Sadi has been described as representing 'the astute, half-pious, half-worldly side of the Persian character'.[10] Setting aside whatever may be meant by 'the Persian character', that seems pretty accurate. Though a contemporary of the two great mystical poets Farid al-Din Attar and Jalal al-Din Rumi, Sadi keeps a foot very firmly planted in this world. He respects the spiritual life and is sometimes mystically inclined, but he's too sharp-eyed to be swept away; this makes him an excellent satirist. His wisdom is rarely lofty; it is homespun, practical and shrewd. He is the great poet of common sense, perhaps the greatest ever; his poetry might even be described as common sense made musical.

All his works, but especially his *Bustan* ('Orchard') and *Gulistan* ('Rose Garden'), offer practical advice in a charming mix of prose and verse, mostly in Persian but with the frequent addition of proverbs and lines of poetry in Arabic – largely, it seems, as a way of showing off. The *Rose Garden* seems puzzling at first sight. It is populated with surly saints and intimidating kings, with conniving merchants and love-struck judges. In one such tale, a tyrant asks a hermit which act of religious devotion would be best for him to perform. The hermit replies, 'For you, it would be to take a nap at noon so that for that one moment at least you won't be vexing your people.' In another, a king cheats his poorest subjects out of firewood which he then gives to his rich friends in a show

---

[10] E.G. Browne, *A Literary History of Persia*, vol. 2: *From Firdawsi to Sa'di* (Cambridge, 1969), p.526.

of generosity. But when his royal palace burns down, the king sits in the ashes and asks where the fire came from. A passerby replies, 'It came from the hearts of the poor.' As this shows, Sadi's rose garden has as many thorns as blossoms.

It also shows something quite essential about Sadi. He isn't afraid to criticise the high and mighty. He is always on the side of the poor and the downtrodden. And he hates hypocrisy. If he is particularly harsh on unjust rulers, he is almost equally so in exposing the failings of hypocritical clerics and phoney saints. In one tale, a king ends up in heaven while a dervish roasts in hell. How can this be? As Sadi explains, 'The king is in paradise because of his devotion to dervishes while the dervish is in hell because of his devotion to kings.' Incidentally, as an illustration of just how smoothly such stories hop from one culture and one language into another, this same little parable was later translated into French and found its way into the *Fables* of the 17th-century French poet La Fontaine; its exotic setting allowed him to get away with satirising his own clergy.

Sadi had good reason to criticise those in power. First of all, this was an old Sufi practice. Sufis frequently scolded kings and governors for their unjust ways, often to their faces, and Sadi was something of a Sufi himself, at least when it suited him. Second, and more importantly, Sadi lived during exceptionally violent times. He and his native city of Shiraz were fortunate in surviving the destruction of the Abbasid dynasty under the onslaught of the Mongols. The *Orchard* appeared in 1257 and the *Rose Garden* in 1258, the very year in which the Mongol conqueror Hulagu Khan (1217–65) ravaged Baghdad. This may help explain why Sadi places such a strong emphasis on good sense and shrewd judgement in his tales and poems, and why he takes so keen a joy in the passing beauty of the world.

The book is divided into eight chapters which range over such topics as the conduct of kings, the character of dervishes, the 'benefits of silence' and the effects of education; a chapter on love is followed by one on the feebleness of old age, and the whole book ends with a discourse on the art of conversation. What unites these scattered chapters is a single unspoken concern: survival in a world that is not only hostile but deceptive. The *Rose Garden* could be seen as a survival manual for terrible times.

E.G. Browne, the great historian of Persian literature, rather disapproved of Sadi. Though he agreed that Sadi was 'essentially an ethical poet', he warned rather primly that 'his ethics are somewhat different from the theories commonly professed in Western Europe'.[11] As examples, he notes that the moral of the very first story in the *Rose Garden* is 'an expedient falsehood is preferable to a mischievous truth', and that the point of another story is that not even the best education can overcome 'inherited criminal tendencies'. This is true enough. But when he wrote this, Browne had forgotten his Aesop which contains much the same sort of advice and is about as 'Western European' as it gets! The ethical advice of Sadi (like that of Aesop) stirs high and low: cunning and street-smarts are considered as valuable as lofty ideas of justice and honour. It is an ethics drawn from life as it is lived rather than from abstract theory. Even so, a deeper vision underlies it.

In the first book of the *Rose Garden*, on the proper conduct of kings, Sadi tells us that once while he was meditating in the Umayyad Mosque in Damascus, an Arab king 'known for his injustice' came to pray. Afterwards he asked Sadi to 'make a thought that will accompany me, for I am vexed by a difficult enemy'. Sadi replied, 'Have mercy on your weak subjects' and concluded with these lines of verse:

The sons of Adam are all limbs of one another
For they were formed of a single essence at creation.
When one limb is hurt by fate, the other limbs cannot find peace.
If you are unconcerned with the troubles of others
You are not fit to be called a human being.[12]

---

[11] Browne, *Literary History*, vol. 2, p.530.
[12] Sa'di, *The Gulistan (Rose Garden) of Sa'di*, tr. W.M. Thackston (Bethesda, MD, 2008), p.22 [translation slightly modified].

Entertainment and Ethics

Along with fables and maxims, poems and proverbs, the literature of Muslim ethics is rich in longer narratives. *The 1001 Nights*
or *The Arabian Nights* (*Alf layla wa-layla* in Arabic) is the most
famous of these. That huge collection of stories, gathered over
centuries by anonymous story-tellers, isn't usually thought of as
an example of 'ethical literature'. When Richard Burton translated
it into English, he called it *The Arabian Nights Entertainment*, and
entertainment appears to be its main purpose. But works of ethical
guidance have always used the devices of entertainment to deliver
their message.

In the preface to *Kalila and Dimna*, Ibn al-Muqaffa has the
Sasanian physician Burzoe, who serves as his mouthpiece, remark,
'As for this book, well, it combines wisdom and diversion. So the
wise choose it for its wisdom while fools choose it for diversion.'
As Nasir-i Khusraw might have said, using one of his favourite
images, here wisdom is 'the pearl' hidden under the 'rough oyster-
shell' of amusing anecdotes. In fact, most if not all the hundreds
of stories in *The 1001 Nights* have a moral. This isn't to say that
the moral is always the point of the story but rather that the moral
is part of the entertainment. That is very different from contemporary narrative, whatever the language. A modern short-story
writer tends to concentrate on the unique situation or the individual psychological profile of his or her characters; it would be
hard to pin down a specific moral from the stories of Chekhov
or James Joyce. I certainly don't want to turn the delightful and
sometimes outrageous stories of *The 1001 Nights* into sermons in
disguise and yet, while the incidents of those tales may thrill and
enchant us, it is their moral, stated or not, which ultimately gives
satisfaction. That moral can take the simplest of forms: justice is
done, the wicked are punished, the good triumph. This is why
Shahrazade tells her stories by night, and it's why we tell our children stories at bedtime: a well-told story sets the world right again
before we fall asleep.

There is a further moral dimension to these ancient tales. The
episodes, from the most humdrum to the most sublime, from the

downright smutty to the impossibly exalted, all take place against a backdrop of eternity. God does not intervene but He is always present. And sometimes (as in Sadi), the most genuinely pious characters aren't the most virtuous; sometimes it's the rascals and tricksters who show the sincerest devotion. It is as though the storytellers – and Shahrazade herself – thought that the world had to be turned upside down before it could be righted again, this time for good. That is why there are so many disguised figures throughout the tales: a beggar is revealed as a prince, a king turns out to be a woman, a wolf ends up as a Sufi saint. Even here there is a message. The things of this world aren't what they seem. Not only is human life tragically brief, it is fundamentally deceptive. We change constantly; only God never changes.

This is not the place to describe the history of the book itself, even if it is as tangled and fantastic as any of the tales it contains.[13] The stories come from many different places and ages; some, the oldest, go back to ancient Iran, others derive from eighth-and ninth-century Baghdad and, especially, the reign of the fifth Abbasid Caliph Harun al-Rashid (786–809); still others reflect the Cairo of the Mamluks (1250–1517). It was under the Mamluks that the stories as we know them, which were originally transmitted by professional storytellers, were finally written down and collected. What holds this enormous grab-bag together is the remarkable personality of Shahrazade, the Persian princess who spins out her tales night after night under the shadow of death.

Shahrazade may be seen as an isolated figure in the long history of Muslim literature. Certainly few women authors are repre- sented there. But Shahrazade may also be seen as standing for many other women of genius whose names have been lost. There were women poets who wrote in Arabic, Persian, Turkish and other languages; only a few of their works have survived. Sometimes their verses are quoted in the medieval anthologies as examples of brilliant improvisation, a skill at which many women at court seem to have been quite expert. But these were impromptu

---

[13] The best introduction is Robert Irwin, *The Arabian Nights: A Companion* (London, 2004).

creations, made for the occasion and seldom recorded; and this is probably true of much poetry composed by women over the centuries. Women were often learned in hadith and consulted for their expertise. In Muslim Spain, they seem to have played a conspicuous part, both as teachers and as bearers of oral traditions. The great theologian Ibn Hazm (c. 994–1064) tells us that he was raised in the harem and that all his teachers, in religious matters as well as in such arts as calligraphy, were women. The Andalusian Sufi master Ibn Arabi (c. 1165–1240) notes that his first two teachers in Sufism were women, whom he mentions by name. It's reasonable to assume that Shahrazade, though probably not a historical personage, stood for an ideal type who was also compellingly familiar: the woman as a clever weaver of tales, with an inexhaustible memory and a special style of wit, at once ironic and tender, and one whose tales have a distinctly ethical edge.

The 1001 Nights uses an ancient narrative device known as a 'frame story'. All the tales are framed by the central story. The tale of the wise king and his three clueless sons is the frame story of *The Panchatantra*. In the frame story of the *Nights*, King Shahrayar and his brother Shahzaman, also a king, have both been betrayed by their wives. Shahrayar vows to take a new virgin bride every night and to have her put to death in the morning. Shahrazade, the wazir's daughter, volunteers to turn the embittered king from this cruel practice and offers herself as his next bride. Once in the king's bed-chamber, however, Shahrazade diverts the king with a tale which she breaks off at dawn; the king will hear the rest of the tale the next evening only if he spares her life. This is the suspenseful situation from which all her stories spring. Of course, the frame story too has a moral aspect. All our stories – which in the end are our lives – are narrated under the inevitable threat of death – 'the destroyer of delights', as Shahrazade puts it. Like her, we buy time with words.

Among the most famous tales is the allegory known as 'The City of Brass'. Here, the moral is plain from the outset. Musa and his companions have been sent on a mission by the caliph. They arrive at a beautiful palace 'whose roofs and walls were inlaid with gold, silver and precious stones'. Over the doorway is an inscription in Greek that Musa has translated:

This people and their works lament the empire they have lost.
The palace brings the last news of its lords, who all lie buried here.
Death parted and destroyed them, throwing to the ground what they
    had gathered in
It is as though they halted here to rest, but then set off again in haste.[14]

There are several inner doorways and each bears a similar message.
Inside, the travellers discover a city of the dead:

The shops were open, with their scales hanging up and the copper pots
arranged in orderly rows; the *khans* were filled with goods of all sorts,
but the traders could be seen dead in their booths with their flesh
desiccated and their bones crumbled away, a lesson for those who could
    learn.

Wherever the travellers go, from the silk market to the jewellers'
shops to the innermost chambers of the palace, they find such eerie
scenes. The merchants are all dressed for business, a princess lounges
on a couch, but all are skeletons, ghosts of the living in a city closed
forever to the world. Even a city of brass cannot stand against time
and death, the story seems to say. Still more frightening, the story
suggests that in a profound sense the dead and the living, viewed
against that backdrop of eternity, are almost indistinguishable. All
the small detail of the market and the shops, so carefully described
('brocade woven with threads of red gold and white silver', 'the
carpets of silk', the perfumes, the beautifully crafted swords and
bows) reinforce this suggestion. We humans are less substantial
than these mere things which will outlast us. God alone endures.

Ethics and the Natural World

Though most popular ethical literature in the Muslim world focussed
on the dilemmas human beings face in their daily lives, from the
ever-present fact of mortality (as in 'The City of Brass') to tricky

[14] *The Arabian Nights: Tales of 1,001 Nights*, tr. M. and U. Lyons (London, 2008) vol. 2, p.523. This is the best English translation of the complete *Nights*.

individual problems (as in *Kalila and Dimna* or Sadi's *Rose Garden*), some writers took a broader view. They were concerned not only with man's place in society but with his larger place in the natural world, or as we would put it nowadays, the environment. What, they asked, is man's role in creation as a whole? What responsibility do we bear for our fellow creatures? Is human dominance over other creatures justified and, if so, on what terms? In particular, such writers puzzled over the problem of the suffering of animals. Animals are not moral beings in our sense; they are not endowed with reason or free will. They are 'innocent' by any definition, legal or otherwise. What meaning, then, could there be in their suffering, either in the natural world or at the hands of man?

This problem troubled theologians, especially those associated with the Mutazilite tradition. That school of theology, which lasted from the eighth century until well into the 12th, tackled the problem of animal suffering for a very specific reason. They upheld a strong conception of God's absolute justice. But if innocent creatures suffered for no apparent reason and not for any sins they had committed, this fact cast doubts on divine justice. The Mutazilites came up with several arguments to explain this unmerited suffering; such animals, they said, would receive a reward in the next life for their pains. This was a doctrinal response to a distressing fact. Other thinkers responded out of simple compassion. The great Syrian poet Abu al-Ala al-Maarri (c. 973–1057), for example, was moved by the plight of fellow creatures. In one of his prose works he raised the following question:

Why do hawk and falcon swoop down on the bird searching for grain? The grouse leaves her thirsty chicks and sets out early to reach water which she would carry to them in her craw, but a hawk finds her far from her chicks and devours her. And so her chicks die of thirst.[15]

---

[15] Quoted in the biography of al-Maarri by Yaqut, *Irshad al-arib*, ed. D. S. Margoliouth (Leiden, 1913), vol. 1, p.199 (my translation). For a translation of the complete passage, see my *Theodicy in Islamic Thought* (Princeton, 1984), p.26.

Al-Maarri was unusual not only in raising such questions but in acting on them; he was, for example, a life-long vegetarian.

Other thinkers at around the same time addressed similar concerns within a wider ethical framework. The most famous of these were the Ikhwan al-Safa or 'Brethren of Purity' who flourished in the 10th century in the city of Basra. It brings us full circle here to note that the name of this group is often explained as deriving from none other than Ibn al-Muqaffa's *Kalila and Dimna* where it is applied to a gathering of 'friendly doves'. The Brethren, a secretive group of philosophically minded intellectuals (evidently with strong Ismaili links), achieved renown through the creation of an ambitious encyclopedia of human knowledge that came to be known as the *Rasail Ikhwan al-Safa* or 'Epistles of the Brethren of Purity'. It contains some 52 'epistles' covering every aspect of learning of the time, from arithmetic and geometry, music and magic, to logic and metaphysics. The *Epistles* aimed to explain all that an educated person may wish to know. In this respect, the work is squarely within the Muslim ethical tradition which consistently stresses the crucial significance of knowledge and intelligence in human moral development, hence serving as a vast manual of self-improvement and summary of human knowledge.

One of these *Epistles* presents a surprising and highly original fable, 'The Case of the Animals versus Man before the King of the Jinn'.[16] Set on the mythical island of Balasaghun 'in the midst of the Green Sea, which lies near the equator', the tale describes a trial held before Biwarasp the Wise, the king of the *jinn*. Since he is neither human nor animal, the king of the *jinn* – one of those beings described in the Quran as made of 'pure fire' – can be impartial. The animals, who have taken refuge on his island to escape human mistreatment, complain that now, with the sudden

---

[16] *The Case of the Animals versus Man before the King of the Jinn: A Tenth-Century Fable of the Pure Brethren of Basra*, tr. L.E. Goodman (Boston, 1978). Some passages of this translation have now been revised in L.E. Goodman, 'Reading *The Case of the Animals versus Man*: Fable and Philosophy in the *Essays* of the Ikhwan al-Safa,' in N. El-Bizri, ed., *The Ikhwan al-Safa' and their Rasa'il: An Introduction* (Oxford, 2008), pp.248–74.

arrival of a group of settlers, they are being enslaved and abused all over again. Each side presents its case. As in *Kalila and Dimna* (to which it is indebted), the animals speak, and at length; unlike those earlier animal fables, however, the animals are not only articulate but eloquent. It is clear that whatever separates man and beast in the world of the Brethren, it is not that 'rational speech' in which humankind takes such pride. The mule opens the arguments. After a magnificent introduction, in which he waxes poetic (and even displays his knowledge of the Quran!), the mule presents his indictment of human ways. The animals, he notes, 'were inhabitants of the earth before the creation of Adam'; they lived in peace and harmony, raising their families and all the while 'praising and sanctifying God, and God alone'. But then,

> Men encroached on our ancestral lands. They captured sheep, cows, horses, mules, and asses from among us and enslaved them, subjecting them to the exhausting toil and drudgery of hauling, being ridden, plowing, drawing water, and turning mills. They forced us to these things under duress, with beatings, bludgeoning, and every kind of torture and chastisement our whole lives long. (p.55)

It is a strong indictment, made even stronger by all the animals who testify afterwards; virtually the entire array of crawling, swimming, flying and stalking creatures takes the stand, from elephants, horses and the lowly pig, to larks and owls, lions and leopards, wolves and foxes, crabs and crocodiles, with all sorts of other slithering and chirping witnesses thrown in. The animals have distinct and often charming personalities. Thus, the crocodile defers to the frog whom he calls 'indulgent, dignified, patient, and pious' and whose 'head is round' and whose 'eyes sparkle'. The humans mount their defence, though none of their arguments impresses either the animals or the puzzled king of the *jinn* who, all the while, behind the scenes, is conferring in secret with his wazirs and courtiers.

The fable is a literary masterpiece, as charming as it is profound. Like all great works it raises more questions than it answers. It has a strangely modern ring. Issues of human stew-

Pl. 1 Cockerel from al-Jahiz's *Book of Animals*, an encyclopaedia of early, often fantastic zoology. Muslim artists and authors took much delight in depicting animals, and their interest was ethical as much as scientific in drawing attention to the traits of individual animals.

Pl. 2 Giraffe from al-Jahiz's *Book of Animals*, which says that the giraffe is thought to be a mixture of a wild camel and a wild cow, with a touch of hyena. The rarity and elegance of the giraffe are emphasized by its exquisite saddle-blanket, the proud demeanour of the keeper who leads him and the pink bird flying up in alarm.

Pl. 3 (a) Harem with Birds, from al-Jahiz's *Book of Animals*; (b) the eunuch is typically cast as frivolous though eager to please, and the women as dignified in contrast.

Pl. 4 Dinar of Umayyad caliph
Abd al-Malik, 695. Obverse: standing
with sword and shahada.
Reverse: modefied version
of Byzantine 'Cross on
steps' (below).

Pl. 5 Gold Byzantine coin.
Obverse: Byzantine emperor
with heir apparent.
Reverse: Symbol of 'Cross
on steps'.

Pl. 6 Dinar of Umayyad
caliph Abd al-Malik,
696–697. Obverse:
shahada and
Quran 9:33.
Reverse:
Quran 112's
proclamation
of God's
uniqueness.

Pl. 7 Lustre bowl depicting lion and hare. Fatimid Egypt, 11th century.

Figural imagery (top) Pl. 8, and non-figural imagery (bottom) Pl. 9, on wall decoration of Mshatta palace, 743–4.

Pl. 10 Emperor Jahangir triumphing over poverty, by Abu'l Hasan, Mughal India, c. 1620–5.

Pl. 11 Calligraphic horse,
parasol and bell.
Iran/India, 19th century.

ardship of the earth, of environmental hazards, even of 'animal rights', are hinted at, if not always broached in contemporary terms. The fable, and the 'Epistles' themselves, were created out of a profound and astonishingly forward-looking consciousness; the work embodies what might be called a cosmic ethics.

In the end, unsurprisingly, the humans prevail. They win the case not because they are smarter or more eloquent than the beasts but because human beings alone enjoy the prospect of immortality. The animals themselves are forced to concede this. 'Ah humans,' they say with one voice, 'Now at last you have come to the truth, you have spoken what is right and answered truly. For such claims as you now speak of are indeed something to boast of . . .'

The truth of human immortality appears to be the final lesson, the moral, of the fable, but it is not the whole moral. Furthermore, it is double-edged. Through the various discourses of the animals, the Brethren launched a sweeping satire against mankind. Compared with the exceptional faculties of animals and the orderly innocence of nature in its patterns and seasons, humans are seen as weak, rough, careless and incompetent; one by one, the animals puncture every human pretension. Only the possibility of an afterlife sets us apart and makes us worthy to rule the animals, intrinsically superior though they are; and yet, this is a possibility which humans must strive for and earn. The fable stands finally as a corrective to human pride. The one thing which distinguishes humans, the promise of immortality, is the one thing of which they remain most ignorant. At the same time, however, unlike the grim moral of 'The City of Brass', 'The Case of the Animals' holds out hope. That perhaps is the final moral of the whole long tradition of Muslim ethical literature. The way of knowledge is also the way of hope.

Further Reading

Goodman, Lenn, 'Reading *The Case of the Animals versus Man*: Fable and Philosophy in the *Essays* of the Ikhwan al-Safa', in *The Ikhwan al-Safa' and their Rasa'il: An Introduction*, ed. Nader El-Bizri. Oxford, 2008, pp. 248–74.

Ikhwan al-Safa. *The Case of the Animals versus Man before the King of the Jinn: A Tenth-Century Fable of the Pure Brethren of Basra*, tr. Lenn Goodman. Boston, 1978.

Irwin, Robert. *The Arabian Nights: A Companion*. London, 2004.

al-Jahiz. *The Life and Works of Jahiz*, ed. C. Pellat. Berkeley, CA, 1969.

Landolt, Herman, Samira Sheikh and Kutub Kassam, eds. *An Anthology of Ismaili Literature: A Shiʻi Vision of Islam*. London, 2008.

Marlow, Louise, 'Advice and Advice Literature', in *The Encyclopaedia of Islam*, ed. M. Gaboriau et al. 3rd edn. Leiden, 2007, vol. 1, pp.1–32.

Nasir-i Khusraw. *Nasir-i Khusraw's Book of Travels (Safarnama)*, tr. Wheeler M. Thackston Jr. Costa Mesa, CA, 2001.

Sadi. *The Gulistan (Rose Garden) of Sadi*, tr. Wheeler M. Thackston. Bethesda, MD, 2008.

4

Ecology

Seyyed Hossein Nasr

Over the centuries, Islam has produced traditions of science, art and literature which dealt with the world of nature. The scientific tradition functioned within an Islamic universe of thought, and has much to offer Muslims today as they seek a language that reflects the ethics of their relationship with the natural environment. Indeed, a contemporary Muslim articulation can contribute to the global quest for a way out of the current environmental crisis. This crisis encompasses the natural ecological system that we all share – including the air we breathe, the food we consume, the water we drink, and even the inner workings of our bodies. It endangers the harmony of the whole fabric of life on earth, physical and spiritual alike.

Islamic art complements Islamic science and its expressions, notably in architecture, landscaping and urban design. These are visible applications and embodiments of the Islamic sciences of nature and cosmology. A careful study of the traditional Islamic arts can be an important source of both knowledge and inspiration for creating human living spaces in harmony, rather than discord, with the natural environment.

Among the Islamic arts is literature, which in the form of poetry has been able to propagate the most profound teachings on the spiritual significance of nature. Various literatures – from Arabic and Bengali to Persian and Swahili – offer a wealth of material on the Islamic view of the relationships between humans and the natural environment. Recall the verse of the poet Abu Nuwas:

> In everything there resides a sign of Him,
> Providing proof that He is one.

And that of Sadi in his *Gulistan*:

> I am joyous in the world of nature for the world of nature is
> joyous through Him; I am in love with the whole cosmos for the
> whole cosmos comes from Him.

Literature remains today an excellent means for the propagation of that view, not only through recourse to classical works but
also through the help of present-day writers and poets, some of
whom could surely turn their attention to this subject if they were
to be made aware of its crucial importance. These scientific, artistic
and literary traditions draw on Islam's foundational sources, which
have much to say about the moral place of humans in the vast-
ness of the natural environment.

Teachings

The Quran in a sense speaks to all of creation, not just to human
beings, in setting forth its foundational teaching. The cosmos
itself is God's first revelation, and upon the leaves of trees, the
faces of mountains, the features of animals, as well as in the
sounds of the winds and gently flowing brooks, are to be found
the signs (*ayat*) of God. This evokes the primordial revelation –
which is why classical thought refers to both the 'cosmic' and the
'recorded' Quran. The verses of the Quran, the phenomena in the
world of nature, and events within the souls of human beings are
all cast as portents or signs of God by the Quran itself, as in the
verse, 'We shall show them our portents upon the horizons and
within themselves, until it becomes manifest unto them that it is
the truth' (41:53). All creatures in the natural world sing the praise
of God. In destroying any of them, we silence God's worshippers.
   Creation in the Quranic vision is sacred but not divine, for
divinity belongs to God alone. Nature is sacred because it is the
effect of the divine creative act, referred to in the verse, 'But, His

command, when He intendeth a thing, is only that He saith unto it: Be! and it is' (36:81). What issues directly from the will (*irada*) of the One and reflects His wisdom (*hikma*) cannot but be sacred. Nature is not only for our use. It is there to reflect the creative power of God; grace or *baraka* flows in the arteries and veins of the universe. Humans are created as a channel of grace for the cosmic ambience around them.

Creatures in nature not only have a relation with humans and through them with God, but also have a direct relation with God and possess spiritual value. The Islamic paradise is full of animals and plants and is not only crystalline. Creatures will speak directly to God on the Day of Judgement. As Rumi says, 'they are silent here but eloquent there.' He adds in another poem:

> If only creatures had tongues [here below],
> They could lift the veil from the divine mysteries.

Like the Quran whose verses have plural levels of meaning, nature too has inner and outward levels of significance. Each phenomenon that we witness has a deeper or noumenal reality which relates to a higher state of being. Nature is not only a physical domain, a source of power and resource. It is above all the abode of spiritual presence and source for the understanding and contemplation of divine wisdom. We need nature not only to feed and shelter our bodies, but also to nurture our souls; for nature complements the Quran itself as revelation.

A central idea in the Quran is *haqq*, which means at once truth, reality, right, law and due. *Al-Haqq* is among the 'names of God', and indeed of the Quran itself. This idea is of utmost importance in grasping the human relationship to the natural environment. Each being exists by virtue of the truth (*haqq*) and is also owed its due (*haqq*) according to its nature. Trees have their due, as do animals and even rivers and mountains. In dealing with nature, human beings must respect and pay what is due to each creature; each creature has its corresponding claims or rights. Islam stands totally against the idea that humans have all the rights and other creatures have none except what we give them. The rights of creatures were accorded by God; they are not to be treated arbitrarily by humans.

The Quran speaks of human beings as both in the service of God (*abd Allah*) and as vicegerents of God (*khilafat Allah*). We may practise our vicegerency on earth on condition that we obey His will and laws. Nowhere does the Quran give humans the right to dominate nature without protecting it and acting as its steward. All claims or rights, in other words, come with responsibilities toward God and His creation.

In word and deed, the daily life of Muhammad, the Prophet of Islam, sought to reflect the teachings of the Quran. He encouraged the planting of trees, forbade the destruction of vegetation even in war, displayed great kindness to animals and encouraged Muslims to do likewise. He established protected areas for natural life, which may be considered Islamic prototypes for contemporary natural parks and nature conservancies. The traditions or hadith of the Prophet show a constant concern about wastefulness of resources such as water, and harm that greed and sheer negligence could inflict on nature. Famously, he pronounced that it was a blessed act even on the day before the end of the world to plant a tree.

What might be called a 'theology of nature' emerges from the philosophical tradition of Islam, which finds particularly strong expression in Sufism. For it is here that the spirit of the inner teaching of the Quran on man and nature is given foremost attention.[1] One illustration is the account that a celebrated Sufi figure, Ibn Arabi (c. 1165–1240), gives about the Prophet. It relates to a well-known tradition about the reclining palm tree of Seville:

> In the vicinity of the Cemetery of Mushka [in Seville] . . . there was a palm tree which, as one could see, was leaning over a great deal. The people in the neighbouring houses, fearing that it might

[1] Seyyed Hossein Nasr, 'The Ecological Problem in Light of Sufism', in *Sufi Essays*, ed. S.H. Nasr (2nd edn, Albany, NY, 1991), pp.152–63; William Chittick, 'God Surrounds All Things: An Islamic Perspective on the Environment', *The World and I*, 1 (1986), pp.671–78.

fall on their homes and damage them, complained to the local ruler who, in response to their concern, ordered it to be cut down. Those who were going to cut it down arrived at the place after the evening prayer and said: 'It will soon be dark. Let us cut it down tomorrow, if God wills' . . .

Now, it so happened that one of our companions [had a vision in which] he saw the Envoy of God—may God bless him and give him peace—sitting in a mosque situated in the middle of the Cemetery of Mushka. [And he saw how] the palm tree in question was ploughing through the ground with its roots until it arrived at his side. It then complained to him that the people wanted to cut it down on account of its curvature, for fear that it might harm their houses, and it said to him, 'O Envoy of God, pray for me!'

The person who had the vision related that the Envoy of God then placed his hand on the palm tree, which immediately straightened, remaining upright and erect, and returned to its place.

In the morning, when the people got up, I went with a group of individuals to establish the veracity of that vision and we all saw that it had straightened up and become erect, without any curvature.[2]

Would that present-day Muslims recall this account when they next wish to cut down a tree for the sake of convenience!

Not surprisingly, this plenitude of teaching finds its way into the practical guidance of the sharia. Natural resources that are used by the community as a whole, such as water and forests, are deemed public property to be suitably conserved. Animals and plants must be treated with proper respect. The ritual killing of animals that can be eaten and whose flesh then becomes *halal* or permissible is of profound import in creating a spiritual bond with the natural world. As well, sharia guidance on economic life – including opposition to wasteful consumerism and to the

---

[2] See Pablo Beneito Arias, 'Life of the Prophet and Miracles of the Palm Tree', *Journal of Muhayiddin Ibn 'Arabi Society*, 30 (2001), pp.88–91. This visionary episode was made famous throughout the Islamic world by its mention in the work of the 13th-century Persian scholar, Zakariya al-Qazwini.

excessive amassing of wealth – clearly have an impact on how humans relate to the larger environment.

All in all, the sharia provides a degree of legitimacy for progressive social conduct toward the environment which secular laws alone can hardly command.

Realities

When one considers the Islamic view of nature and humankind's relation to it, as well as how classical Muslim civilisation created urban settings largely in harmony with nature, the situation in the Muslim world today does not compare well. For those uprooted from rural settings, there are often squalid conditions in larger towns and cities where the healthier ecological practices of earlier generations no longer prevail. Yet in most of the Muslim world, where all ethics have a religious basis, Islam as a faith is robust. Mosques are teeming, and on Fridays thousands listen to preachers on various secular as well as religious matters. Books and media programmes dealing with Islam have a vast readership and audience. What, then, are the challenges to knowing and putting into practice the ecological traditions and teachings of Islam?

The present environmental crisis is directly related to the use of modern technology and the various applications of modern science. One can see this in problems as far apart as the rise in population due to the practice of modern medicine and global warming caused by a set of complex industrial factors. Modern science and technology also provide those who possess them with power – which is why, of course, the West is globally dominant at this time. Muslim governments and many Muslim individuals want to gain better access to this science and technology. Yet they are at the receiving end of what is constantly changing and needs to be borrowed anew. There is no pause in the development of newer forms of technology which might allow Muslim societies to 'humanise' certain aspects of it, and tame its negative environmental impact.[3]

---

[3] Ivan Illich's observations a generation ago still hold true: see his *Tools for Conviviality* (New York, 1980).

Consider, for example, biotechnology, which the West has recently developed. Already the global impact in the fields of medicine and agriculture is obvious. Muslims did not invent the problems arising from genetically altered crops. But they must now grapple with them, as they must grapple with the ethical consequences of cloning. Muslims, like nearly all other non-westerners (except perhaps the Japanese), have to accept the fact that here too the West runs the playing field. This poses a huge challenge to Muslim societies if they wish both to implement Islamic principles involved and to play the game. If they choose not to do so, external pressures become so great as to force them to enter the playing field. Only smaller units may in some cases remain separate and not participate in the game of the day.

A culture of 'scientism' is now commonplace both in the West and beyond: in this view, scientific method is the only reasonable way to understand reality, and hence in giving us access to truth. This makes science (and technology) an end in itself. Although the number of advanced scientists in the Muslim world is relatively small, scientism has a fairly substantial following there as well. They tend to see the Islamic tradition of science simply as a prelude to modern science, not as a different science with a special view of nature.[4] Besides, even so-called fundamentalists are in favour of the propagation of modern science and technology, as a means of partaking in its global advance. There is little appreciation of the need to cultivate once again an Islamic ethic in science.

On a more practical level, there is the problem of mass migration to urban areas, with the high cost mentioned earlier for how the environment is treated as a result. This global phenomenon is no less serious in the Muslim world. Survival is such a challenge for most of these urban migrants and their families, that their physical habitats receive little attention. Trees, water flows, soil conservation and the like are luxuries; municipal measures in this regard are, all too often, simply ignored. Among the most

---

[4] See Seyyed Hossein Nasr, *Science and Civilisation in Islam* (Chicago, 1968) and *The Encounter of Man and Nature* (London, 1978).

conspicuous examples of this reality today are the old city in Fez in Morocco, and the heart of Cairo; both are plagued by the ecological debris of modernity. There was a time in the lives of migrants when in their rural environment, a tree outside was *their* tree to be protected, and a stream flowing by their house was *their* stream, not to be polluted. That ethic no longer holds for them in the towns and cities that they inhabit.

In confronting these challenges, governments in the Muslim world are too ready to follow models of development that are western.[5] There has lately been a rise in 'green groups' among citizens in countries such as Iran, with some success in resisting the destruction of the environment. But in many Muslim societies, such groups have limited public space for opposition to official policies. Indeed, even where they do, the agendas of such groups frequently tend to ignore indigenous traditions – including Islamic ones – of conservation. Yet these are not only practically relevant, but also have strong legitimacy.

This brings us finally to the issue of public education. One notes the lack of awareness and preparation of the *ulama* or traditional scholars, who have the ear of so many Muslims in all matters, secular and religious alike. Historically, the *ulama* often spoke to congregations about kindness to animals and the virtue of planting trees as the Prophet had commanded. But issues of biodiversity and global warming require an education on their part that is attuned to contemporary social and economic affairs, and this is generally lacking. Challenges of cultural and political identity are at the forefront of 'modern' education, as a result of colonialism and its legacy. Today, the effects of globalisation tend to draw out the same dominant concern. A number of eminent *ulama* – such as the late grand mufti of Syria, Shaykh Ahmad Kuftaro – have spoken on the need for environmental responsibility. To be fair,

---

[5] Recall the experience of the Egyptian architect Hasan Fathy (1900–89), whose pioneering housing projects for the poor encountered limited success amid lack of support from both public officials who were attached to standard western models, and also from the beneficiaries themselves. See his *Architecture for the Poor: An Experiment in Rural Egypt* (Chicago, 1973).

even in the West, Christian and Jewish thinkers only recently turned their attention to the 'theology of nature'. One can only encourage these trends, given the scope of the influence that traditional scholars can exercise in influencing public opinion.

What Is to Be Done?

The scientism that is so widespread today not only in the West but beyond, needs urgent correction if we are to respond seriously to the challenges posed by the environmental crisis. A sacralised vision of nature is central to Islam. Retrieving this way of seeing the world means clearing the ground of ruinous materialist ideologies that cloud our thinking. Only then can we come to grips once again with the tradition of respect for the natural environment and our place in it. This requires articulation in the clearest possible way, so that it is accessible to Muslims at large. Neither the philosopher nor the cobbler and the peasant must feel left out. Poetry, sermons and metaphysics all have their role in this process. Much already exists in this regard, but has not as yet been widely disseminated.

In the training of those who govern societies and exercise leadership in civil society, it is critical to introduce courses on the environment at all levels, as well as to include themes relating to the environment in the teaching of other fields. For example, it is almost criminally negligent to teach engineering without drawing attention to the environmental impact of various projects. Likewise, economic planning should never be taught without consideration of the environmental costs involved. The West has been more successful in this matter in recent years than the Muslim world, because modern educational institutions in the Muslim world simply emulate the West and are therefore usually a step behind.

Nor should such initiatives be limited to secular educational institutions. Places of traditional learning such as *madrassas*, where future community and religious leaders are often trained, should be part of the trend. The effect on the way in which these leaders then relate to governments and ordinary Muslims alike will surely be enormous. Yet for this educational effort to succeed there is the need to teach these matters by drawing on Islamic as well as contemporary western perspectives. Favourable starts have been made in this regard here and there, but not in any organised manner that puts the environment at the core of traditional curricula across the Muslim world.

The media has a key role to play in all educational initiatives, secular and religious. *Ulama* in the Muslim world give sermons on television, radio and the internet, where environmental teaching can become critical. True, the amount of freedom that they have is not unlimited, but ways need to be found for political authorities to see such initiatives as integral to good governance. Indeed, government officials, civil society leaders and scholars can use the media themselves to get the word out. And so can responsible media itself through documentary films and talks.

Nongovernmental organisations (NGOs) and less formal associations, both local and global, have begun to have an impact in the Muslim world and should play a robust role here.[6] They are a sign of healthy civil society, whether devoted exclusively to issues of conservation or to sensitivity to the environmental impact of specific public or private projects. In the West, civil society groups have played a vital part in shaping public opinion; some have gone as far as to establish trusts that acquire pristine land and forested areas in order to preserve such natural resources. There is no reason why such civil society groups cannot expand in the Muslim world, including such institutions as religious endowments or *awqaf*, rather then simply imitating western models. There are many such endowments for the creation of mosques, schools and hospitals. Why should they not also safeguard water, soils, trees and animals?

Initiatives are also required for new respect for the use of indigenous technologies, in the face of our blindness to the perils of so many modern technological choices. This is true of areas ranging from irrigation to medical drugs. Alternative technologies that need less energy and have a more benign impact on the natural environment are already sought actively (though not adequately,

---

[6] See Richard Foltz, ed., *Environmentalism in the Muslim World* (New York, 2005).

of course) even in advanced industrial societies. This is entirely in keeping with an Islamic approach to nature, and needs plenty of encouragement in Muslim contexts by civil society groups and governments.

Among the various forms of encouragement that are used today to further the cause of what the government or society or religious establishments consider to be important is the use of awards of recognition. They may be local, national and global. In the Muslim world, such awards are given for artistic creation, books and services to the cause of Islam. But rarely is there an award of recognition for services to the environment. Surely it is time for this to happen, mindful of what it can also do to raise and educate public consciousness.

Conclusion

It cannot be only governments that have responsibility for the environment, and the ethics that go with it. It is true that they wield more power than anyone else, but these are matters for all of society. No transformations in society ever take place simply from the top down. On the contrary, it is usually a small number of committed individuals and groups that take the lead. Ultimately, a new ecological consciousness and changed social behaviour will require civil society as well as the state to pull together. One hopes that the realisation of the urgency of this will be timely.

Above all, the environmental crisis calls for us to recognise not just its outward effects, but also its spiritual and religious dimensions. A perspective that is true to Islamic teachings needs to be articulated with rigour and clarity. There are forgotten traditions to be retrieved and fresh ways of understanding and applying them today. Only then can we speak properly of an 'ethics of the environment'. For Muslims, one of the names of God is *al-Muhit*, the All-Pervading – or, in the present context, quite literally, our 'environment'.

Further Reading

Deen, Mawil Y.I. *The Environmental Dimensions of Islam.* Cambridge, 2000.

Dwivedi, O.P., ed. *World Religions and the Environment.* New Delhi, 1989.

Folz, Richard. *Animals in Islamic Tradition and Muslim Cultures.* Oxford, 2006.

—— Frederick Denny and Azizan Baharuddin, eds. *Islam and Ecology: A Bestowed Trust.* Cambridge, MA, 2003.

Haq, Nomanul. 'Islam', in Dale Jamieson, ed. *A Companion to Environmental Philosophy.* London, 2001, pp.111–29.

Helminski, Camille, ed. *The Book of Nature: An Anthology of Spiritual Perspectives on Nature.* Chicago, 2006.

Khalid, Fazlun M. and Joanne O'Brien, eds. *Islam and Ecology.* New York, 1992.

Nasr, Seyyed Hossein. *Man and Nature: The Spiritual Crisis of Modern Man.* Chicago, 1967.

—— 'Islam and the Environmental Crisis', in S. Rockefeller and J. Elder, eds. *Spirit and Nature: Why the Environment is a Religious Issue.* Boston, 1992, pp.83–108.

Peterson, Anna L. *Being Human: Ethics, Environment, and Our Place in the World.* Berkeley, CA, 2001.

5

Art

Fahmida Suleman

To oversee [the potters] there shall be appointed a trustworthy man who knows their craft and their corrupt practices . . . The porcelain must be of even texture, of the accustomed mould, perfectly glazed . . . They must be sound so that food can be placed in them without their breaking in the hand of any person holding them . . . [Pottery kilns] must not be heated with human or other dung, which is unclean, but with esparto grass, rice husks or similar things . . . If a customer comes to purchase a hundred vessels from a porcelain-maker he must not confine himself to displaying a single vessel and afterwards deliver something different. That is fraudulent . . . [Painters] similarly must swear not to provide adulterated goods and that they will paint three times anything which they sell to the public and will expose it to the sun before delivery to the owner . . . They must be forbidden to paint pictures. The Apostle cursed painters of figures. According to a tradition, he said: 'Those who fashion images will be punished and commanded on the Day of Resurrection to bring their creations to life.'[1]

The 14th-century counsel quoted here is typical of what the manual of a market inspector (*muhtasib*) set forth on the proper public

---

[1] Quoted in Reuben Levy, ed., *The Ma'alim al-qurba fi ahkam al-hisba of Diya' al-Din Muhammad ibn Muhammad al-Qurashi al-Shafi'i known as Ibn al-Ukhuwwa (d.1329)* (Cambridge, 1938), pp.89, 96.

behaviour of artisans and other vendors. Every Muslim was to uphold the essential ethic of 'commanding right and forbidding wrong' (Quran, 3:104); and it was the inspector's role to apply this in supervising the marketplace. The *muhtasib* was a man known for his integrity as well as his competence in matters of law. He ensured that every aspect of the sale and purchase of goods was – from the accuracy of scales to the quality of workmanship and the state of hygiene – beyond reproach. After an initial reprimand, more serious penalties that the *muhtasib* could impose included beating and a parade in disgrace through the streets, the confiscation of incorrect weights and faulty products, and a full veto on trading.

Indeed, the inspectorate also took a lively interest in how artisanal goods were decorated. According to the manual quoted above, the painting of pictures was forbidden, and the Prophet is alleged to have cursed painters of figures – presumably human and animal figures. Yet, if we survey the plurality of medieval Islamic artefacts and architecture from across the Iberian Peninsula to Central Asia, we find an abundance of human and animal imagery. The very fact that the prohibition against the depiction of figural imagery was specifically mentioned in this manual from Mamluk Egypt attests to the practice. Moreover, the discussion of the ethics and permissibility of figural art in Islam was not merely a medieval problem; the debate has continued relevance in society today.

In 2001, the destruction of the monumental rock-cut Buddhas of Bamiyan by the former Taliban government of Afghanistan was justified by the regime as follows: 'These statues have been and remain shrines of unbelievers and these unbelievers continue to worship and respect them. God Almighty is the only real shrine [*taghut*] and all fake idols should be destroyed.' The institution that was responsible for carrying out the destruction of these and other statues in the region was the 'Ministry of the Promotion of Virtue and Suppression of Vice', a title that recalls the *muhtasib*'s duties of moral policing. There was widespread Muslim condemnation of this defiling of an ancient heritage; yet the consequences of the Taliban's actions were summed up by the art historian

Finbarr Flood: 'There can be little doubt that the destruction of the Buddhas will define "Islamic iconoclasm" in the popular imagination for several decades to come and it will reinforce the widespread notion that Islamic culture is implacably hostile to anthropomorphic [human figural] art.'[2]

What gave rise to this widespread idea of an Islamic aversion to figural art? How does it square with the history of Muslim attitudes toward figural representation? Is it more accurate to describe Islam as 'aniconic', that is, as being averse to idols and similar images, rather than being opposed to figural art as such? This chapter turns for answers to the foundational periods of Islam, to grasp the particular contexts in which important choices were made about the use of figural art. It becomes evident that the ethical codes which guided artisans, patrons, consumers and the *muhtasib* in the past were richly varied in the practices of Umayyad, Fatimid and Mughal societies. This in turn allows us to locate modern perspectives and choices in their proper cultural, social and theological settings.

Images and Icons

In describing Muslim attitudes to the arts, the terms 'aniconism' and 'iconoclasm' are often used as if they mean the same thing. Iconoclasm (Greek *eikon*, 'image', 'likeness' + *klas*, 'to break') is about the breaking of images, and doctrines that seek to justify this. An iconoclast is a person who destroys or mutilates existing figural images. In contrast, aniconism (Greek *an-*, negative prefix, 'without' + *eikon*, 'image', 'likeness') means 'without images', or the absence of any representations. Which of these appropriately describes early Muslim attitudes to figural art?

The Holy Quran does not provide explicit guidance on representational art. But it does mention the use of idols in worship in this verse (6:74) about the prophet Ibrahim (Abraham):

---

[2] Finbarr Barry Flood, 'Between Cult and Culture: Bamiyan, Islamic Iconoclasm, and the Museum', *The Art Bulletin*, 84 (2002), pp.641, 655.

And when Ibrahim said to his father, Azar: 'Do you take idols [*asnam*] for gods? Surely I see you and your people in manifest error.'

The Arabic word *asnam* is taken to mean images or statues, perhaps in the shape of animals and humans, that could be used as idols. In this context, the Quran clearly opposes the adoration or worship of idols. It does not reject representational art as such, nor the making of images, only their worship.

One of the 99 Beautiful Names of Allah *(al-Asma al-husna)* is *al-Musawwir*, which invokes God's attribute as 'the Fashioner' or 'the Bestower of Forms and Shapes'. The attribute *al-Musawwir* and its verbal forms appear several times in the Quran, uniquely with reference to the divine creative impulse:

He it is who shapes you [*yusawwirukum*] in the wombs as He likes; there is no god but He, the Mighty, the Wise. (3:6)

He is Allah the Creator [*al-Khaliq*], the Maker [*al-Bari*], the Fashioner [*al-Musawwir*]; His are the most excellent names; whatever is in the heavens and the earth declares His glory; and He is the Mighty, the Wise. (59:24)

It is sometimes argued that God's power as creator and giver of life must not be mimicked through representational art. In this vein, the artist that dares to depict living creatures is deemed an impious fraud who chooses to compete with the incomparable *al-Musawwir*. Oliver Leaman, a scholar of Islamic philosophy, recalls the teaching of the Andalusian polymath Ibn Rushd (Averroes) (c. 1126–1198) in rejecting this view:

God's pivotal role as creator does not invalidate human attempts at creation, although no doubt what we mean by creation when it is carried out by human beings is very different from divine creation . . . [Ibn Rushd argues that] God as creator, then, represents the perfect example of creator, in that he is entirely unconstrained in his creation . . . His creatures, by contrast, can create

but we are very limited, we need something to create out of and
our ideas about what to create are limited.[3]

We have from the lifetime of the Prophet accounts that have
been interpreted both in favour of and against the idea of a fresh
stance on figural representation. A well-known example relates to
the idols in the Kaaba, a legacy of its pre-Islamic importance as
a place of worship. One of many accounts of an episode in 630
holds that Muhammad destroyed several hundred of the idols but
left an image of the Virgin Mary with baby Jesus intact. This
suggests that figural representations as such did not pose a theological problem to him, though worshipping them clearly did.

In another incident, the Prophet's wife, Aisha, is said to have
hung a curtain with images of winged horses (or birds) on a wall
of their house, which prompted the Prophet to say: 'Take this
thing away: every time I enter it makes me think of this world.'
According to a variant of this account, the Prophet said: 'Take this
thing away, I keep thinking of the images on it while I am praying.'
Aisha reportedly took down the curtain and cut it into pieces to
sew cushions out of it, implying that images on cushions were
less obtrusive and hence permissible. There are other such narratives from Muhammad's household. The upshot is that figural
images appear to be problematic when they distract – not merely
because they exist. This provides a plausible basis for the long-
standing practice of decorating the interiors and exteriors of
mosques with calligraphic, geometric and vegetal designs while
avoiding the use of both human and animal imagery.

Yet there are accounts of a stricter view of images. Typical
examples of hadiths that have an iconoclastic tone have the Prophet
saying: 'Angels do not enter a house in which there is a dog, an
image, or a ritually impure person.' In a similar vein, Muhammad
is said to have proclaimed: 'Those who will be severely punished
on the Day of Judgement are the murderer of a prophet, one who
is put to death by a prophet, a false imam who leads men astray,
and a maker of images or pictures.' A third example: 'Those who

---

[3] Oliver Leaman, *Islamic Aesthetics: An Introduction* (Edinburgh, 2004), p.47.

make images will be punished on the Day of Resurrection and they will be called upon to breathe life in them, but they will not succeed in this task.'[4]

Traditions of this kind may have been a factor historically in encouraging acts of iconoclasm. But it is unclear how widespread these ideas were during the earliest periods of Islam, since hadith material was only compiled from the mid-eighth and ninth centuries – at least a century after the Prophet's death – and reflects in part the judgements and attitudes of a later time. Could the issue of the permissibility of figural art have arisen in the eighth century because many jurists and hadith collectors were taking up secular occupations in the arts and crafts? These 'day jobs' included decorating walls, roofs and furniture, trades that were frowned upon by scholars such as al-Ghazali because of their link to figural art.[5]

On balance, a reading of the Quran and at least some hadith suggests that there was indeed a concern with the worship of images, rather than with the idea of figural representation. Although some hadith express iconoclastic sentiments and the Prophet is reported to have destroyed images in the Kaaba, he did not after all destroy the image of the Madonna and Child there. Nor did he appear to be disturbed by figural art in home life if they did not interfere with religious practice. One may conclude that the earliest Islamic attitudes were more likely aniconic with respect to religious contexts, not iconoclastic. We turn next to material evidence from the reign of the Umayyads, the first Muslim dynasty.

Sacred and Secular: The Umayyads

The ancient city of Damascus became the capital of the Umayyad caliphate in 661, until the ascent of the Abbasids in 750. We know

---

[4] These hadiths and their variants are discussed in Dan van Reenan's fine study, 'The *Bilderverbot*, A New Survey', *Der Islam*, 67 (1990), pp.27–77, esp. pp.42–4, 51.

[5] See H.J. Cohen, 'The Economic Background and the Secular Occupations of Muslim Jurisprudents and Traditionists in the Classical Period of Islam (Until the Middle of the Eleventh Century)', *Journal of the Economic and Social History of the Orient*, 13 (1970), pp.16–61, at p.31.

from the extant wall paintings and sculpture found at the Umayyad desert palace ruins in Jordan and Palestine that figural imagery flourished in Muslim art and architecture at this time. There may well have been hadith circulating then which cautioned against icons, but this appears not to have discouraged secular figural art. In contrast, religious architecture such as the Dome of the Rock in Jerusalem and the Great Mosque of Damascus was entirely devoid of animal and human imagery. Why did the early Muslims favour vegetal and geometric designs over figural ones in mosques?

According to Oleg Grabar, the public or official art of early Islam – which includes coinage and religious architecture – should be understood as aniconic.[6] The private arts, on the other hand, could be energetically iconic. During the first decade of his reign, the fifth Umayyad caliph Abd al-Malik (r. 685–705) experimented with a variety of figural images and symbols for his official coinage (Pl. 4). However, in 696–7, he revolutionised the appearance of Muslim coinage by adopting a purely epigraphic (i.e. calligraphic) or aniconic design in order to publicly distinguish the now well-established polity from the Byzantine and former Sasanian empires.

Up until this time, Muslim rulers had continued to circulate coinage of the former regimes that featured ruler portraits combined with Christian or Zoroastrian symbols (Pl. 5). Abd al-Malik's newly conceived coinage – using legible Arabic Kufic script – included the Muslim profession of faith or *shahada*, that there is no god but Allah and Muhammad is His messenger, alongside specific Quranic verses about Muhammad's mission as the chosen and final messenger of the omnipotent deity (Pl. 6). This design distinguished Muslim coinage both visually and doctrinally from existing Byzantine and Sasanian coinage and remained the standard template of Islamic coinage for centuries.

Umayyad choices in artistic design, from the abstract vegetal wall mosaics in the Dome of the Rock to epigraphic coinage, were likely influenced by what was seen as Quranic guidance against using figures in worship but not against all representation. This

---

[6] Oleg Grabar, 'Islamic Attitudes Toward the Arts', in Oleg Grabar, ed., *The Formation of Islamic Art* (New Haven and London, 1987), pp.72–98.

attitude is most neatly exemplified at the Umayyad palace complex of Mshatta in the Jordan desert, built in the eighth century. The external walls of this building are covered in stone-carved representations of humans, animals and elaborate vegetal motifs (Pl. 8). But no figural motifs appear on the external wall that corresponds to the *qibla* wall (facing Mecca) of the mosque inside (Pl. 9). Clearly, the avoidance of figural representation in a sacred or religious context was deliberate and systematic. It would not be accurate to see this as an iconoclastic response to images, since the remaining walls of the Mshatta complex include images of birds, beasts and humans.

The absence of figural representations in mosques was to become the norm across the Muslim world, though this did not always extend to other religious buildings, such as shrines. For example, the 13th-century star-and-cross lustre tiles from the Imamzadeh Jafar shrine at Damghan in northeastern Iran are decorated with animals and verses from the *Shahnameh* (Book of Kings) of Firdausi.[7] In a similar vein, with the exception of illuminated Qurans, religious manuscripts such as Sufi tracts and stories about the lives of the prophets have traditionally included figural images to accompany the texts. Thus, an illustrated text of the 12th-century Sufi epic *Mantiq al-Tayr* (Conference of the Birds) of Farid al-Din Attar was donated by the Safavid ruler Shah Abbas to his dynastic shrine at Ardabil in northwestern Iran. Another vibrant example is an Uighur Turkic manuscript, dated 1436, with depictions of the Prophet's ascension (*meraj*) to the heavens.[8]

---

[7] Admittedly, this was not universally approved of; on occasion, even images of birds have been defiled, presumably as profane. See Venetia Porter, *Islamic Tiles* (London, 1995), p.36.

[8] Sheila Canby, *Shah 'Abbas: The Remaking of Iran* (London, 2008), pp.170–1; Marie-Rose Séguy, *The Miraculous Journey of Mahomet: Mirâj Nâmeh* (London, 1977).

A Flowering of Figural Imagery: The Fatimids

Give your attention to the merchants and artisans and your best
consideration to their submissions . . . they are the source [of well-
being] of the people. The people profit from their products and
from what they import for their use and comfort . . . Thus these
classes have their own rights and dignity, which need protection.[9]

Admonitions against images in art are nowhere to be found in the
10th-century legal compendium of the Fatimid state, *Pillars of
Islam*, composed by the dynasty's leading official jurist, Qadi
al-Nu'man. On the contrary, innovative artists appear to have enjoyed
an elevated status during the Fatimid period (909–1171). The sources
even recount an episode at court when a painting contest was
organised by the wazir al-Yazuri during the reign of the Caliph-
imam al-Mustansir billah in the eleventh century. Two renowned
painters, an Egyptian and an Iraqi, competed to produce images of
dancing girls in a three-dimensional style so that they appeared to
be entering into and emerging out of a wall. Both painters were
publicly rewarded with robes of honour and bags of gold.[10]

In his famous 11th-century book on optics, Ibn al-Haytham
(Alhazen), the great physicist and mathematician who worked in
Cairo, wrote of painters whose clever use of coloured pigments
and skilled draughtsmanship allowed them to reproduce three-
dimensional figures on smooth two-dimensional surfaces. He
argued that by including realistic details such as 'hair, the pores
and wrinkles on their skin, and the creases in their clothes . . .

---

[9] Qadi al-Nu'man, *Da'a'im al-Islam*, tr. Asaf A.A. Fyzee, revised by Ismail
K. Poonawala (New Delhi, 2002), vol. 1, p.453.
[10] Richard Ettinghausen, 'Painting in the Fatimid Period: A Reconstruction',
Ars Islamica, 9 (1942), pp.112–13. The Persian emissary Nasir-i Khusraw
describes al-Mustansir's dais at the palace as decorated with 'hunting and
sporting scenes' and 'marvellous calligraphy', and banquet tables with 'thousands of images and statuettes in sugar': Nasir-i Khusraw, *Safar-nama*, tr.
W.M. Thackston Jr, *Naser-e Khosraw's Book of Travels (Safarnama)* (New
York, 1986), pp.56–7.

pictures [of individual people] will be perceived to be like the
forms they represent if those who made them were skilled in the
art of painting'.[11]

The large number of signed pieces of Fatimid Egyptian lustre
pottery with both figural and nonfigural designs may also indicate
artists' heightened sense of pride in their work and the public recognition of individual potters. Much of the art produced during this
period is characterised by a lively style of depiction and an inventive use of designs. The most notable and best-preserved artefacts
range from carved woodwork, ivory and rock crystal to woven
textiles, gold jewellery and glazed ceramics. Artisans drew inspiration from a variety of sources including contemporary urban and
courtly culture, oral and written literature, in addition to artistic
traditions beyond the Mediterranean world. Epigraphic decoration
was also included in the repertoire with timeless words of wisdom
inscribed on objects, such as 'Forgive [others] and you will be forgiven
[by God]' and 'Be happy with a little and you will have a lot'. Objects
also included benedictions such as 'perpetual glory and prosperity',
'blessings [*baraka*] to the owner' and 'perfect health and happiness'.

The use of moral phrases as decorative inscription is not unique
to the arts of Fatimid Egypt.[12] However, the Egyptian lustre potter
deftly coupled such inscriptions with skilful line-drawn designs,
such as on a bowl featuring a lion and a hare (Pl. 7). Animals, birds
and fantastic creatures abound in Fatimid art and are often interpreted as emblems of good fortune. The image on this particular
bowl was likely inspired by fable literature.[13] This calls attention

---

[11] Ibn al-Haytham, *The Optics of Ibn al-Haytham, Books I–III: On Direct
Vision*, tr. Abdelhamid Sabra (London, 1989), Book 3, p.39.

[12] Among the most accomplished works bearing such aphorisms are Samanid
epigraphic wares produced in Eastern Iran or Transoxiana in the 10th and
11th centuries. See Oya Pancaroğlu, *Perpetual Glory: Medieval Islamic Ceramics
from the Harvey B. Plotnick Collection* (New Haven and London, 2007), pp.64–
71.

[13] See Esin Atil, 'Humor and Wit in Islamic Art', *Asian Art & Culture*, 7
(1994), pp.15–16; and Fahmida Suleman, *The Lion, the Hare and Lustre Ware:
Studies in the Iconography of Lustre Ceramics from Fatimid Egypt*, unpub-
lished DPhil thesis (Oxford, 2004).

to the use of figural images as tools of ethical instruction in the medieval Muslim world – parallel to the use of storytelling for ethical ends, discussed in Eric Ormsby's chapter in this volume.

Instructive Images

Ibn al-Muqaffa's purpose in translating and adapting the Pahlavi text of the *Kalila wa Dimna* into Arabic in the eighth century was manifold. He sought to engage the youth through the vehicle of animal fables; to delight the hearts of princes through richly illus-trated depictions of the tales; to entice kings and common folk everywhere to acquire their own copies and thus benefit the painters and scribes; and to engage the philosophers in the wisdom of its tales. Already at this early stage in Islamic history, figural paint-ings as illustrative accompaniments to entertaining and didactic literary texts went hand in hand. Medieval scholars also expounded on the power and positive aspects of images, such as the thera-peutic benefits attained through gazing at beautiful pictures. Authors presented figural images – in two- and three-dimensional forms – as means of ethical instruction, sources of talismanic wonder and products of divine inspiration.

One exemplar was Muhammad b. Mahmud b. Ahmad-i Tusi, who was active in 12th-century Iran under the Seljuk dynasty. For Tusi, images could alter one's emotional state so that a person would be reminded of eternal truths, such as death. While he denounced the veneration of images, in line with the Quranic ethos, Tusi 'relates the danger of idolatry to a weakness of the human will and not to the images themselves'. He refers to the Buddhas of Bamiyan, which were believed to smile when the sun shone on them since, like other benevolent talismanic images, they were attuned to God's will. Tusi describes them thus:

In the region of Bamiyan, there is a place called 'Astar Bahar'. They have made two statues, each one 250 cubits tall with crowns on their heads. They call one 'White Idol' [*khing but*] and the other 'Red Idol' [*surkh but*]. In their nose, pigeons have nests. When the sun rises, they both smile. This I have seen in many books but the meaning of their smiles is not known, God knows best. This smile should not be [thought] strange, for whatever the sun shines on cheerfulness and joviality appear in it and that thing inclines toward the sun.[14]

In other words, the Bamiyan statues are understood as reflections of divine grace that are meant to cause wonder and amazement. Although they are not products of an Islamic culture, they function and are appreciated as among God's signs for all humankind. Interestingly, medieval Islamic society did not develop a strong tradition of three-dimensional sculpture. Rather, calligraphy and the arts of the book were accorded special importance and reached great heights.

The arts of the book, in all their expressive power, took on extraordinary significance under the patronage of the Safavid, Mughal and Ottoman dynasties. Several traditions of Islamic figural painting had developed by this time and artists worked together to produce manuscripts of the highest quality in the royal workshops. One of the hallmarks of Mughal painting was a seamless blending of Persian, Indian and European artistic idioms. The emperors encouraged creative collaborations among their Muslim and Hindu artists, which helped foster an eclectic style. A sample from a 17th-century album illustrates how the Mughal emperor Jahangir effectively used figural imagery to assert his claim as the embodiment of a just and ethical ruler (Pl. 10).[15]

In this allegorical painting, a haloed Jahangir firmly stands on top of a globe and aims a second arrow at a dark enemy across from him – having successfully pierced his target's forehead with the first one. The gaunt naked figure with long grey hair and a beard represents the embodiment of poverty. A number of winged

---

[14] Quoted in Oya Pancaroğlu, 'Signs in the Horizons: Concepts of Image and Boundary in a Medieval Persian Cosmography', *Res: Journal of Anthropology and Aesthetics*, 43 (2003), p.34–5; the article includes a full discussion of Tusi's discourse on images.

[15] I have relied here on Robert Skelton's study of this painting, 'Imperial Symbolism in Mughal Painting', in Priscilla P. Soucek, ed., *Content and Context of Visual Arts in the Islamic World* (Pennsylvania and London, 1988), pp.177–91.

cherubs also feature in the scene. One holds the emperor's arrows, two others bear his divinely conferred crown, and a fourth one grasps a chain of bells embellished with Mongol yak tails (customarily hung from the palace for the benefit of any civilian who wished to raise a complaint to his majesty). Jahangir, whose name translates as 'World-seizer', rests his feet on top of a docile lion that nuzzles cosily next to an unperturbed sheep, symbolising a utopian age. The globe rests on the back of a fish upon which Manu, the legendary Hindu law-giver, stretches out reading his codebook, symbolising the harmony between Muslim and Hindu laws under Jahangir's just rule. The painter, probably the famous court artist Abul Hasan, added a descriptive label below the flying cherubs: 'The auspicious likeness of his Exalted Majesty, who casts economic sickness [penury] from the universe with his beneficent arrow and refashions the world with his justice and equity.'

Whether or not Jahangir was the true embodiment of justice and equity is arguable. Yet the world in which he and contemporary Muslim rulers operated was filled with richly complex figural imagery which conveyed Islamic ideals of governance.

Conclusion

This short survey of Islamic art spanning over nine centuries suggests that artistic expression within the context of the mosque remained aniconic, to avoid distraction when praying to God as well as the peril of image worship. This is in keeping with the spirit and letter of the Quran and hadith. At the same time, Muslim attitudes toward figural representations in secular contexts have been largely welcoming. Images were frequently regarded as instruments for moral, ethical and scientific teaching and learning. Despite isolated cases of iconoclasm in Muslim history, figural representation has thrived over the centuries in both secular and religious settings (Pl. 11).

Principles of ethical guidance and practice, such as compassion, equity, generosity and honour, broadly impacted the arts – beginning with the integrity of artistic production and trading.

Responses to ethical codes found expression in the inscribing of Quranic verses on buildings, textiles and coins, as well as the use of moral aphorisms in calligraphy on daily objects. These ethical notions were also articulated as figural representations in the form of ruler portraits with rich iconographic meanings. Finally, figural paintings also accompanied important religious and literary texts, such as the poems of Jalal al-Din Rumi and Farid al-Din Attar and the tales of *Kalila wa Dimna*. The legacy of this creative interface of aesthetic and moral drives plays itself out today in remarkable expressions of what we call 'Islamic art' the world over, in forms both traditional and contemporary.

Further Reading

Ali, Wijdan. *Modern Islamic Art: Development and Continuity*. Gainesville, FL, 1997.

Allen, Terry. 'Aniconism and Figural Representation in Islamic Art', in Terry Allen, ed., *Five Essays on Islamic Art*. Sebastopol, CA, 1988, pp.17–37.

Baker, Patricia L. *Islam and the Religious Arts*. London and New York, 2004.

Behrens-Abouseif, Doris. *Beauty in Arabic Culture*. Princeton, 1999.

Beaugé, Gilbert and Jean-François Clément, eds. *L'image dans le monde arabe*. Paris, 1995.

Blair, Sheila and Jonathan Bloom, 'Art and Architecture: Themes and Variations', in John Esposito, ed. *The Oxford History of Islam*. Oxford, 1999, pp. 215–67.

Bloom, Jonathan M. *Arts of the City Victorious: Islamic Art and Architecture in Fatimid North Africa and Egypt*. London and New Haven, 2007.

Grube, Ernst J., ed. *A Mirror for Princes from India: Illustrated Versions of the Kalilah wa Dimnah, Anvar-i Suhayli, Iyar-i Danish, and Humayun Nameh*. Bombay, 1991.

Kana'an, Ruba. *A Brief Introduction to Islamic Art*. London, 2009.

King, Geoffrey R.D. 'Islam, Iconoclasm and the Declaration of Doctrine', *Bulletin of the School of Oriental and African Studies*, 48 (1985), pp.267–77.

6

Gender

Zayn Kassam

Does the Quran cast women as inferior to men in how they relate to God? What of the social order that is envisioned by the scripture, and how it has played out in Muslim societies? Leading feminist scholars such as Laila Ahmed, Asma Barlas, Riffat Hassan, Azizah al-Hibri and Amina Wadud argue that the sexes clearly enjoy moral and spiritual equality in the revelation, which is key to respect for their human dignity. This chapter is not an appraisal at large of the locus of women in Muslim ethics. Rather, it focuses on contemporary practices that shed light on an enduring tension between basic teaching and actual conduct toward women in Muslim communities. There follows a reflection on ways in which 'ethical resources' are brought to bear by those aiming to reorient practice, amid the challenges of a globalised world in which Muslim women are increasingly confronted.

Text and Context

The sura *Nisa*, the Quran's chapter on women, opens with a robust assertion of the inherent worthiness of men and women, and the 'like nature' of male and female (4:1). She does not spring from 'Adam's rib'. On the contrary, she is deemed to merit special esteem as the giver of birth, and as one who often finds herself among the oppressed. Solidarity is the proper response of the community amid life's challenges, in the eyes of the Creator 'who cares for all' (4:130). A latter passage offers a celebrated affirmation that charity, constancy, devotion, discipline and humility are not female virtues but for all 'Muslim men and women' (33:35).

At the same time, the Quran does in some cases distinguish between the sexes in the economic and legal sphere. Women are to inherit half the bequest allotted to men (4:11), and half their testimony counts at law (2:282). Men are 'a degree above' women in a verse that clearly relates this to men's responsibility as typical breadwinners (4:34). Scholars such as Amina Wadud and Azizah al-Hibri have argued that the term for 'a degree above', *qawwamuna ala*, implies no intrinsic superiority at all. Further, that the inheritance and testimony provisions must be read in the specific setting of family and contract relations of the time.[1] By comparison, the value of inherent equality in the eyes of God is timeless.

As in much of the discourse on religious ethics, a central issue here is about how one should read the Quran. Are the verses equally binding for all Muslims for all time, or do they speak to their historical context as modern jurists and thinkers like Muhammad Abduh (1849–1905), Fazlur Rahman (1919–88 CE), Abdolkarim Soroush (1945 –) and Khaled Abou el Fadl (1963 –) have argued? After all, the particular directives at issue come mainly from medieval law books that draw on sources which include not only scripture, prophetic traditions and practice but also scholarly consensus (*ijma*), analogical reasoning (*qiyas*) and local custom (*adat*). One recalls the figure of Khadija, wife and confidant of Muhammad when he received the first revelations, whose life involved a career of leadership not only within the umma but also in the wider sphere of trade.

How, then, did the scriptural vision of equal dignity and respect for women unfold among those to whom it was revealed? First, the rapid spread of Muslims into the Byzantine and Persian empires meant close contact with societies that had long been patriarchal. This shaped the Muslim reading of scripture and the nature of

---

[1] A. Wadud, *Qur'an and Woman: Rereading the Sacred Text from a Woman's Perspective* (Oxford, 1999), pp.63–93; A. al-Hibri, 'Women and Social Change', in A.B. Sajoo, ed., *A Companion to the Muslim World* (London, 2008), pp.139–47.

social institutions, just when the Muslim schools of law were emerging. We have strong evidence of this in the work of scholars such as Barbara Stowasser, Leila Ahmed and Asma Barlas. A case in point is that Eve in the Quran has no part in Adam's fall, nor is his inferior – yet is treated in the commentaries (*tafsir*) no differently than in the Biblical ones. Muslim writers drew on the *asbab al-nuzul* literature which elaborated on the settings in which revelation was thought to have occurred, and the *qisas al-anbiya* literature which told moral stories about pre-Islamic prophets and other scriptural figures. Both of these literary modes kept the attitudes to women (along with narrative details) found in Biblical texts and discourses.

Now the legal schools saw fit to emulate the veiling and seclusion of women in societies that Muslims had conquered, where such practices marked high cultural status. True, the Quran enjoins women 'to draw their scarves [*khumur*][2] around their bosoms' (24:31) and 'to draw their cloaks [*jilbab*] around themselves [when outdoors] so that they may be recognised and not be harassed' (33:59); it asks that the wives of the Prophet be approached 'from behind a curtain' (*hijab*) (33:53). But these verses were used to turn a limited physical barrier into a portable barrier (the veil) for all Muslim women in all public encounters. It became, variously, a status symbol consistent with Byzantine and Persian practice, as well as a tool of male social control; both influenced a claim to piety that may have had little to do with scriptural intent. In a similar vein, polygamy was put forward as a right on the strength of the Quran's statement that men may marry up to four women if they could treat them equally, ignoring its warning that such treatment was not achievable with the best of intentions (4:129). The ethics, then, was trumped by other preferences.

Another major trend was that Islamic legal development came under the control of state administration, despite the original idea

---

[2] The text does not explicitly call for head coverings, so either the practice was so commonplace as to require no mention, or the adoption of veiling when Muslims emulated Byzantine and Persian practices became a guide to reading the verses.

of an independent class of jurists or *ulama* as 'keepers' of the law. In the Persian, Mughal and Ottoman empires, what remained under the control of the *ulama* were laws on ritual obligations, family matters and, to a point, charitable endowments (*waqf*). During British rule in India, new uniform administrative, financial, criminal and civil codes did away with prior laws; yet the colonial power upheld religiously established family laws for various Indian communities on the supposed basis of their sanctity.[3] This had the effect of bringing family relations under the control of laws actually tied to ethnic custom, though regarded by their adherents to be part of Muslim tradition (rightly or wrongly); it also revitalised Islamic family law.

Some countries such as Morocco, Tunisia and Egypt modified their legal codes on personal law to reflect to a small degree the changing nature of society, including more equitable treatment of women (which is consistent with the moral and religious egalitarianism found in the Quran). Other states have utilised the instrument of 'Islamisation' to legitimate political power. Under General Zia ul-Haq in Pakistan, this meant a patriarchal stance toward women backed by the legal system in the name of Islam. In 1979, Zia had the constitution amended to include specialists in Islamic *fiqh* or jurisprudence in the high courts and the Supreme Court. Also in 1979, the Hudood Ordinances declared that a man and woman not validly married to each other were guilty of *zina* or adultery if they engaged in sexual relations; four male witnesses were required to prove this. It made rape difficult to prove, since women's testimony was denied legal weight and the unborn child of a woman so impregnated was evidence of illicit intercourse. For her, this turned rape into adultery, for which the penalty could be stoning or death. Many women fought back, through organisations such as the Women's Action Forum and the Pakistan Human Rights Commission, which sought to defy the institutionalisation of medieval codes of practice.

---

[3] Srimathi Basu, 'Cutting to Size', in Rajeswari Sunder Rajan, ed., *Signposts: Gender Issues in Post-Independence India* (New Delhi, 1999), pp.254–7.

Akbar Ahmed has shown in his work among tribal societies in northwest Pakistan that ethnicity or tribal affiliation, religion and nationality are identities that are held concurrently. There can be much tension among these identities, further complicated by class and literacy issues. Beyond Zia's Pakistan, attempts at Islamisation have ranged from Afghanistan under the Taliban to Nigeria. In most cases, the result has included the veiling or reveiling of women. Leila Ahmed notes that in the wake of colonisation, the narrative of resistance to colonialism went through an ironic twist. The veil, whether enforced or voluntary, 'came to symbolise in the resistance narrative, not the inferiority of the culture and the need to cast aside its customs in favour of those of the West, but, on the contrary, the dignity and validity of all native customs, and in particular those customs coming under fierce colonial attack – those customs relating to women – and the need to tenaciously affirm them as a means of resistance to Western domination.'[4]

This also means a retrenchment of patriarchal elites. 'The position of women in Muslim society mirrors the destiny of Islam: when Islam is secure and confident so are its women; when Islam is threatened and under pressure, so too are they.'[5] The campaign for 'Islamisation' makes its target the family, and by this it means women, who are made the moral bearers of what is felt to be a Muslim identity under threat.

Social Practice

Two issues that afflict women in Muslim communities – but are not restricted to them – merit concern as a matter of practical ethics: female genital mutilation and honour killings. Only a small portion of the estimated 650 million Muslim women globally experience these practices. Yet the killing of a single woman on mere

---

[4] Leila Ahmed, *Women and Gender in Islam* (New Haven, CT and London, 1992), p.164.
[5] Akbar S. Ahmed, *Discovering Islam: Making Sense of Muslim History and Society* (New York, 1989), p.184.

suspicion of adultery is one crime too many. When so many of the afflicted happen to be Muslim, we are obliged to inquire into what accounts for the behaviour, and the ethical implications in the secular as well as religious domain.

Female Genital Mutilation

The practice of female genital mutilation (FGM), also known as 'cutting' or 'circumcision', did not originate with Islam. It is practically unknown in Arabia and its environs, and there is no mention or sanction of female (or male) circumcision in the Quran. Early sources attest that Muslims adopted male circumcision in keeping with the covenant made with the common progenitor of the Semitic monotheisms, Abraham. Not surprisingly, he is also made the source of female circumcision in Muslim traditional literature. Taken by Muslims to be the first monotheist, Abraham is the husband of Sarah who cannot bear children; with Sarah's permission he has a child, named Ishmael, by Sarah's handmaiden Hagar. Ibn Kathir, a 14th-century historian and Quranic commentator, mentions that Hagar grew haughty with Sarah, which provoked Sarah to vow to cut 'three limbs' off Hagar. Thereupon, Abraham ordered Hagar to pierce her ears and circumcise herself.[6] But there is no record of such attribution in the highly regarded hadith collection of Bukhari.[7]

The practice is unknown in Central and South Asia where large numbers of Muslims live, many with histories going back to Islam's earliest centuries; it is also entirely alien to many parts of the Middle East. Yet a series of classical Muslim legal works came to treat circumcision, male and female, as standard. For the Shafii school of law, which predominates in Egypt and Sudan, this generally entailed an obligation; for the Hanbali, Hanafi, Maliki and Jafari schools,

---

[6] Barbara Freyer Stowasser, *Women in the Qur'an, Traditions, and Interpretation* (New York, 1994), p.47.

[7] See Noor Kassamali, 'When Modernity Confronts Traditional Practices', in H.L. Bodman and N. Tohidi, eds, *Women in Muslim Societies: Diversity Within Unity* (Boulder, CO and London, 1998), p.44.

markedly less so.[8] Why was male circumcision extended to include female circumcision, a pre-Islamic practice from outside the heartland, in Islamic religious prescriptions? When in 1994 social activists in Egypt sought to outlaw the practice, a senior Muslim legal scholar declared that the hadith accounts of female genital mutilation were of unsound provenance, and there was no basis for the practice in Islam. But the then head of Cairo's Al-Azhar, the premier training ground for Sunni *ulama*, claimed that 'female circumcision is a part of the legal body of Islam and is a laudable practice that does honour to the women'.[9] Finally in 2008, with the endorsement of another senior cleric, Grand Mufti Ali Gomaa, Egypt declared the practice forbidden by Islam and also a threat to public health. Marie Assad notes that some Islamic jurists still approve of female circumcision not only as a tradition endorsed by the Prophet, but also for 'its effect on attenuating the sexual desire of women and directing it to the desirable moderation.'[10]

The sociological evidence is that FGM is a feature mainly of regions that include Egyptian Copts, Jews and Muslims, parts of the Near East, down to eastern Africa in Somalia, Kenya and Uganda, and also Southeast Asia. It predates the advent of Islam in Africa by at least a millennium, for it is known from Pharaonic times. In its most extreme form, it involves infibulation that excises the clitoris and the labia, as well as vaginal narrowing; this makes coitus, childbearing and urination painful and difficult. The reasons for the practice have also been explored. 'Honour' in patrilineal societies is thought to be at stake in reducing female libido, with genital discomfort discouraging women from taking extramarital partners. Often it is an essential rite of passage to

---

[8] Nuh Keller, ed. and tr., *Reliance of the Traveller: A Classic Manual of Islamic Sacred Law* (Beltsville, MD, 1999); E.K. Hicks, *Infibulation: Female Mutilation in Islamic Northeastern Africa* (New Brunswick, NJ, 1996); W. Walther, *Women in Islam: From Medieval to Modern Times* (Princeton, NJ, 1993)

[9] Quoted in Kassamali, 'When Modernity Confronts Traditional Practices', p.43.

[10] Marie B. Assad, 'Female Circumcision in Egypt: Social Implications, Current Research, and Prospects for Change,' in *Studies in Family Planning*, 11 (1980), pp.3–16.

adulthood, which may explain why the negative health and sexual effects are overlooked.

Grass roots organisations use educational strategies to raise awareness of the health risks at stake, and to address the larger issues of women's poverty and status in social settings where group membership involves male views of honour and shame. Kurdish activists in Iraq have mobilised *ulama* and politicians alike to have the practice outlawed. In Somalia, the campaign against FGM announces that the practice is 'not healthy, not clean, not Islamic, and [does] not even guarantee virginity'. Meanwhile, migrant communities from Somalia and other parts of eastern Africa have found themselves caught on both sides of the divide.

From Canada and the United States to Italy, thousands have been known to continue the practice, sometimes defended as a 'cultural right'. Activist organisations and clerics from the same communities have worked in solidarity with mainstream human rights groups against FGM. Doctors from within and outside the communities are reluctant to be involved. The result is an underground market of exploitation and severe physical and psychological health risks.[11] Criminalising the practice has proven less than satisfactory, when not supported by wider networks of resources for vulnerable migrant families and communities. What is least helpful is the portrayal of FGM as somehow pointing up the backwardness of Islamic cultures. Aside from being wrongheaded, such an approach sparks a defensive denial on the other side and makes the work of reformers more difficult.

Honour Killings

Another issue that is closely bound to patriarchal control and 'tradition' is that of honour killings, notably in the Middle and

---

[11] See P. Gallo, L. Araldi, F. Viviani, and R. Gaddini, 'Epidemiological, Medical, Legal, and Psychological Aspects of Mutilation/At-Risk Girls in Italy: A Bioethical Focus', in G.C. Denniston et al., eds, *Male and Female Circumcision: Medical, Legal, and Ethical Considerations in Pediatric Practice* (New York, 1999), p.242.

Near East and South Asia. Diaspora communities in Europe and North America have also experienced numerous such killings. In the particular context of South Asia, the practice is reminiscent of Indian 'dowry-burnings', as both tend to be cast as 'kitchen accidents' where the victim is severely burnt with kerosene, or disfigured with acid. A painful death is often the result. Hard data on the incidence of honour killings is lacking, but a conservative United Nations estimate put the global figure at 5000 such crimes each year.[12]

Typically, a woman is killed by her in-laws or by her own family on the basis of allegations about an extramarital relationship seen as bringing shame on the family's honour. The decision is made by the family or in some cases by a tribal council (*jirga*). It is usually males who do the killing; but as with genital cutting, women themselves play a role in the process, sometimes directly in the burning or disfiguring of 'dishonourable' women. Law enforcement and judicial authorities treat the crime lightly, with the perpetrator(s) facing a minimal sentence or none; the matter may also be treated as 'domestic violence' rather than as murder.

Explanations for such crimes generally focus on patriarchal ideas of familial status, with women being regarded as bearers of honour. Economic deprivation can add to the 'competition' among male members of the community to preserve such honour. There can be other mundane motives, too. The victim's removal can allow another marriage to take place that will bring further bride-wealth. As well, the use of women to settle scores with other men is a feature of such killings.[13] In this form of vigilante or tribal justice, the sharia-related norm of bringing forward four witnesses who can testify to the woman's sexual misdemeanour in court is rarely observed.

---

[12] UN Commission on Human Rights, *Report of the Special Rapporteur, Ms. Asma Jahangir: Submitted Pursuant to Commission on Human Rights Resolution 1999/35* (E/CN.4/2000/3) (New York, 2000).

[13] Amnesty International (London), 'Pakistan: Honour Killing of Women and Girls' (1999), accessible at: http://web.amnesty.org/library/Index/engASA330181999.

Once again, nothing in the verses of the Quran lends the slightest support to such behavioural choices. On the contrary, the text strongly upholds the sanctity of life, the honour of women, and integrity in delivering justice. Yet there can be no denying perceptions among communities where honour killings are practised that they are consistent with 'religious' traditions. Even in the diaspora context, a 2006 poll of 500 British Muslims, Hindus, Christians and Sikhs revealed that 10 per cent of respondents would expressly condone the killing of a relative to protect family honour.[14] Legal, political and religious institutions in Muslim societies (and beyond) have long failed to effectively counter the practice, despite the strenuous efforts of human rights and women's advocacy groups.[15]

In her efforts to address the complexity of honour killings, Riffat Hassan has created the International Network for the Victims of Violence in Pakistan (INRFVVP) to raise awareness of violence against women and raise funds for burn units, health care, medicine for burn victims, and shelters for survivors of attempted honour killings. She worked to convince Pakistan's former president, Pervez Musharraf, that honour killings should be criminalised and dealt with appropriately by the justice system. Musharraf called for a review of the Hudood Ordinances, and in 2005 saw through a change to criminalise the practice (but without removing the customary option of 'blood money' that can allow perpetrators to go unpunished).[16]

Such legislative reforms are certainly vital in reorienting how justice systems deal with honour crimes, especially in the Middle East. Yet far more is required for a significant shift in social behaviour, given the cultural legitimacy that the practice enjoys. Amina

---

[14] BBC Asian service poll, cited in Joan Smith's introduction to Ayse Onal, *Honour Killing* (Beirut and London, 2008), p.11.

[15] See Onal, *Honour Killing*, on attitudes across a broad spectrum of systems; and Tracy McVeigh, 'Ending the silence on "honour killing"', *The Observer*, 25 October 2009: http://www.guardian.co.uk/society/2009/oct/25/honour-killings-victims-domestic-violence.

[16] Owais Tohid, 'Pakistan outlaws "honor" killings', *Christian Science Monitor*, 25 January 2005: http://www.csmonitor.com/2005/0120/p06s01–wosc.html.

Wadud and Asma Barlas, for example, have drawn attention to popular as well as scholarly readings of Quranic verses as sanctioning men's superiority over women, or the claim that women should be obedient to men, as feeding old patriarchal attitudes about the permissibility of 'keeping women in line'. Khalid Abou El Fadl suggests that purported hadith narratives which demean women need scrutiny:

> If one adopts the faith-based conviction that the Prophet was not sent by God to affirm and legitimate conservative and oppressive power structures, traditions that affirm the hegemony of patriarchy would have to pass the strictest level of scrutiny. However, applying this level of scrutiny to these traditions would reveal that there were too many patriarchal vested interests circulating, advocating, and embellishing these types of [hadith] reports.[17]

Recent trends in Islamisation, noted earlier, tend to reinforce traditionalist views about the place of women that can legitimise violence against them in assorted settings. Often such trends respond to the perceived need to resist the influence of western cultural models, by holding on to or retrieving 'authentic' identities and practices. Examples include the adoption of stricter dress codes, bans on the sale of alcohol, the use of religious spaces to advance militant ideologies, and restrictions on the public role of women. The economic and social effects of globalisation only compound the situation, and not in Muslim settings alone. True, women have greater participatory opportunities in a globalised public sphere; but they have borne the brunt of the exclusionary impact of rapid transitions, with the 'feminisation of poverty' and of direct contestation with men. Nativist responses to globalisation, in the form of nationalism, fundamentalism and other expressions of local identity, too often reinforce patriarchy instead of challenging it in the shared quest for civil society.

---

[17] Khalid Abou El Fadl, *Speaking in God's Name: Islamic Law, Authority and Women* (Oxford, 2003), pp.246–7.

Conclusion: An Ethical Reflection

A positive outcome of the privations caused by the impact of globalisation is the emergence of feminist or women's organisations that are transnational in their concerns and strategies. Their agendas cover issues ranging from social violence and maternal-child health to education, poverty and the environment. Such organisations also critique the patriarchy of nationalistic and religious ideologies, whether on the part of the state or otherwise. Equitable access to justice as well as equity under the law are among the most serious obstacles, for they affect how women fare on matters such as rape, honour crimes, divorce, child custody and inheritance. Beyond calls for legal reform, a number of approaches have been advocated that aim to shift the ethical terms of the discourse and the practical ways in which the problems are addressed.

Muslim feminists in Iran have been at the forefront of taking on the task of re-reading the Quran and the hadith against patriarchal interpretations. In many cases, they have promoted a 'parallel universe' in which women can play a fully active role in banking, the civil service, educational institutions (including seminaries), health care, publishing, sports and even the cinema. Legal reform is high on their agenda, but in the meantime, a gender-segregated life with strict dress codes and other constraints is regarded as at the very least superior to one of public exclusion.

What they share with Muslim gender activists in less traditional settings – such as Laleh Bakhtiar, Asma Barlas, Zainab al-Ghazzali, Azizah al-Hibri, Fatima Mernissi, Asifa Qureishi and Amina Wadud – is a commitment to re-reading the scripture and hadith which they see as richly supportive of their emancipatory aims. For them, this is not merely a strategy for social and legal reform but an essential part of their identity as 'believing women' (a popular phrase which echoes sura 33:35). Riffat Hassan, whose work on honour crimes in Pakistan was noted, sees engagement with theology as a promising route to reshaping the law. Hassan derives a specific list of rights from the Quran, in parallel with the secular 1948 Universal Declaration of Human Rights. These include the rights to life, freedom (including to 'responsible dissent'), privacy, sustenance and mobility, but also a compound right to live a 'good life' that protects human developmental and spiritual choices.

Others such as Maha Azzam, Asma Jahangir and Mehrangiz Kar have drawn on more secular tools for reform, though the issues they face as women are very similar. Often it is the particular setting that determines what strategies are adopted; some stay away from theological matters because they can be divisive or bring unwelcome attention (including in western contexts). It is not unusual in practice for women activists to straddle the secular–religious divide. The Iranian Nobel laureate Shirin Ebadi, for example, is a human rights lawyer and former judge who freely professes her faith in a liberating Islam.

'Islam's ethical vision is stubbornly egalitarian, including with respect to the sexes', notes Leila Ahmed; what Islam says about women is 'embedded in and framed by the new ethical and spiritual field of meaning that the religion had come into existence to articulate.'[18] In sum, ethical resources that range from scriptural texts to networks of solidarity offer a potent critique of prevailing social practices that erode the dignity of women. These resources can also bridge the divide of 'religious' and 'secular' in dealing with social practices. The evidence suggests that economic, cultural and ideological factors have much to do with society's failures in diverse settings. Ethical traditions can summon social legitimacy in ways that are unique, in reshaping the secular and religious landscape that is shared by communities of women and men.

Further Reading

Ahmed, Leila. *Women and Gender in Islam: Historical Roots of a Modern Debate*. New Haven, CT and London, 1992.

Badran, Margot. *Feminism in Islam: Secular and Religious Convergences*. Oxford, 2009.

Barlas, Asma. *'Believing Women' in Islam: Unreading Patriarchal Interpretations of the Qur'an*. Austin, TX, 2002.

---

[18] Ahmed, *Women and Gender in Islam*, p.63.

Bayes, Jane H. and Nayereh Tohidi, eds. *Globalization, Gender, and Religion*. New York, 2001.

Bodman, Herbert L., ed. *Women in Muslim Societies: Diversity Within Unity*. Boulder, CO and London, 1998.

Hassan, Riffat. 'Are Human Rights Compatible with Islam?' *The Religious Consultation on Population, Reproductive Health and Ethics*. Louisville, KY, 1994: http://www.religiousconsultation. org/hassan2.htm.

al-Hibri, Azizah Yahia. 'Women and Social Change', in Amyn B. Sajoo, ed. *A Companion to the Muslim World*. London, 2009, pp. 133–55.

Kar, Mehrangiz. *Crossing the Red Line: The Struggle for Human Rights in Iran*. Costa Mesa, CA, 2006.

Mernissi, Fatima. *The Veil and the Male Elite: A Feminist Interpretation of Women's Rights in Islam*, tr. Mary Jo Lakeland. Reading, MS, 1991.

Moghadam, Valentine M. *From Patriarchy to Empowerment: Women's Participation, Movements, and Rights in the Middle East, North Africa, and South Asia (Gender and Globalization)*. Syracuse, NY, 2007.

Onal, Ayse. *Honour Killing: Stories of Men who Kill*. Beirut and London, 2008.

Wadud, Amina. *Inside the Gender Jihad: Women's Reform in Islam*. Oxford, 2006.

7

Health Care

Abdallah Daar and Ahmed Al-Khitamy

An 18–year-old Muslim man sustains severe head injuries in a traffic accident while riding his motorcycle. He is declared brain dead. The transplant co-ordinator approaches the grieving mother to obtain consent for organ donation. At first, the patient's mother is shocked at this approach. She then requests waiting for her family to arrive before making a decision.

A 38–year-old Muslim woman is found to have a rapidly growing carcinoma of the breast. She requires surgery and post-operative chemotherapy. She is five weeks into her first pregnancy and is advised to terminate the pregnancy before the chemotherapy.

Human beings in the vision of the Quran are the crown of creation and are God's vicegerents on earth (2:30). They are endowed with reason, choice and responsibilities, including stewardship of other creatures, the environment and their own health. Muslims are expected to be moderate and balanced in all matters, including health. Illness may be seen as a trial or even as a cleansing ordeal, but it is not viewed as a curse or punishment or an expression of divine wrath. Hence, the patient is obliged to seek treatment and to avoid being fatalistic.

Muslim health care ethics is intimately linked to the teachings of the Quran and the tradition of the Prophet Muhammad, and thus to the interpretation of religious law. In other words, deliberation on the ethics of health care is inseparable from the religion itself, which emphasises continuities between body and mind, the material and spiritual realms, and between ethics and jurisprudence. The Quran itself has a surprising amount of detail regarding the development of the human embryo, which informs discourse on the ethical and legal status of the embryo and fetus before birth.[1]

Muslim ethical teaching stresses the importance of preventing illness as an individual as well as a societal duty. When prevention fails, it provides guidance not only to the practising physician but also to the patient. The patient must be treated with respect and compassion, and the physical, mental and spiritual dimensions of the illness experienced must be taken into account. The Muslim physician understands the duty to strive to heal, while acknowledging God as the ultimate healer.

The values of the Hippocratic Oath, central to modern medical practice, are reflected in Muslim health care ethics. However, the invocation of multiple gods in the original version, and the exclusion of any god in later versions, has led Muslims to adopt the Oath of the Muslim Doctor, which invokes the name of Allah. It appears in the Islamic Code of Medical Ethics, formally approved in 2004 after many years of deliberation, dealing with issues such as organ transplantation and assisted reproduction.[2]

Principles

In Islam, life is sacred: every moment of human life has value, even if it is not of the highest quality. The saving of life is a duty, and the unwarranted taking of life a grave sin.[3] The Quran affirms this reverence in reference to a similar commandment given to other monotheistic peoples: 'On that account We decreed for the

---

[1] Maurice Bucaille, *Human Reproduction: The Bible, the Qur'an and Science* (Indianapolis, IN, 1979), pp.198–210; M.A. Albar, *Human Development as Revealed in the Holy Qur'an and Hadith* (Jeddah, 1996).

[2] Commentary and text at http://www.islamonline.net/English/News/2004-12/15/article04.shtml, and http://www.islamset.com/ethics/code/main.html. See also Amyn B. Sajoo, *Muslim Ethics: Emerging Vistas* (London, 2004), pp.16–17, 108–17.

[3] See generally Jonathan E. Brockopp, ed. *Islamic Ethics of Life: Abortion, War and Euthanasia* (Columbia, SC, 2003).

Children of Israel that whosoever killeth a human being . . . it shall be as if he had killed all humankind, and whosoever saveth the life of one, it shall be as if he saved the life of all humankind' (5:32). This passage legitimises medical advances in saving human lives and justifies the general prohibition against both suicide and euthanasia or 'mercy killing'.

The Oath of the Muslim Doctor includes an undertaking 'to protect human life in all stages and under all circumstances, doing [one's] utmost to rescue it from death, malady, pain and anxiety. To be, all the way, an instrument of God's mercy, extending . . . medical care to near and far, virtuous and sinner, and friend and enemy.'

Islamic bioethics is an extension of the sharia – the traditional corpus of ethics and law – which is itself based on two principal foundations. These are the Quran ('a healing and a mercy to those who believe': 41:44), and the sunna, or guidance based on the Prophet's words and acts. Development of the sharia in the Sunni branch of Islam over the ages has also required *ijma* (consensus) and *qiyas* (analogy), resulting in four major Sunni schools of jurisprudence. Where appropriate, consideration is also given to *maslaha* (public interest) and *urf* (local customary precedent).

The Shia branch of Islam has in some cases developed its own interpretations, methodology and authority systems, with special importance on the role of the imam as temporal and spiritual guide. On the whole, Shia ethical rulings on health care do not differ fundamentally from the Sunni positions. Broadly in Islam, the determination of valid religious practice and hence the resolution of ethical issues in diverse settings is undertaken by qualified scholars of religious law, who provide rulings on whether a proposed action is forbidden, discouraged, neutral, recommended or obligatory.

Islamic scholars have been writing about issues in medical ethics for a very long time. Not surprisingly, the flourishing of medicine and science at large in the medieval Muslim world period was an especially fertile time for reflection on the ethics of health care: among the luminaries were Zakariya al-Razi (864–930), Ibn Sina (980–1037) and al-Nafis (1213–88). The four key principles of contemporary bioethics – autonomy, beneficence, nonmalfeasance and justice – were discussed by Muslim scholars as early as the 13th century.[4]

To respond to new medical technology, Muslim jurists informed by technical experts have regular conferences at which emerging issues are explored and consensus is sought. Over the past few years, these conferences have dealt with such issues as organ transplantation, brain death, assisted conception, technology in the intensive care unit, and even futuristic issues such as testicular and ovarian grafts. More widely, there has been work on human embryonic stem cell research, organ transplantation, triage, informed consent, end of life decision-making, abortion, assisted reproduction and genetic testing, nursing and pharmacy. The Islamic Organisation for Medical Sciences (IOMS), based in Kuwait, holds conferences and publishes the *Bulletin of Islamic Medicine*.[5] Nevertheless, most Muslim societies would tend to defer to the opinion of their own recognised religious scholars.

Many medical schools in countries with Muslim majorities have bioethics curricula. There are established mechanisms for addressing emerging biomedical and bioethics issues, and curricula are updated accordingly. One example is the Aga Khan University's Medical College and the School of Nursing in Karachi, which collaborates with leading global centres in developing a contemporary orientation in ethical codes that are sensitive to local cultural as well as broader Islamic principles.[6]

Islam is not monolithic and there is a plurality of views on health care ethics. This diversity stems not only from the various schools of jurisprudence that have evolved historically, but also from the multiple socio-cultural backgrounds and varying levels of religious observance.

There is little that is strange or foreign in Islamic bioethics for western physicians, who are often surprised at the similarities of

[4] Sahin Aksoy and Abdurrahman Elmai, 'The Core Concepts of the "Four principles" of Bioethics as Found in Islamic Tradition', *Medicine and Law*, 21 (2002), pp.211–24.
[5] IOMS website at http://www.islamset.com/.
[6] See respectively http://www.aku.edu/medicalcollege/ and http://www.aku.edu/SON/.

approach to major health care ethical issues among the monotheistic religions, and especially particularly between Islam and Judaism. Secular western health care ethics are in the main rights-based, with a strong emphasis on the individual. Muslim ethics derive largely from duties, such as with regard to the preservation of life and to seek treatment. However, rights that pertain to the individual, the community and to God do feature in Muslim health care ethics – as does a call to virtue (*ihsan*), which informs the principle of the public good (*maslaha*) in approaches to health policy.[7]

Practice

For many of the world's more than 1.5 billion Muslims, including those in Europe and North America, religion is deeply woven into every aspect of their lives. They invoke the name of God in daily conversation, and live a closely examined life in relation to what is right or wrong behaviour – believing their actions to be accountable and subject to ultimate judgement. For ethical guidance, Muslims draw often on the Quran, the traditions of the Prophet and the teachings of imams, as well as on the rulings of Muslim jurists and scholars.

It is certainly understood that one may not be able to perform all one's religious duties when suffering from injury and illness; yet many Muslims will seek to practise their faith as normally as possible even when admitted to hospital or other care facilities. An appreciation of some of the fundamentals of Islamic ethics would enhance the health care of such individuals, wherever the situation arises in our globalised world.

There are varying degrees of observance of traditional Muslim beliefs and practices. Health care professionals and others need to be sensitive to this diversity and avoid a stereotyped approach to all Muslims in their care. At the practical level, one should be mindful that the provision of simple measures can make an immense difference to one's Muslim patient or charge. Quite aside

---

[7] For perspectives on *maslaha*, see J.E. Brockopp and T. Eich, eds. *Muslim Medical Ethics: From Theory to Practice* (Columbia, SC, 2008).

from an appreciation of the religion and culture, there are some practical considerations that apply to matters ranging from diet and privacy to the giving of informed consent. These attest to the wide-ranging scope and implications of the ethics of health care in the daily lives of Muslims.

Diet

Muslim dietary rules relate to well-established ethical traditions. Pork is forbidden. Meat should be processed in special ways (*halal*). Alcohol is prohibited, though it can be applied externally for health purposes. The rationales for these rules are about clean consumption, humane animal slaughter for food, and maintaining one's sobriety and balance by avoiding intoxication. In situations of extreme necessity (*darura*), such as lack of alternative food sources, the rules can be relaxed. A common example of this is recourse to *kosher* meat and *kosher* food in general where *halal* choices are unavailable.

Privacy

When it comes to exposing the body, propriety tends to rank high for most Muslims. In a faith tradition where veiling is common, it will come as no surprise that women are often reluctant to uncover. If possible, physicians should ask female patients to uncover one area of their body at a time; they should be particularly careful when examining breasts or genitalia, and explain in advance what they are about to do. As far as possible, a chaperone should be present if the physician is male. Many Muslim families will prefer to have a female physician for the female family members, especially for gynecological examinations, and a male physician for the male members, if circumstances permit.

Religious observance

In general, health concerns override all religious observances. However, the more devout Muslims and those who are physically able, along with their companions, may wish to continue some religious observances in hospital. They would need running water for ablutions and a small quiet area to place a prayer mat facing Mecca. Health care staff should avoid disturbing them during the ten minutes or so that it takes to pray, whether three or five times a day. Some patients will also frequently recite silently from the Quran or appear to be in meditation. During the month of Ramadan, Muslim patients may ask about fasting, even though they are not required to fast when ill. Muslims regard both fasting and praying as being therapeutic.

Consent

Essentially, the principles and components of informed consent that have become part of global medical practice apply no differently to Muslims. However, depending on their cultural as well as educational background, they may wish to consult closely with family members and religious advisors before consenting to major procedures. Particular sensitivity should be exercised when the consent involves abortion, end of life questions, or sexual and gynecological issues. These are matters that can engage one's deepest ethical convictions, and perspectives can vary significantly even among Muslims themselves.

Hygiene

Muslims are on the whole very conscious of matters pertaining to bodily functions and hygiene. Bodily discharges such as urine and feces are often considered ritually unclean and must, therefore, be cleaned in certain ways. Ablutions are especially important before prayers, and so it is crucial to provide running water close to the patient, with sandals to wear in the toilet. Muslim patients may resist having a colostomy because it makes ritual cleanliness for prayers difficult to achieve. Physicians might therefore need to spend more time than usual explaining the medical need and the steps that can be taken to minimise soiling.

Illustrative Cases

The first case mentioned at the beginning of this chapter raises the issue of organ transplantation, which is practised in most countries with Muslim majorities. This generally involves kidney donations from living relatives, but cadaveric (after death) donation is increasing. Many Muslim scholars favour cadaveric organ donation. The Quranic affirmation of bodily resurrection has determined many religious and moral decisions regarding cadavers.[8] Traditionally, mutilation is prohibited in Islam as disrespectful to the integrity of the body, which one is endowed with as a divine favour. Historically, this has tended to discourage carrying out autopsies – but they are increasingly becoming common, especially when there is suspicion of foul play.

Death is considered to have occurred when the soul has left the body, but this exact moment cannot be known with certainty. Death is therefore diagnosed by its physical signs. The concept of brain death was accepted by a majority of scholars and jurists at the Third International Conference of Islamic Jurists in 1986. Most, but not all, countries with Muslim majorities now accept brain death criteria. In Saudi Arabia, for example, about half of all kidneys for transplantation are derived from cadavers, with the application of brain death criteria.

The mother of the recently deceased boy in the intensive care unit was initially shocked because she did not expect an approach so soon after her son's death. The co-ordinator, however, has been specifically trained and is very experienced and culturally sensitive. She allows the mother time to reflect and wait for her family to arrive. The mother's faith has taught her that God decides when a life is to end, and although she is grieving she knows that nothing could have saved her son when the moment of death arrived. A friend of the family, a professor of Islamic studies at a local university, arrives and confirms that it is acceptable in Islam to donate organs under such circumstances. The family jointly agrees to the

---

[8] See Abdulaziz Sachedina, 'Islam', in W.T. Reich, ed., *Encyclopedia of Bioethics* (New York, 1995), pp.1289–97

donation. The surgical team is made aware of the Muslim require-
ment to bury the body on the same day and arranges for the
organs to be removed that afternoon.

The second case raises issues of the commencement of life. The
general Islamic view is that, although there is some form of life
after conception, full human life, with its attendant rights, begins
only after the ensoulment of the fetus. On the basis of interpretations of passages in the Quran and the sunna, some Muslim
scholars agree that ensoulment occurs at about 120 days after
conception, while other scholars hold that it occurs at about 40
days after conception.

Muslim legal scholars differ in their opinions about abortion.
Abortion has been allowed after implantation and before ensoulment in cases in which there were adequate juridical or medical
reasons. Accepted reasons have included rape. However, some Shia
and Sunni authorities have generally not permitted abortion at
any stage after implantation, even before ensoulment, unless the
mother's life is in danger. Abortion after ensoulment is traditionally
forbidden by Islamic authorities, but the vast majority make an
exception to preserve the mother's life. If a choice has to be made
to save either the fetus or the mother, then the mother's life would
take precedence. She is seen as the root, the fetus as an offshoot.

In the case presented here, chemotherapy is necessary for the
mother's health, although it might cause a miscarriage or severe
developmental abnormalities in the fetus. The pregnancy itself
may worsen her prognosis. These are medical indications for termination. Some contemporary Muslim authorities have ruled in
favour of prenatal diagnosis and accept severe congenital anom-
alies and malformations as a reason for termination before ensoulment.[9] Two physicians certify that chemotherapy and abortion are
necessary, and the pregnancy is terminated with the consent of
the patient and her husband.

The couple says that they would dearly love to have a child in

[9] See, for example, Muslim World League Conference of Jurists, 12th Session,
Regarding Termination of Pregnancy for Congenital Abnormalities (Mecca,
1990).

the future and inform the physician that Islam permits *in vitro* fertilisation. They ask if it is possible before chemotherapy to retrieve and freeze her ova, to be fertilised later. This would be permissible provided the sperm, with certainty, came from her husband, and that at the time of fertilisation they are still married and the husband is alive. The option of surrogacy is broached by the physicians as an alternative. On checking with their local religious scholar, the couple is informed that, in Islamic legal tradition, the birth mother, not the ovum donor, would be the legal mother. The couple decides not to pursue surrogacy.

Conclusion

As applied in Muslim settings, the ethics of health care is a field with a record that stretches over some fourteen centuries. Its central teachings and practice have much in common with major eastern as well as western traditions, given their overlapping histories and shared ethical outlook in multiple respects. A vast body of literature in a variety of languages speaks to those key teachings; numerous web-based resources are also available. Perhaps the most significant development at a global level in the field of bioethics is the UNESCO Universal Declaration on Bioethics and Human Rights, which was adopted by UNESCO's General Conference on 19 October 2005.[10] The long development of this declaration took into account different cultural perspectives, including those of Muslim communities, successfully negotiating the tension between universality, on which much of human rights discourse and practice has been predicated, and cultural traditions, on which local ethical positions may largely depend. There is now an active programme to develop teaching materials and curricula that are specific to various regions but draw on the principles of the Declaration. UNESCO's office in Cairo is spearheading this effort in the Middle East and North Africa region.

---

[10] Full text at http://portal.unesco.org/en/ev.php-URL_ID=31058&URL_DO=DO_TOPIC&URL_SECTION=201.html

In practical terms, an appreciation by health care providers of the small number of ethics-related needs of Muslim patients will do much to enhance the quality of treatment and care. It would allow Muslim patients to feel more comfortable in health care settings, and make it possible for them to practise – to the extent allowed by their medical condition and the physical circumstances – their quite straightforward religious observances. Ultimately, this wider ethic of care is part of the essential link between medicine and human dignity that the global community affirmed in the UNESCO Declaration, in calling for 'moral sensitivity and ethical reflection' as integral to our encounter with biomedicine and the sciences at large.

Further Reading

Antes, Peter. 'Medicine and the Living Tradition of Islam', in Lawrence E. Sullivan, ed. *Healing and Restoring: Health and Medicine in the World's Religious Traditions.* New York, 1989, pp.173–202.

Beauchamp, Tom L. and J.F. Childress. *The Principles of Biomedical Ethics.* 6th edn, Oxford, 2009.

Brannigan, Michael C. and Judith A. Boss. *Healthcare Ethics in a Diverse Society.* Mountain View, CA, 2001.

Brockopp, Jonathan E. and Thomas Eich, eds. *Muslim Medical Ethics: From Theory to Practice.* Columbia, SC, 2008.

Chipman, Leigh N.B. 'The Professional Ethics of Medieval Pharmacists in the Islamic World', *Medicine and Law*, 21 (2002), pp. 321–38.

Daar, Abdallah, Tarif Bakdash and Ahmed B. al-Khitamy. 'Islamic Bioethics', in Peter A. Singer and A.M. Viens, eds, *The Cambridge Textbook of Bioethics.* Cambridge, 2008, pp.408–15.

Guinn, David E., ed. *Handbook of Bioethics and Religion.* Oxford, 2006.

Moazam, Farhat. *Bioethics and Organ Transplantation in a Muslim Society: A Study in Culture, Ethnography, and Religion.* Bloomington, IN, 2006.

Nanji, Azim, 'Medical Ethics and the Islamic Tradition', *Journal of Medicine and Philosophy,* 13 (1988), pp. 257–75.

Padela, Aasim, 'Islamic Medical Ethics: A Primer', *Bioethics,* 21 (2007), pp.169–78.

Rahman, Fazlur. *Health and Medicine in the Islamic Tradition: Change and Identity.* New York, 1987.

Sachedina, Abdulaziz. *Islamic Biomedical Ethics: Principles and Application.* Oxford, 2009.

8

Economy

Rodney J. Wilson

Being Muslim implies concern with the ethics of social justice. This extends as fully to economic relations as to all other aspects of one's life. Ethical concern here springs from the very basic principles of Islam, such as the giving of alms (*zakat*) and the prohibition of usury (*riba*), as essentials of a just economic order. It applies no less to contemporary concerns about poverty and sustainable development. What Muslims call *fiqh muamalat* or civil jurisprudence has much to say about the propriety of one's behaviour in economic relations. This chapter is a reflection on the development of that rich tradition and some of its key implications for our time.

We will begin with an Islamic perspective on the nature of economic cycles and their impact on human conduct. The great Muslim philosopher of history, Ibn Khaldun (1332–1406), offered a moral theory of the rise and decline of economies, where decline was ascribed to greed and corruption resulting in social breakdown. Islam as a religion stresses social responsibility, which is in danger of being neglected at the peak of economic cycles. Peaks are often accompanied by individual excesses and government complacency, for it is wrongly assumed that the boom will continue. History, noted Ibn Khaldun, teaches otherwise; yet its lessons are too often ignored.

Indeed, many today assume that economic downturns will be followed by upswings that will leave most people better off than they were before the decline. However, the notion of continuous

material development dates back just over 200 years to the era of
Adam Smith (1723–90) and the origins of classical economics. In
terms of material wealth, the majority of Muslim societies may
rank as poor, but using other measures of development, especially
those based on social capital, the picture becomes more complex.
What are the objectives of economic development from an Islamic
perspective – and does economic prosperity facilitate or distract
from spiritual fulfilment?

We will inquire as well into Islamic guidance on economic
policy, which involves decisions on taxation and public spending.
Should tax systems be redistributive and aim at a more equitable
distribution of income and wealth, or should the priority be low
taxation to reduce economic costs and free individuals to make
their own choices on resource allocation? Islam has its own traditional system for redistribution through *zakat*, one of the pillars
of the faith; is this a substitute for or an addition to state taxation and compulsory social insurance contributions? There is also
the provision of *waqf*, charitable trusts, the income from which
is assigned to social welfare spending. A wider issue is whether
religiously motivated charitable donations ameliorate the hard-
ships of the poor or, like many secular welfare systems, simply
create a culture of dependency.

'Islamic finance' has become the area of greatest interest to
Muslim economists who ask how the principles of their faith may
be applied to commercial transactions. To what extent is Islamic
finance ethical? A key concern is to ensure financial contracts are
just, so that none of the parties are exploited. Interest or *riba* is
regarded as exploitative, as is *gharar* or contractual uncertainty.
Gharar may cause misunderstandings for clients that could be
taken advantage of by financial institutions. Islamic finance is not
only concerned with the methods of financing, but also with how
money is used. Finally, we will consider the parallels and differences between Islamic (or 'sharia compliant') and secular 'socially
responsible' finance, with regard to a variety of choices in economic
behaviour.

Cycles of Economic Life

There have always been ups and downs in economic activity that imply uncertainty, which for many will result in loss of income and employment. There are ethical and moral issues with such cycles, not least because the gains and losses vary considerably within most societies. A privileged minority tends to enjoy the greatest gains during upswings, while the poor and those in marginal employment suffer most in the downswings. Economic cycles are a human phenomenon. They are not inherently bad, though they can be associated with exploitative behaviour, with opportunists gaining most during periods of growth, and perhaps being more adept at protecting themselves during contractions.

Economists and economic historians have proposed many theories to explain these cycles: a common idea is that a failure to control the supply of money can result in price bubbles which ultimately burst. Such explanations are morally neutral. Ibn Khaldun, writing in the late 14th century, proposed a theory of the economic cycle in which moral standards in society were not merely influenced by the phases of the cycle, but were in fact the cause.[1] For Ibn Khaldun, credit or blame for events was attributable to the ruler or government, as those in charge were finally accountable to God for their acts. A just government must seek to establish stability in which commerce would prosper and artisans might specialise and embark on long-term projects, without the risk of not being paid for their labour.

Ibn Khaldun lived in an era when most governments were autocratic, with much power residing with the ruler, though this did not preclude rulers from being benign. Indeed, a just and God-fearing ruler might set an example to the people and encourage society to be peaceful and productive. But as material output rose, the temptation to be corrupt could also grow, undermining the spiritual virtues of the society. Ibn Khaldun was especially critical of rulers and governments that sought profit at public expense

---

[1] Ahmed El-Ashker and Rodney Wilson, *Islamic Economics: A Short History* (Leiden, 2006), pp.275–83.

– for example, by paying private agricultural suppliers as little as possible, then selling the goods with a high mark-up. It was unjust for governments to abuse their command status to exploit their populations, and indeed Ibn Khaldun sees this as one of the causes of economic recessions, which ultimately can undermine the greatest empires and cause their eventual demise.

These writings are vital in understanding how Muslims came to view market economies and the role of the state. Markets are seen as natural venues for commercial transactions, places where buyers and sellers interact, and social and economic bonds are formed. Most of the great centres of Muslim civilisation, including Mecca, Medina, Damascus, Cairo, Istanbul and Isfahan, owed their existence to trade, which was celebrated rather than seen as a source of conflict and division. However, Ibn Khaldun recognised that markets could not be entirely left to run themselves: a kind of trading standards authority or *hisba* had to ensure that market participants did not exploit each other. There are numerous writings on the functions and role of the *hisba*, most notably by Ibn Taymiyya, a 14th-century scholar who greatly influenced Ibn Khaldun. The state oversees the *hisba*, with a state official, the *muhtasib*, responsible for ensuring that the market functions fairly and efficiently. The *muhtasib* is like a regulator, though in dealing with complaints and disputes among traders, he is also like a modern ombudsman.

Economic cycles should be viewed not as a problem to be overcome, but as an ordinary aspect of human interaction and need. The growth phase of a cycle, often triggered by a technological innovation, is linked to work, energy and increasing material achievement. Then, society may suffer from exhaustion and need time to contemplate what direction it should take. For Muslim thinkers the effort of *ijtihad* was needed, to work out how moral teaching could be adapted to new circumstances. This effort may lag behind material developments and new forms of human activity; the innovations themselves, such as new methods of financing or biomedical breakthroughs, might need time to be evaluated from a sharia perspective.

Traditionally, openness to trade is favoured over what we would now call protectionism. The great Muslim civilisations always traded extensively with predominantly non-Muslim economies such as those of China and Europe. Today, the Organisation of the Islamic Conference (OIC) would like to see more trade between Muslim countries, an aspiration also of its subsidiary, the Turkish-based Standing Committee for Economic and Commercial Cooperation (COMCEC). At the same time, the future direction of trade is likely to favour commerce with China and India, two largely non-Muslim countries, though with large Muslim minorities.

Development and Ethics

Most countries with Muslim-majority populations are ranked as developing nations, on the basis of material indicators such as gross domestic product (GDP) per capita, level of industrialisation, and use of cars and telephones. On such measures, Muslim countries like Bangladesh fare badly, while others such as the oil-rich Gulf nations are among the most affluent in the world (though their GDP per capita varies enormously according to whether only local citizens are counted or the entire population, most of whom are migrant workers). Now the relationship between national economic wealth and political power and influence is important – and Islam is certainly respectful of human material endeavour. But to measure human development in terms only of these indicators is to leave out a whole dimension of public welfare and the social good.

Indicators such as the degree of literacy and the general level of education add usefully to the picture. Traditionally, Muslim societies gave high priority to learning, religious and secular, with *madrassas* attached to mosques as the key institutions. During the 20th century, there was a huge expansion in state education in most Muslim countries resulting in virtually universal primary education and high levels of literacy and numeracy. Primary school completion rates reached 99 per cent in 2007 in Indonesia, the world's most populous Muslim country, while the comparable figures were 98 per cent for Egypt, 96 per cent for Turkey and

93 per cent for Saudi Arabia, with virtually no gender gap remaining.[2] A majority also benefited from secondary education, and university education became accessible to many. Most contemporary Muslim societies recognise the empowering effect of education, with higher education viewed as a way of ensuring that there will be better-informed citizens. Yet academic standards vary considerably, as do literacy levels and gender equity in access to learning, and there is a significant lag overall vis-à-vis western standards.[3]

Measures of life satisfaction and ecological wellbeing figure prominently on the London-based New Economic Foundation's 'Happy Planet Index' (HPI).[4] Here, predominantly Muslim societies (along with Latin American ones) rank far higher than most western 'developed' economies: Egypt is ranked 12th in the world, Saudi Arabia 13th with an extremely high life satisfaction score, and Indonesia 16th. In contrast the United Kingdom ranks 74th and the United States 114th on the HPI, reflecting not only heavy carbon footprints but also low life satisfaction scores. There are fewer family breakdowns in most Muslim societies, and high levels of social capital which in many poorer countries tends to compensate for the lack of physical capital. Whether social capital and harmony can be preserved as societies become more affluent is an open question.

There has been much interest among economists searching for 'Islamic solutions' to the problems of poverty and economic disempowerment. Ways to effective solidarity are sought as a practical expression of the concept of *tawhid* (unity under the one and only God).[5] In Islam there is no virtue in poverty and no equivalent

---

[2] World Bank, *World Development Indicators Database* (Washington, DC, April 2009).

[3] Anil Khamis, 'Cultures of Learning', in Amyn B. Sajoo, ed. *A Companion to the Muslim World* (London, 2009), pp.237–62.

[4] The HPI is sponsored by the New Economic Foundation (London): http://www.happyplanetindex.org/.

[5] See M. Umer Chapra, *Islam and the Economic Challenge* (Leicester, UK, 1992), pp.199–212.

to the monks in Buddhism or Christianity, who not only forgo material aspirations for a life of prayer but also expect to be supported materially by fellow believers who work and earn income. Opting out of worldly pursuits is seen as trying to escape reality; believers must contribute to society through their capacity to work, which after all is an endowment of their Creator.

These premises also apply to the nation state or the Muslim community within a state. Although the ultimate purpose of life is to serve the Almighty, not personal and social material enrichment, successful Muslim states that have advanced economically are seen as better role models. During the early centuries of Islam, when this new religion spread rapidly from its Arabian heartland as far as the Atlantic and Central Asia, the adoption of Islam was associated with increasing commerce as barriers to trade and movements of people in the new territories were reduced or eliminated and converts enjoyed prosperity. Merchants played an important role in the spread of Islam to South Asia and across the Indian Ocean to Malaysia and Indonesia. This was not surprising given that Mecca and Medina themselves were significant trading centres, and that in the Quran the virtues of honest trade are stressed and contrasted with the evils of usury which is viewed as exploitative.

The stress on the benefits of trade in Islamic economic literature has parallels in the work of Adam Smith, for whom free trade was an engine that drove the wealth of nations. Smith saw little need for intervention in markets, as the rationalising 'invisible hand' would ensure efficient outcomes.[6] Muslim writers have been concerned not only with efficiency but also justice, much like today's advocates of fair trade. Farmers, labourers and consumers deserve a fair price and should not be exploited. Traditionally, as noted, this was the responsibility of the *hisba*. Its mandate was comprehensive, including selling practices, with a prohibition on

---

[6] Smith does lay stress on the ethical side of market behaviour in *The Theory of the Moral Sentiments* (1759), which is tied to 'sympathy' that is innate to human nature. But he was confident that this too would ultimately be rationalised by the market's 'invisible hand', which would produce benevolent social organisation.

monopoly behaviour that could result in consumers being taken advantage of. Weights and measures were inspected for accuracy; food safety and hygiene were to be ensured. As such, there were obvious parallels with trading standards authorities today.

Despite the historical emphasis on the importance of trade in Muslim economic thought, contemporary Muslim states do not rank highly in the World Economic Forum's competitiveness index. This is largely based on measures of economic openness that are viewed as essential for market efficiency and economic growth. Qatar emerges as the most competitive Muslim state, ranked 22nd overall, with the United Arab Emirates 23rd, Malaysia 26th and Saudi Arabia 28th – but Egypt finishes 70th, Algeria 83rd, Syria 94th and Pakistan 101st. Factors affecting performance include the efficiency of markets for labour and goods, with favourable ratings for the speed with which businesses can be started, lack of bureaucratic procedures and low tariffs and ease of trade. In many Muslim countries, the inefficient bureaucracy is a legacy of post-colonial nationalist or socialist policies that were unrelated to Muslim traditions which favoured trade and open economy policies long before European colonialists entered the picture.

Again, the World Economic Forum's rankings reflect the material priorities of political economy, not ethical considerations. This is less the case when it comes to perceptions of corruption as indexed by Transparency International, which samples the number of times bribes are required to facilitate business transactions, licences or planning approvals. Qatar emerged as the least corrupt Muslim country and in 2008 ranked 28th globally, while the UAE was ranked 35th. Egypt was ranked 115th, Sudan 173rd, Afghanistan 176th and Somalia 180th. Islamic teaching, of course, abhors corruption and lauds honesty and morality in commerce. Bribery is singled out for particular condemnation and contrasted with reward for honest work. Not surprisingly, one of the appeals of Islamist political parties is the perceived honesty of their members despite living in societies where corruption is rampant. As with other states, there seems to be an inverse relationship between the degree of corruption and the level of development of Muslim countries, which may be because a high level of corruption impedes progress. The notion that material advance encourages corruption is not borne out by the data on Muslim states; the most developed are the least corrupt.

Countries which are more developed have the power to influence the global political agenda. Throughout the 20th century it was largely non-Muslim states that were in the ascendancy and determined the international agenda, but with the defeat of Fascism in the Second World War, the collapse of the Soviet Union, and the limitations of the subsequent global hegemony of the United States increasingly apparent, economic and political power is becoming more diffuse. In particular, the group of 20 industrialised nations (G20) which accounts for 80 per cent of global economic activity has become the major forum for international economic decision-making, including over development issues. Three Muslim countries are represented on the G20 – Saudi Arabia, Turkey and Indonesia – the first time Muslim states have had a say over the direction of international economic policy since the demise of the Ottoman Empire. Although so far these three Muslim states have not advocated an 'Islamic' economic agenda, they can represent the interests of Muslim banks and other sharia-compliant institutions in the debates on global economic reform.

The presence of those three nations in the G20 will also raise awareness of global issues in the Muslim world, which may result in a widened agenda for *ijtihad*, the process of dynamically applying sharia principles to changing circumstances. Muslim economists have been giving much attention to the analysis of the global financial crisis of 2008, and its implications for sharia-sensitive finance. At the same time, there is growing concern within the G20 and other global forums about the issue of climate change and what it could imply for economic and social wellbeing. Clearly, Muslim societies share with all others in the stakes with regard to the ethical handling of resources, both ecological and economic.

Practice

On matters of economic policy such as the role of the state and the nature of taxation (fiscal policy), opinion varies widely among

Muslim writers and activists as to what is ethically appropriate. But there is wide agreement that equity in the distribution of income and wealth as well as in access to resources is a moral imperative.[7] Equitable distribution does not mean equal distribution, which would be inefficient and detrimental to the interests of society, as the ability to manage assets varies according to one's intellect, knowledge and integrity. Those with control over more resources have greater accountability to their Creator; equity is defined in terms of the balance between rights and duties. This means ensuring that resources are used not only for personal consumption and gratification but for the benefit of the wider community. Yet consumers need not feel guilty about their possessions or lifestyle – as long as they are not the fruit of exploitation. Rather, this is viewed as part of the bounty of the Creator for which one should be properly grateful. Serving the needs of others is one way of expressing that gratitude (though one is encouraged to do this as a basic aspect of membership in the umma or civic community).

Traditionally, there were four major forms of taxation levied in Muslim societies: *kharaj* or land taxation, *jizya* or head tax, *fai* or levy on war booty, and *zakat*, a form of wealth tax. Land taxation has obviously been vital in rural societies where it can provide an incentive for agricultural production; if land is left fallow, the owner incurs the same tax liability as the more productive farmer. There is also an equitable and redistributive aspect to *kharaj*, as those owning more land will pay more. Applying *jizya* may be more controversial from an ethical perspective, as a head tax where everyone pays the same amount is arguably regressive and inequitable. The rationale is that if everyone benefits from the resultant spending, as with street lighting for example, then this demands an equal contribution. However, the poor are usually exempted from *jizya*, as are women and children.

The idea of individuals gaining from the booty of war is repugnant in most modern societies, but in traditional societies this

---

[7] Syed Nawab Haider Naqvi, *Perspectives on Morality and Human Well-Being: A Contribution to Islamic Economics* (Leicester, UK, 2003), pp.143–83.

was regarded as quite normal. The application of *fai* in Islamic societies served to reduce individual gains, and meant that a proportion of the booty would accrue to the state, which would be appropriate if the war served a just cause.

The role of *zakat*

While none of the other traditional taxes is applied in contemporary Muslim societies, *zakat* remains vital in Islam, an obligation for all the faithful. *Zakat* is generally an annual levy, in the amount of one-fortieth of the value of assets of each Muslim. Since the purpose is entirely one of wealth-sharing and charity, it should arguably be classified not as a tax but rather as alms-giving, which benefits not only the recipient but also the donor as wealth is purified through such giving.

There is much debate over which assets are liable for *zakat*, how it should be collected, the use of the proceeds and whether it should be a substitute for secular taxes such as income or value added tax.[8] Usually *zakat* is regarded as applying to financial assets such as funds in bank accounts and securities such as bonds or their Islamic equivalent, *sukuk*. *Zakat* is not levied on owner-occupied property; whether it should be applied to private rented property or commercial real estate can be debated. If immovable property and equity investment are exempt from *zakat*, this may encourage holdings of these types of assets and discourage excessive monetary holdings in bank accounts and debt instruments.

A government ministry is responsible for *zakat* collection and disbursement in most Muslim countries. In Saudi Arabia, for example, there is a Department of Zakat and Income Tax, and in Indonesia, where *zakat* collection used to be decentralised, there is now a national *zakat* agency.[9] In the United Arab Emirates, a state Zakat Fund was established in 2003 as an independent agency

---

[8] Timur Kuran, *Islam and Mammon: The Economic Predicaments of Islamism* (Princeton, NJ, 2004), p.105.

[9] Arskal Salim, *The Shift in Zakat Practice in Indonesia: From Piety to a Socio-Politico-Economic System* (Bangkok, 2008), pp.17–60.

from the Ministry of Justice, Islamic Affairs and Endowments. A similar position exists in Malaysia where a Zakat Collection Centre was established in 1991, and in Pakistan where the Ministry of Religious Affairs has exercised responsibility for the organisation of *zakat* collection and distribution since independence. In the United Kingdom there is no state involvement in *zakat* collection but there are several voluntary agencies administrating *zakat* as registered charities. These include Jamiat Ihyaa Minhaaj Al Sunnah (JIMAS), or the Association to Revive the Way of the Messenger, and the Malay Community Association of the United Kingdom. The Zakat Foundation of America has played a similar role in the US since 2001. All these organisations have websites.

Is *zakat* collection and disbursement better undertaken by the state or voluntary organisations? Where the ministries or agencies of national governments are honestly run and maintain proper records, preferably independently audited, there is a strong case for them being involved in *zakat* administration. Democratic legitimacy is not necessarily a prerequisite, but transparency and good governance of *zakat* funds are essential, as is effective management. Where voluntary organisations are involved, it seems preferable for them to be registered charities rather than profit-making commercial organisations. Where professional asset management is required, this can be outsourced to financial institutions – but the charities should maintain overall control and responsibility to *zakat* payers. In most jurisdictions, registered charities must submit annual independently-audited accounts to a state regulator as a condition for taxation benefits.

Zakat revenue must be used for social expenditure for the benefit of the poor and needy; it cannot be used for general government spending on investments in infrastructure or defence. Defining who qualifies as poor and needy is a debatable issue, as poverty is relative: a poor person in the UAE or Qatar may have a much higher income than a poor person in Afghanistan or Bangladesh. There is also the issue in countries with large expatriate populations, such as those in the Gulf, of whether *zakat* should be disbursed only to local nationals or to foreign workers who are generally poorer. In the UAE, the needy are defined as those with little income: orphans, widows, divorcees, the elderly, those who are ill or incapacitated, students, the unemployed, and families of prisoners and missing people. Inevitably, similar questions arise with *zakat* disbursements as with other social security spending. For instance, should it be used to support broken families who may have some responsibility for their own predicament, and might this produce a dependency culture?

Organisations such as JIMAS confine *zakat* disbursements to within the United Kingdom, though they also assist asylum seekers who have already arrived, as well as Muslim students having problems in paying tuition fees. The Zakat Foundation of America focuses on emergency relief as well as long-term sustainable development through the funding of water wells, education and skill training, access to heath care and microfinance for those who cannot obtain bank funding for lack of collateral assets or a regular income.

As *zakat* is fixed, it cannot be used as a tool of fiscal policy (like taxes on spending or income, which can be raised or lowered in response to varying economic circumstances). *Zakat* revenue rises in a boom and falls in a recession, though it is during recessionary times that more *zakat* disbursement may be required. This highlights the need to maintain reserves in *zakat* funds rather than simply balancing current receipts with current expenditure during a boom. *Zakat* funds should be cautiously handled and not fall into deficit, as payment for borrowing from financial institutions would not constitute a legitimate use of *zakat*.

Waqf charitable trusts

Another tradition with a strong ethical purpose is *waqf*, a charitable trust usually created through bequests in wills on death. Islam prescribes that inheritance be subject to a fair and equitable distribution that recognises the rights and obligations of each of the beneficiaries of an estate. Each beneficiary has discretion over how one-third of their estate may be distributed. It is usually from this portion that a *waqf* is established; but it can also be created through a lifetime donation. Once funds are designated for *waqf*, the donor no longer has ownership over them. Commonly, a *waqf* is used to fund the building of mosques and *madrassa*s, as well as public health care institutions.

A *waqf* is an endowment where the initial donation can generate income which can continue in perpetuity. Although a cash *waqf* may be set up which invests in ethical securities that yield dividends and capital gains, most *waqf*s involve real estate with rent as the major source of income. Where *waqf*s are situated in prime urban locations, some of the land may be occupied by a mosque while the remainder is leased for commercial or residential use. Often, property developers will pay a substantial sum to acquire a leasehold on such land, with the ensuing rental income shared with the *waqf*. Such arrangements unleash the income-generating potential of *waqf*s and increase the funds available for charitable causes.

As with *zakat* administration, there has been much debate over the governance of *waqf*s. Historically, most were private endowments linked to individuals or families. But in many countries, especially those with socialist policies in the post-colonial era, *waqf*s were taken under the control of the state and run by special ministries. Such policies were pursued in Egypt, Syria and Turkey. For example, recent Turkish law has allowed greater autonomy for *waqf*s and tax incentives for the foundation of new ones. Many Islamists resented the interference of the state in *waqf* affairs, though it should be noted that in Ottoman times a register was maintained of *waqf* property and state courts dealt with disputes. Indeed, many of today's debates echo those of previous centuries, as is shown by a detailed study of *waqf*s in Ottoman Algeria.[10]

Ethical Finance

Parallels are often drawn between 'Islamic' finance and 'socially responsible' investment practices. This has long applied to such services as mortgages and mutual funds, but in the wake of the

---

[10] Miriam Hoxter, *Endowments, Rulers and Community: Waqf al-Haramayn in Ottoman Algiers* (Leiden, 1998).

financial crisis of 2008 there has been strong interest in alternatives to conventional banking at large. Could Islamic banks provide a model for a fairer and sounder type of financial institution to the benefit of both Muslims and non-Muslims?

A key contrast between Islamic and conventional banking is the traditional prohibition of *riba* or interest. For those who espouse Islamic finance, this tends to apply to all interest-based transactions. The rationale for the prohibition is essentially ethical: usury is exploitative for borrowers, and even where interest rates are more modest, the client must yield to the rate that the financial institution offers. Nor is the interest payment scheme related to the client's capacity; if he suffers a loss of income, there will be no respite from the interest payments and debt obligations. If rescheduling of a loan is allowed, this will usually entail higher interest payments, as the period of the debt will be lengthened.

Islamic finance is based on the principle of risk-sharing, in which the financial institution takes on a higher degree of risk to justify its return. For example, in financing trade, *murabaha* comes into play: the bank buys a commodity on behalf of a client before reselling it to the client at a profit which is disclosed. The profit is justified as the bank assumes ownership; if the goods are defective, the client could sue the bank for damages. With conventional trade finance, there is no such recourse; the client must bear the full risk of unsatisfactory goods. For longer-term finance, Islamic banks offer *ijara* contracts, based on operating leases over assets such as buildings or equipment. The bank is responsible for the insurance and at least partial maintenance. By comparison, in conventional practice such burdens are transferred to the lessee.

Risk-sharing is also a feature of Islamic insurance or *takaful*. Participants pool the risk by bearing each other's burden: donations to the *takaful* fund are socially rather than individually motivated. The monies are invested in a sharia-compliant manner that avoids any *riba*-related profit, and the interests of the management company are kept separate from those of the policy holders, who alone have a claim on the *takaful* fund. By contrast, in conventional insurance the policy holder seeks to transfer the risk to the insurance company, since the motive is simply to protect oneself.[11]

Islamic finance can also be used for microcredit, which involves funding for the poor who cannot offer collateral or qualify for bank loans for lack of a regular source of income. To safeguard the funds, microfinance relies on peer pressure among the recipients to repay their loans. Often microfinance is provided through credit unions, with participants encouraged to save and their modest savings used to fund co-participants in the scheme. The administrative cost of providing many small loans is high, so there is often a subsidy from aid agencies. For sharia-compliant microfinance institutions, the subsidy may come through *zakat* proceeds or *waqf* endowments, which can ensure sustainability; *riba* is not involved at any stage. The Grameen Bank in Bangladesh, through which the Nobel-laureate Muhammad Yunus pioneered modern microcredit (especially for poor women) in the mid-1970s, does involve *riba* in its funding.

By far the largest network for microcredit in the Muslim world is the Aga Khan Agency for Microfinance (AKAM), which serves both rural and urban communities in Central Asia, the Middle East and sub-Saharan Africa. As a non-profit and non-denominational initiative, AKAM is geared toward the most vulnerable members of society.[12]

Aside from the standard microcredit to individuals and groups for small to medium-sized enterprises, loans are offered for education and housing as well as for insurance to protect health, crops and other assets at risk. In Pakistan, AKAM recently partnered with national postal outlets (the largest public or private network

---

[11] See Rodney Wilson, 'Concerns and Misconceptions in the Provision of *takaful*', in Sohail Jaffar, ed., *Islamic Insurance: Trends, Opportunities and the Future of Takaful* (London, 2007), pp.72–85.

[12] The agency is part of the Aga Khan Development Network (AKDN), whose mandate is 'underpinned by the ethical principles of Islam – particularly consultation, solidarity with those less fortunate, self-reliance and human dignity'. See http://www.akdn.org/akam.asp.

in the country) to broaden its reach – which already included microinsurance for nearly 400,000 individuals among the poor in 2008.

Beyond microcredit, two traditional forms of financing have been revived in recent years, though the high risks for the financier have limited their popularity. *Mudaraba* involves a partnership in which one side contributes the effort and the other the funding, with profits divided according to an agreed percentage but losses borne by the financier alone. In practice, *mudaraba* has largely been applied to bank deposits, with the depositor being the financier. This enables depositors to earn a profit share rather than the interest which accrues on conventional savings, viewed as *riba*. As the profit is a reward for risk-taking it is regarded as ethical, unlike gains for simply hoarding funds in an account. The risk for the *mudaraba* depositor relates not only to the variable profit rate but also potentially to the loss of the funds deposited, since these cannot be guaranteed. Most banks reinvest some of the profits in reserve funds that can be used for contingencies, which helps protect the value of deposits.

Partnership is also involved in *musharaka*, where all the parties invest and share profits as well as losses in proportion to their investment. In other words, those contributing more capital have more assets at risk, but they also have a greater capacity to absorb losses. *Musharaka* often involves sharia-compliant investment companies rather than banks, as they are more lightly regulated than banks and can take on the risks which direct investment inevitably involves. *Musharaka* is particularly useful for injecting private equity capital into small or medium-sized family businesses to enable their expansion. The sharing of risk is regarded as preferable to taking on significant amounts of additional debt for unproven ventures with a limited track record.

'Sharia-compliant' and 'socially responsible' funds

While *musharaka* may be used for private equity investment, mutual funds are the usual vehicle for pious Muslim investors who wish to have exposure to the shares of quoted companies listed on stock markets. Mutual funds were not a traditional vehicle for Islamic financing, but the general rule is that choices are permissible unless explicitly forbidden, and there is no prohibition on this method of financing. Indeed, as mutual funds involve sharing risks and rewards, they are arguably just from an Islamic perspective.

The advantage of investing through a fund from both an Islamic and general ethical stance is that the stock acquired can be screened. Portfolios only include companies which are identified as being engaged in *halal* activities, or in the case of ethical investments as being socially responsible.[13] Usually for Islamic funds, screening methods are approved by a sharia board appointed for this purpose; ethical funds will have an independent body accountable to the investors. Islamic funds do not invest in companies involved in the production and distribution of alcohol, pork products or tobacco, nor in conventional banks involved in *riba* transactions. Ethical funds often use sustainability criteria and will not invest in companies which pollute heavily and contribute to global warming, or companies with suppliers that exploit low-cost labour or employ children who should be at school rather than engaged in sweatshop factories. Ultimately, what Islamic funds can and cannot invest in is determined by religious teaching, whereas the ecological or socially determined criteria used by ethical funds are an outcome of investors' consciences and preferences.

Islamic funds are also concerned with how the businesses are financed and the types of assets they hold. For example, it is recognised that most listed companies will have bank borrowings on which interest is payable; Islamic funds do not invest in heavily leveraged companies where the ratio of debt to asset value exceeds one-third. Companies earning more than five per cent of their income from interest on treasury holdings are also excluded from sharia-compliant investment portfolios.

---

[13] See Rodney Wilson, 'Screening Criteria for Islamic Equity Funds', in Sohail Jaffer, ed., *Islamic Asset Management: Forming the Future for Sharia-Compliant Investment Strategies* (London, 2004), pp.35–45.

Ethical funds do not use financial screening criteria, but they do apply other positive and negative screens. For example, sustainable energy sources such as wind farms or solar panels are viewed as desirable types of business from an ecological perspective. It has been suggested that Islamic funds should invest in companies that create employment in the Muslim world where unemployment and poverty are major issues, in contrast to the preference today for investments in developed economies.

Conclusion

During the last half century there has been mounting interest in the ethics of economic choices, which has intensified in the aftermath of the 2008 global financial crisis. This coincides with the 'rediscovery' of traditional teachings in the Muslim world on economic behaviour, and the efforts of scholars to apply this through *ijtihad* to modern banking and financial activity. From Malaysia and Indonesia to the European diaspora and the Middle East, economists and finance specialists are as engaged with religious scholars as with the latest global trends in seeking effective ways of putting principles into practice.

As well, there is a strong interest in altruism in economic behaviour, in the wider context of proper motivation for economic choices. Those involved in 'socially responsible' and Islamic finance have much to learn from one another. Again, when it comes to social as well as economic development – notably with respect to poverty alleviation and equitable distribution, environmental sustainability and the fair flow of trade – secular and religious ethics share a robust concern. A convergence in this regard is already evident in the work of many Muslim organisations and activists who recognise the inescapably global nature of economic life.

Further Reading

Boatright, John R. *Ethics in Finance*. 2nd edn, Oxford, 2007.
Gasper, Des. *The Ethics of Development*. Edinburgh, 2004.

Iqbal, Munawar and Rodney Wilson, eds. *Islamic Perspectives on Wealth Creation.* New York, 2005.

Jaffer, Sohail, ed. *Islamic Wealth Management: A Catalyst for Global Change and Innovation.* London, 2009.

Saeed, Abdullah, 'Islamic Banking and Finance: In Search of a Pragmatic Model', in Virginia Hooker and Amin Saikal, eds. *Islamic Perspectives on the New Millennium.* Singapore, 2004, pp. 113–29.

Thomas, Abdulkader, ed. *Interest in Islamic Economics: Understanding Riba.* London, 2006.

Tripp, Charles. *Islam and the Moral Economy: The Challenge of Capitalism.* Cambridge, 2006.

Wilson, Rodney, 'Islam', in Jan Peil and Irene van Staveren, eds. *Handbook of Economics and Ethics.* Cheltenham, UK and Northampton, MA, 2009, pp. 283–90.

Yunus, Muhammad. *Banker to the Poor: Micro-lending and the Battle against World Poverty.* New York, 2003.

9

Dispute Resolution

Mohamed Keshavjee

From the outset, the just resolution of disputes became in Islam an ethical virtue inspired by the Quran and the life of Muhammad as prophet and statesman. A non-adversarial approach that led to a negotiated settlement or *sulh* was the ideal. At the heart of this approach was the matter of fairness, or what has come to be called 'equity', over and above a literal application of legal rules. Indeed, equity is the key to the practice of alternative dispute resolution (ADR), a modern response to the limits of the civil justice system in resolving all the cases that come before it. Principles of equity have also remained vital in dispensing justice to disputants in the various Muslim schools of law. This chapter proposes that in considering the idea of equitable resolution as an ethical good, ADR in Muslim settings can serve both to deliver formal remedies *and* to be seen as doing so by the disputants – provided it is conducted competently and fairly.

During the last few centuries, European colonialism imposed new laws on Muslim societies, which led to systems such as Anglo-Muhammadan law in India and *Droit Musulman* in Algeria. There was a rupture not only in the practice of traditional law, but also in the collective memory of that law. With decolonisation, national constitutions and legal codes were based on western models, whether inherited from the colonial powers or otherwise borrowed to meet modern needs. These new legal systems often included aspects of the sharia, as locally interpreted, in such matters as family law and inheritance. More recently, especially since the

1970s, many Muslim countries have witnessed the 'Islamisation' of their laws. This trend is generally tied to nationalism and other political and social factors. The result is that some of the newly adopted laws have at times come into conflict with international legal norms and practices, including those related to protecting the rights of the individual. This chapter will touch on the complex nature of such conflict.

ADR is not a solution for all ills. Yet creatively applied, it can play a vital role in bridging Muslim tradition and legal modernity. ADR offers the prospect of revisiting some of the essential tenets – *maqasid* – that underlie Muslim teachings and jurisprudence on the protection of religion (*din*), personhood (*nafs*), offspring (*nasl*), property (*maal*) and reason (*aql*). Tradition can become a rich resource for contemporary legal systems that must respond to the demands of justice, with due respect for the plurality of customs and values of Muslim communities. How does this relate to the resolution of disputes as an ethical good?

Foundations

The principle of resolving disputes peaceably outside the legal arena (*sulh*) is enshrined in the Quran itself. For the homestead, it proclaims:

> *If you fear a breach*
> *Between them [husband and wife],*
> *Appoint two arbiters,*
> *One from his family,*
> *And the other from hers;*
> *If they wish for peace,*
> *Allah will cause their conciliation:*
> *For Allah hath full knowledge,*
> *And is acquainted with all things.* (4:35)

More broadly, the Quran proclaims:

> *Allah doth command you*
> *To render back your Trusts*
> *To those to whom they are due;*
> *And when ye judge*
> *Between man and man*
> *That ye judge with justice;*
> *Verily, how excellent*
> *Is the teaching which He giveth you!*
> *For Allah is He who heareth*
> *And seeth all things.* (4:58)

There are numerous hadith that offer daily narratives where the virtues of forgiveness, trust, compassion and consensus-building are extolled, especially with regard to resolving disputes. A classic instance relates to the Prophet taking a daily route on which, as he passed, a woman would empty her dustbin from her balcony over his head. Muhammad would merely continue on his way. On one occasion, when she failed to do the deed, he inquired about her and was informed that she was ill. He sought permission to visit her and, on finding that she was unable to even sit up for a drink of water, helped her do so. The woman asked the Prophet's forgiveness, which he duly offered; touched by this, she embraced the faith.

Another instance attests to Muhammad's capacity for building consensus. In the reconstruction of the Kaaba in Mecca, a sharp quarrel arose over the setting of the *Hajar al-aswad*, the Black Stone. Each one of the four Quraysh leaders in dispute was eager not to be outdone in having the honour. To break the impasse, one of the leaders proposed that the first to arrive in the sacred sanctuary the next morning could place the Stone. As it transpired, the Prophet was that person – but not wishing to have the privilege alone, he asked for a representative from each tribe to come forward. Muhammad then spread a sheet of cloth on the floor, put the Stone upon it and asked each representative to hold one end and together raise it for placement. This averted any further conflict among the tribes.

In the year 658, the fourth caliph and first Shia imam, Ali b. Abi Talib, dispatched a remarkable document on the art of governance to Malik al-Ashtar on his appointment as governor of Egypt. It sets forth systematically the ethics of public administration, notably with regard to the entitlements of the citizens to be served. Hence, justice is defined here as 'bringing to everyone what is his due'.[1] It requires serving 'the people, as against yourself, your near ones and those of your subjects for whom you have liking'. Elaborating on the qualities of those who arbitrate, the caliph-imam writes: 'You must be very judicious in selection of officers for dispensation of justice among your people. For this purpose, you should select persons of excellent character, superior calibre and meritorious record, that is from among the best available in merits and morals.' Such arbitrators 'should not be satisfied with superficial enquiry or simple scrutiny of a case till everything for and against it has been thoroughly examined; when confronted with doubts and ambiguities, they must pause, go for further details, clear the points and then give the decision.' As a further word of caution, he exhorts: 'Do not make haste to arrive at decisions before the time is ripe. Similarly, do not delay decisions and actions when the time is ripe and opportune.'

In his *Compendium of Fatimid Law* (1969), the noted jurist Asaf Fyzee devotes an entire chapter to the proper conduct of judges. Drawing on the teachings of the leading Fatimid theologian and jurist, al-Qadi al-Nuʿman (c. 903–974) in his *Daʿaʾim al-Islam* ('The Pillars of Islam'), Fyzee observes that a judge 'should have patience; not show his displeasure to any party; not accept any present from any party, and should not hold court and perform his functions while he is angry or hungry or sleepy.' Moreover, judicial processes should always be open to the prospect of a less formally negotiated settlement (*sulh*) among the parties.[2] This

---

[1] Translation in Reza Shah-Kazemi, *Justice and Remembrance: Introducing the Spirituality of Imam ʿAli* (London, 2006), Appendix 2, with an insightful commentary in Chapter 2.

[2] See Aida Othman, 'And Amicable Settlement Is Best: Sulh and Dispute Resolution in Islamic Law', *Arab Law Quarterly*, 21 (2007), pp.64–90.

was evident, for example, in the context of the Ottoman courts:

> *Muslihun* [those who help negotiate compromise and reconcilia-
> tion] were regular features of the court. Often, litigants reported
> to the court that *Muslihun* had negotiated *sulh* between them,
> indicating that a compromise had been accomplished away from
> the court.[3]

Indeed, *sulh* is embedded in the family law codes of various
Muslim countries. For example, the Jordanian Law of Personal
Status (1976) has an elaborate procedure on reconciliation and
arbitration. Article 132 outlines in great detail the actual procedure to be followed and provides for two arbitrators of upright
character to intervene to bring about reconciliation. Arbitrators
must be persons of experience, integrity and ability to effect reconciliation. Similar provisions also exist in the personal law codes of
countries such as Algeria, Egypt, Iraq, Iran, Kuwait, Libya, Malaysia,
Morocco, Syria, Tunisia, Iran, Iraq, and in the Muslim Family Law
Ordinance of Pakistan. As noted earlier, this foreshadows the modern
practice of alternative dispute resolution (ADR).

Alternative Dispute Resolution (ADR)

In one form or another, ADR has a long global history. A celebrated illustration comes from South Africa in 1893, where two
Indo-Muslim businessmen had a commercial dispute. One of them
wrote to the head office in Porbander in India to request a lawyer
who could serve as an intermediary between himself and his
European lawyers in South Africa, mindful of the cultural gap to
be bridged between lawyer and client. The Porbander office
dispatched a young, freshly trained barrister by the name of
Mohandas Karamchand Gandhi (1869–1948), who agreed to go
on a one-year contract (but actually stayed for 21 years). Gandhi
managed to settle the case out of court by drawing on the Indian

---

[3] Ronald Jennings, 'Kadi Court and Legal Procedure in the 17th century
Ottoman Keysari', *Studia Islamica*, 48 (1978), pp.133–72.

Lok Adalat (people's justice) tradition. This tradition had the esteem
of the disputants, alongside the principle of *sulh* or negotiated
settlement extolled in Islamic teachings.

A century later, in the same vein, the people of South Africa
sought an approach to justice in settling demands that no formal
legal system could deliver: a fair deal for all citizens after the end
of the apartheid system that had imposed massive inequity upon
the black majority. With the prospect of civil war imminent in
the 1990s, leaders such as Nelson Mandela and Archbishop
Desmond Tutu were able to draw upon an indigenous tradition
– *ubuntu* – for an ethical solution. Tutu describes *ubuntu* as a mix
of the ethics of generosity and compassion with clear implications for equity:

> [M]y humanity is caught up, is inextricably bound up, in theirs.
> We belong in a bundle of life. We say 'a person is a person through
> other people'. It is not 'I think, therefore I am'. It says rather: 'I am
> human, because I belong, I participate, I share'. A person with
> *ubuntu* is open and available to others . . . for he or she has a
> proper self-assurance that comes from knowing that he or she
> belongs in a greater whole and is diminished when others are
> humiliated or diminished, when others are tortured or oppressed,
> or treated as if they were less than who they are.[4]

The upshot was that a Truth and Reconciliation Commission
(TRC) emerged in 1995 as a forum where deep political and social
grievances could be publicly heard and, in many instances, medi-
ated. Tutu was to play a key role in the TRC, which was a form
of ADR widely credited with helping to avert violent conflict.
More broadly, *ubuntu* contributed an ethical vision that informed
the country's political agenda in the difficult transition to a viable
and vibrant democracy.

One finds indigenous ADR traditions in this vein across civilisations, from China and the Roman Empire to the Middle East.
As with *ubuntu*, they appeal to a conciliatory ethic that is less

---

[4] Desmond Tutu, *No Future Without Forgiveness* (London, 1999), pp.34–5.

individualistic. But they also share a distrust of formal litigation that is captured in such popular Chinese aphorisms as 'win your lawsuit, lose your money' and 'let householders avoid litigation, for once you go to law there is nothing but trouble'.[5]

Various faith communities today have their own ADR systems. Faced with the daunting prospect of clogged secular courts and high legal fees, some in Canada today have turned to religious forums with robust traditions of effective dispute resolution among their adherents.[6] These include the Jewish community's *Beit Din*, which involves an arbitration panel not only for religious matters but also civil issues such as divorce and the restitution of property. Since 1946, Roman Catholics in Canada have been availing themselves of marriage tribunals, which decide whether a union may be annulled if either party wishes to remarry within the church. These tribunals have lawyers with expertise in canon law and all cases are reviewed by the Canadian appeal tribunal in Ottawa. Ismaili Muslims in Canada may refer a range of civil cases to their Conciliation and Arbitration Boards (CAB), within the framework of the law of the land. Such CABs now exist in a number of countries and, over the past decade, panellists have been trained in the latest techniques of mediation.

What is ADR today?

Since the term emerged in the 1970s, ADR has evolved into a global response to the limits of formal civil justice systems. In essence, there must be a voluntary willingness on the part of the disputants to reach a negotiated solution. ADR uses a number of

---

[5] See Simon Roberts and Michael Palmer, *Dispute Processes: ADR and the Primary Forms of Decision Making* (Cambridge, 2005).

[6] See Marion Boyd, 'Dispute Resolution in Family Law: Protecting Choice, Promoting Inclusion', Toronto, 2004 (Report for the government of Ontario, Canada), available at: http://www.attorneygeneral.jus.gov.on.ca/english/about/pubs/boyd/. On Muslim ADR in the diaspora generally, see John Bowen, 'Private Arrangements: "Recognizing sharia" in England', *Boston Review* (March/April 2009), available at: http://bostonreview.net/BR34.2/bowen.php.

standard approaches in doing so. The most widely known is *arbitration*, which is closest to the judicial adjudication of disputes. Less formal are *mediation* and *conciliation*. All three involve a third-party intervener – impartial and neutral – who helps the disputants reach an agreement.

Arbitration is a centuries-old approach, notably in matters of commerce. In most types of arbitration, an independent third party (which could be a panel of more than one person) hears all sides of a dispute. Hearings are private and generally informal, which means that a more relaxed approach is taken to the strict rules of procedure and 'due process of law' than would apply in a judicial hearing. However, the process is final and binding; there are generally very few grounds allowed for appeal.

In mediation, an impartial third party helps reach a negotiated agreement among the disputants or their representatives. It is not the role of the mediator to impose a decision, but rather to facilitate communication and problem-solving by the parties themselves. Again, there may be more than one mediator, especially in matrimonial disputes (which for Muslims would also be in keeping with the spirit of the Quranic injunction in sura 4:35 quoted earlier). Mediation draws much support as an approach that empowers the parties and improves communication between them, especially where spousal relations continue. Unlike arbitration, the parties themselves can decide whether the outcome will be legally binding and on recourse to appeal.

Conciliation involves an impartial third party who plays a more direct role, by offering an opinion on how the parties may resolve their dispute. It has much in common with mediation and the two terms are often used interchangeably. But a conciliator must be prepared to guide the parties in particular directions at various stages in the process. The outcome is not binding on the parties, and they may subsequently choose to use other means to reach a satisfactory resolution.

While arbitration, mediation and conciliation are quite distinct processes, in practice they may well depart from their 'standard' distinctions, such as the role of the third-party intervener, or the binding nature of the settlement. Indeed, all three processes may at various stages of a dispute come into play. After all, the ultimate purpose of ADR is to arrive at a negotiated solution. Such flexibility is still more necessary across cultural boundaries. For John Lederach, one of the world's leading authorities in cross-cultural ADR, there is much to learn from groups that have experienced significant cultural change and transition. In multicultural settings, says Lederach, one should facilitate a group process rather than act as an 'expert' in conflict resolution. This allows one to draw on 'valid and important insights and knowledge about the problem, the possible options . . . and the viability of proposed solutions'.[7]

ADR, the Sharia and Legal Modernity

To fully understand the role that ADR can play in Muslim civil dispute resolution, one needs an appreciation of how ADR relates to the sharia, past and present. The term sharia literally means 'path' or 'way' to the water source. Daily access to water was prized by the communities of desert dwellers that largely characterised the Prophet's Arabia. The sharia emerged as the body of ethical principles for 'right living' found in the Quran and the teachings of the Prophet – which came to be supplemented later by the interpretive teachings of eminent jurists and, for Shia Muslims, those of their imams.

Over the course of time, this body of ethical principles has informed the development of law in Islam, variously derived by scholars with expertise in *fiqh* or jurisprudence. The Quran, the primary source of the sharia, is not a code of law, though a fair number of its verses deal with matters from which law is derived. Where it enjoins certain moral acts and forbids others, the Quran holds individuals ultimately accountable to God. In effect, then, Quranic precepts inform the 'code of conduct' that is the sharia and give it its high moral character.

In his lifetime, the Prophet was not only the medium of reve-

---

[7] John P. Lederach, *Preparing for Peace: Conflict Transformation Across Cultures* (Syracuse, NY, 1995), pp.109–18.

lation but also its interpreter. The nascent Muslim umma routinely brought to him their disputes for authoritative rulings. His companions or *sahaba* were also approached for their wisdom, as were the Prophet's four successors as the *khulafa rashidun* or 'rightly-guided caliphs'. In their wake, amid a plurality of views in the growing Muslim community about who could exercise legitimate authority over them, it was theologians and jurists – the *ulama* and *fuqaha* – who took on the role of interpreting the sharia and the derivative body of law or *fiqh*. Shia and Sunni scholars alike developed a dynamic corpus of ethical and legal guidance that found particular expression in their respective *madhhab*s or schools of thought. An expanding Islamic empire needed a sophisticated and adaptive approach to the practice of faith and governance.

As with all theological and legal traditions, however, a period of conservatism set in, marked by the declining fortunes of the major dynasties in the face of both intra-Muslim rivalry, and then the catastrophic Mongol invasions from the early 1200s onward. Rigidity in doctrine and decreased scope for innovative thinking was to become widespread. As Coulson puts it, 'the spring of juristic speculation, which had supplied the rapidly-moving stream of Islamic jurisprudence in its early stages, gradually ceased to flow; the current slowed, until eventually and inevitably, it reached the point of stagnation'.[8] This is what is often referred to as the 'closure of the gate of *ijtihad*' or independent reasoning.

Whether or not such a 'closure' took place in any formal manner, there can be little doubt that a rather long period of stagnation in legal and theological development ensued in much of the Muslim world. There were important exceptions, to be sure. Mughal rule in India, the Ottomans in the Near East and Europe, and the Safavids in Iran were markedly creative in legal and religious thought in the 1500s; Sultan Suleyman (r. 1520–66) was known to his Ottoman subjects as *al-Qanuni*, 'the Law-giver'. But in most areas of public and private law, it was the societies of Europe that began to respond more effectively to the fresh challenges of

---

[8] Noel Coulson, *A History of Islamic Law* (Edinburgh, 1964), p.73.

early modernity. The rise of European colonialism affirmed the hegemony of western approaches far beyond their borders into the Muslim lands of the Middle East, Asia and sub-Saharan Africa.

From the 19th century onward, we begin to see laws of European origin being adopted in various areas of the Muslim world, not only in civil and mercantile affairs but also in constitutional and administrative law. European law – commercial and criminal – already had a foothold in the 19th-century Ottoman Empire through the system of 'Capitulations', by which the western powers ensured that their citizens and often also their co-religionists in the Middle East would be governed by their own laws. It was to the laws applied under this system that local authorities turned when the desire for efficiency and progress seemed to necessitate going beyond traditional practices. Large-scale reception of European law was effected by the Ottoman *Tanzimat* (reorganisation) of 1839–76. This was to have a snowball effect across the region: the codification of laws and new reformist constitutions became a mark of modernity.

Outside the Middle East, the infiltration of western law into Muslim societies was tied to the politics of occupying colonial powers. This was evident in Algeria with the French conquest in 1850, in Indonesia where Dutch public and penal laws were similarly imported, and in British India, where codification of considerable portions of the civil law on an English basis ensued. In the Indian subcontinent, as elsewhere, Islamic law was now confined to family matters and related personal law. So pervasive was the colonial influence even in the application of sharia and *fiqh* principles that an 'Anglo-Muhammadan Law' emerged in British India. Its impact was felt as far afield as colonial East Africa.

In the latter part of the 20th century, nationalism and the quest for 'authentic' cultural/religious identity led to a backlash against the legacy of colonialism in many societies. For Muslims, this sometimes found expression in calls for the 'Islamisation' of laws and for a 'return of the sharia'. The phenomenon was given impetus by such events as the Arab oil crisis of the early 1970s, followed in 1979 by the Iranian Revolution, and the Soviet invasion of Afghanistan in 1980. They were to unleash deeply felt post-colonial grievances, which related to a gamut of economic, political and social injustices.[9] Some of those grievances were linked directly to the actions of former and neo-colonial powers, others to succeeding local elites. There was a sense that indigenous identities and sovereignties had to be reclaimed, often by reaching for customs, rules and practices anchored in a distant time and place, 'unspoilt' by the ideologies of modernity.

Thus 'religion' may become a repository of fresh rhetorical claims in a bid for legitimacy, whether by aggrieved communities or by a defensive state. The results can be vexing for some of the hard-won gains of legal and political modernity, notably in matters of individual human rights and civil society. Applied as 'sacred law' and without the safeguards of legal due process, the sharia in practice can become a barrier to its own *maqasid* or higher ethical commitment to equity.[10] The issue, as Mashood Baderin persuasively shows in *International Human Rights and Islamic Law* (2003), is not merely one of compliance with global rules but of a sensible dialogue that enhances 'a common understanding' of human dignity and autonomy.

ADR 'in the shadow of the Law'

To serve as an effective medium for broad social access to justice outside the limits of formal legal systems, ADR itself must function in harmony with the latter. Or as two leading scholars, Robert Mnookin and Lewis Kornhauser, famously put it, in successful ADR 'negotiations always take place in the shadow of the law'.[11] Even as it offers an alternative to formal justice, ADR requires

---

[9] See John L. Esposito, 'Contemporary Islam', in J.L. Esposito, ed., *The Oxford History of Islam* (Oxford, 1999), pp.643–90.

[10] Illustrative are the widely reported cases of Abdul Rehman in Afghanistan (2006), where apostasy was alleged against a background of poor traditional and constitutional protection of religious freedom; and Amina Lawal in Nigeria (2002), where a conviction for adultery resulted in a sentence of death by stoning, which was ultimately reversed by a sharia appeal court.

[11] R. Mnookin and L. Kornhauser, 'Bargaining in the Shadow of the Law: The Case of Divorce', *Yale Law Journal*, 88 (1979), pp.950–97.

careful regulation under public law to ensure that it meets the highest standards of propriety and fairness. Further, dispute resolution modes and systems will only serve the increasingly complex demands of the public if they offer 'state of the art' sophistication, in terms of the quality of human and institutional resources that provide such services. Alternative justice cannot be inferior justice.

In Muslim settings, this means a creative process of adapting 'traditional' and customary legal norms and practices to serve not only contemporary expectations of fair play and respect for human rights, but the overarching ethical purposes of the sharia itself. Indeed, given the growing importance of public religion in societies across the world, including in such 'secular' domains as commercial and public law, the sophistication of faith-based frameworks of law and ADR will likely become vital. This implies that dispute resolvers in Muslim communities will need to be knowledgeable about what 'the sharia' really is, as an ethico-religious system that has inspired the making of law. After all, today's global marketplace calls for sharia-sensitive intervention not only in matters of family and inheritance disputes, but also in matters of banking, insurance and a host of financial products. A key sharia principle here is the prohibition of usury or *riba*, rooted in the Quran's recurrent concern with social equity. How exactly this principle is to be interpreted today is a subject of much debate among scholars,[12] with implications for dispute resolution at various levels, including arbitral awards at the international level.

One obstacle to the creative modernising of Muslim dispute resolution processes is the popular view that customary practices (*urf*), which tend to reflect local traditions, are somehow universal and timeless. Examples in the area of personal law are the linking of practices like forced marriages, female circumcision and crimes of honour with the sharia, when they are in fact tribal customs

---

[12] See Rodney Wilson, 'The Development of Islamic Economics: Theory and Practice', in Suha Taji-Farouki and Basheer Nafi, eds, *Islamic Thought in the Twentieth Century* (London, 2004), pp.195–222.

that have nothing to do with Islam and run afoul of the ethics of the sharia.[13] Yet the evidence shows that the sharia – like the body of *fiqh* derived from it – has time and again been capable of creative change, driven by the principles of *darura* (necessity) and *maslaha* (public interest). It is these principles that have made the role of the sharia and *fiqh* so vibrant in contemporary commercial matters, as Rodney Wilson's chapter in this volume makes evident.

Conclusion

'Alternative dispute resolution', by its very nature, has a limitless remedial imagination. We have seen the potency of that imagination in early Muslim history, driven by the ethical teaching of the Quran as well as the Prophet and his successors. The legacy includes not only the principles and rulings of the sharia and *fiqh*, but also the lived traditions of negotiation and settlement in Muslim communities. Drawing on the full panoply of these resources – including the larger worldview of Islam – is essential for Muslim ADR to be a modern success, notes the legal scholar and activist, Amr Abdalla. Relying on *fiqh* and formal jurisprudence alone, he notes, is not sufficient in meeting the range of human needs.[14] Thus, dispute resolvers must bring to their task fresh ways of understanding and applying traditional principles, along with a command of the latest techniques in the practice of ADR.

Yet there is also the issue of conservatism among Muslim communities, notably in matters of Muslim personal law. Dispute resolvers, however well disposed, can hardly impose 'progressive' ADR on an unwilling clientele. Such resistance is perhaps explained

[13] Ahmed E. Souaiaia, *Contesting Justice: Women, Islam, Law, and Society* (Albany, NY, 2008).

[14] Amr Abdalla, 'Principles of Islamic Interpersonal Conflict Intervention: A Search Within Islam and Western Literature', *Journal of Law and Religion*, 15 (2000), pp.1–2, pp.151–84. In the same vein, see Mohamed Abu-Nimer, 'Conflict Resolution in an Islamic context: Some Conceptual Questions', *Peace and Change*, 21 (1996), pp.22–40.

by fears that relate to preserving cultural identity: questions of family law and the status of women surely fall in this category. Modern ADR may be seen as 'invasively western' in matters of personal law, where it is felt to 'disturb' traditional social arrangements. Far less resistance is evident when it comes to western institutional offers of 'sharia-compliant' financial products or dispute resolution techniques. But in an increasingly globalised world, with large-scale Muslim migration across cultural frontiers, shared ethical values are becoming more keenly evident among religious and secular communities alike. ADR is an arena where pluralist ethics can flourish, if cultural sensitivities are respected on all sides.

This is in fact consistent with the spirit that animated Islam's foundational age. For a leading 20th-century Muslim thinker, Fazlur Rahman (c. 1919–1988), the ethical sharia needs to be retrieved from the legalistic cloak in which it has come to be wrapped historically.[15] Rahman's call for the higher principles (*maqasid*) of the sharia to serve as guiding lights for reform today finds wide sympathy among activist thinkers like Tariq Ramadan, Mohamed Talbi, Abdolkarim Soroush, Mohamed Shahrour, Ebrahim Moosa and Abdullahi An-Na'im. Such an approach locates reform squarely within 'tradition', while treating that tradition itself as dynamic rather than as merely a received body of opinion. As such, the legitimacy of this reform process also depends on how well it situates itself within public narratives that are both familiar and progressive. Among the fields in which this endeavour unfolds, ADR may well serve as a practical area of application – an exercise in the creative use of ethical wisdom to resolve human conflict.

Further Reading

An-Na'im, Abdullahi A., ed. *Islamic Family Law in a Changing*

---

[15] Fazlur Rahman, 'Law and Ethics in Islam', in R.G. Hovannisian, ed., *Ethics in Islam* (Malibu, CA, 1985), pp.3–15. More generally, see his *Islam and Modernity: Transformation of an Intellectual Tradition* (Chicago, 1984).

World: A Global Resource. London, 2002.

Baderin, Mashood A. *International Human Rights and Islamic Law.* Oxford, 2003.

Hallaq, Wael. *The Origins and Evolution of Islamic Law.* Cambridge, 2004.

Haque, Tatjana, et al. *In Search of Justice: Women's Encounters with Alternative Dispute Resolution.* Dhaka, 2002.

Keshavjee, Mohamed. 'Alternative Dispute Resolution in a Muslim Community: The Shia Imami Ismaili Conciliation and Arbitration Boards', in Prakash Shah and Werner Menski, eds, *Migration, Diasporas and Legal Systems in Europe.* London, 2006, pp.74–85.

—— 'Alternative Dispute Resolution in a Diasporic Muslim Community in Britain', in Prakash Shah, ed. *Law and Ethnic Plurality: Socio-Legal Perspectives.* Leiden, 2007, pp.145–75.

Lederach, John P. *Preparing for Peace: Conflict Transformation Across Cultures.* Syracuse, NY, 1995.

Roberts, Simon and Michael Palmer. *Dispute Processes: ADR and the Primary Forms of Decision Making.* Cambridge, 2005.

Rosen, Lawrence. *The Anthropology of Justice: Law as Culture in Islamic Society.* Cambridge, 1989.

Saeed, Abdullah. 'Fazlur Rahman: A Framework for Interpreting the Ethico-legal Content of the Qur'an', in Suha Taji-Farouki, ed., *Modern Muslim Intellectuals and the Qur'an.* Oxford, 2004, pp.37–66.

10

Tolerance

Reza Shah-Kazemi

In our time, one commonly hears the claim that tolerance is an outcome of secular 'rationality' and 'neutrality'. Indeed, secular tolerance is seen as a hallmark of western modernity – in contrast to the supposed intolerance of traditions and civilisations that take religion too seriously, including the pre-modern West itself. How else to explain the events of 11 September 2001, and their aftermath, if not as a painful reminder of the perils of religious intolerance? Yet this view rests on a mistaken view of history, and of what tolerance amounts to both in precept and practice.

This chapter will argue that religious traditions, with specific regard to Islam, offer rich layers of ethical teaching requiring a positive disposition toward the Other. There is no shortage of historical evidence here – even if the failure of human beings to adhere to these teachings is obvious, as indeed it is in the wars and genocides of secular modernity. I intend to draw attention to the scope of Muslim teaching and practice on diversity as not only inspiring toleration but also celebration. Toleration on the outward, legal and formal plane; celebration on the inward, cultural and spiritual plane.

As with secular tolerance, one encounters here an open-minded attitude that enables policies and laws of a tolerant nature toward the religious Other. But this derives from an appreciation of the Other as part of an unfolding divine vision, not simply an inconvenience to be put up with grudgingly or condescendingly. For one can be tolerant in a secular sense, outwardly and legally, without

sincere regard for the faith of the Other. Moreover, a purely secular
approach carries the risk of falling into a corrosive relativism of
the 'anything goes' variety. It can lead to the particularity of one's
own faith being diluted, if not sacrificed, for the sake of a political or social scheme.

For Muslims, tolerance of the Other is integral to the practice
of Islam. It is not an optional extra, a cultural luxury. The Quran
sets forth an expansive vision of diversity and difference, plurality
and indeed of universality. This is all the more ironic since the
practice of contemporary Muslim states, not to mention extra-
state groups and actors, falls lamentably short of those expectations as well as of current standards of tolerance set by the secular
West. In response, many within and outside the Muslim world
advocate a western approach as an antidote to tradition and religiosity. A more fruitful response is to see such tolerant codes of
conduct as expressions of the universal principle of tolerance, and
to discern this principle at the very heart of the vision of Islam
itself: a vision in which the plurality of religious paths to the One
is perceived as a reflection of the spiritual infinity of the One.
Tolerance of human diversity is a moral outcome of this plurality,
becoming an expression of the wisdom of the One. In this framework, tolerance involves a duty and a right: an ethical duty to
permit people of different faiths to practise their own specific
ways of embodying these universal values, and the spiritual right
to benefit from the varied cultural expressions of these universal
values oneself. Hence the Quranic injunction:

> O mankind, We have created you male and female, and We have
> made you into tribes and nations in order that you might come
> to know one another. Truly, in the sight of God, the most honoured
> amongst you is the most pious amongst you. (49:13)

When asked 'which religion is most loved by God?', the Prophet's
reply was to highlight what is required for a religion to become
'the most beloved' of God: *al-hanafiyya al-samha* or 'the primordial, generously tolerant faith'. In accordance with the implication
of verse 49:13, the Prophet emphasises the equality of all believers,

the sole moral hierarchy within humanity being that based on virtue, not gender or tribe or nation or religion. In this framework of equality and the belief in revelation as a universal phenomenon (no community being deprived of divine guidance), intolerance of the Other has no place. It is against this normative standard that we may judge historical lapses, large and small, in what has generally been an impressive narrative of Muslim esteem for the ethic of tolerance.

Roots of Liberal Tolerance

The idea of tolerance as it emerged in secular modernity has a family tree larger than is generally appreciated. History offers some intriguing insights into how its roots stretch well beyond the West. John Locke, one of the founding fathers of modern liberal thought, wrote his famous 'Letter Concerning Toleration' in 1689. This letter is viewed as instrumental in the process by which the ethical value of religious tolerance was transformed into a universal ethical imperative for the individual conscience, and into a legal obligation for the upholders of state authority. It is evident from this letter that Locke was deeply struck by the contrast between tolerant 'barbarians' – the Muslim Ottomans – and violently intolerant Christians. Locke ruefully reflected that Calvinists and Armenians were free to practise their faith if they lived in the Muslim Ottoman Empire, but not in Christian Europe: would the Turks not 'silently stand by and laugh to see with what inhuman cruelty Christians thus rage against Christians?'[1]

Locke passionately argued for 'universal tolerance', whatever one's religious beliefs, and in the prevailing Christian climate, *despite* one's beliefs. Following logically from this principle was the right of non-Christians, including Jews and Muslims, to enjoy 'civil rights' in England. This strict separation between religion and politics, church and state, so often viewed only as part of the evolutionary path of western secularisation, must also be seen in

---

[1] Quoted in N. Matar, 'John Locke and the Turbaned Nations', *Journal of Islamic Studies*, 2 (1991), p.72.

the light of the historical interface between mutually intolerant Christian states and denominations, on the one hand, and a vibrantly tolerant Muslim polity, on the other. The current freedom of religious belief and worship in the western world is not simply a corollary of secular thought. It is a principle inspired, at least in part, by the influence of Islam.

Muslim Ottoman tolerance was something to which Christendom was accustomed: 'Better the turban of the Sultan than the mitre of the Pope', was a well-worn saying among Eastern Orthodox Christians, acutely aware of the fact that their rights were more secure under the Ottomans than under their Catholic co-religionists. Ottoman conquest was followed almost without exception by an attitude of religious tolerance toward the conquered communities. According to (Reverend) Dr Susan Ritchie, 'Tolerance was a matter of Ottoman policy and bureaucratic structure, and an expression of the Ottoman interpretation of Islam, which was in most instances stunningly liberal and cosmopolitan.' She argues convincingly that this Ottoman tolerance decisively influenced the process leading to the famous Edict of Torda in 1568, issued by King John Sigismund of Transylvania (which was under Ottoman suzerainty), an edict hailed by western historians as expressing 'the first European policy of expansive religious toleration'.[2]

It is hardly surprising that Norman Daniel, in his *Islam, Europe and Empire* (1966), should make the simple – and, for many, startling – claim that, 'The notion of toleration in Christendom was *borrowed* from Muslim practice' (emphasis added). Ottoman attitudes toward the Jews provide an illuminating contrast with the anti-Semitism of Christendom, which resulted in the regular pogroms and 'ethnic cleansing' by which the medieval Christian world was stained. Many Jews fleeing from persecution in Central Europe would have received letters like the following, written by Rabbi Isaac Tzarfati just before the Ottoman capture of Constantinople in 1453, in reply to the call for help from Central European Jews:

---

[2] Susan Ritchie, 'The Islamic Ottoman Influence on the Development of Religious Toleration in Reformation Transylvania', in *Seasons* [Semiannual Journal of the Zaytuna Institute], 2 (2004), pp.62, 59.

Listen, my brethren, to the counsel I will give you. I too was born in Germany and studied Torah with the German rabbis. I was driven out of my native country and came to the Turkish land, which is blessed by God and filled with all good things. Here I found rest and happiness . . . Here in the land of the Turks we have nothing to complain of. We are not oppressed with heavy taxes, and our commerce is free and unhindered . . . every one of us lives in peace and freedom. Here the Jew is not compelled to wear a yellow hat as a badge of shame, as is the case in Germany, where even wealth and great fortune are a curse for the Jew because he therewith arouses jealousy among the Christians . . . Arise, my brethren, gird up your loins, collect your forces, and come to us. Here you will be free of your enemies, here you will find rest . . .[3]

At the very same time that the Christian West was indulging in periodic anti-Jewish pogroms, the Jews were experiencing what some Jewish historians themselves have termed a kind of 'golden age' under Muslim rule. As Erwin Rosenthal writes, 'The Talmudic age apart, there is perhaps no more formative and positive time in our long and chequered history than that under the empire of Islam.'[4] One particularly rich episode in this 'golden age' was experienced by the Jews of Muslim Spain. As has been abundantly attested by historical records, the Jews enjoyed not just freedom from oppression, but also an extraordinary revival of cultural, religious, theological and mystical creativity. Such great Jewish luminaries as Maimonides and Ibn Gabirol wrote their philosophical works in Arabic, and were fully 'at home' in Muslim Spain. With the expulsion, murder or forced conversion of all Muslims and Jews after the *reconquista* of Spain – brought to finality with Granada's fall in 1492 – it was to the Ottomans that the exiled Jews turned for refuge and protection. They were welcomed across Muslim North Africa, joining the settled and prosperous Jewish communities already there.

---

[3] Quoted in S.A. Schleifer, 'Jews and Muslims: A Hidden History', in *The Spirit of Palestine* (Barcelona, 1994), p.8.

[4] Quoted in Schleifer, 'Jews and Muslims', p.5.

As for Christians under Muslim rule in Spain or Andalusia, we have ample testimony of their flourishing in *la convivencia* (the Coexistence). An astonished Catholic nun from Saxony, Hroswitha of Gandersheim, famously described Cordoba in the mid-10th century as the 'ornament of the world'. At about the same time, embassies were exchanged between the court of Otto I of Germany and the court of Cordoba. One such delegation was led by John of Gorze in 953, who thus records the words of the resident bishop of Cordoba during the Muslim conquest: 'in the depths of such a great calamity, they do not forbid us to practise our own faith . . .'[5]

Even so fierce a critic of contemporary Islam as Bernard Lewis cannot but confirm the facts of history as regards the character of such intercommunal relations until recent times. In his *The Jews of Islam* (1984), he writes that even though there was a certain level of discrimination against Jews and Christians under Muslim rule,

> Persecution, that is to say, violent and active repression, was rare and atypical. Jews and Christians under Muslim rule were not normally called upon to suffer martyrdom for their faith. They were not often obliged to make the choice, which confronted Muslims and Jews in reconquered Spain, between exile, apostasy and death. They were not subject to any major territorial or occupational restrictions, such as were the common lot of Jews in premodern Europe. (p.8)

This pattern of tolerance characterised the nature of Muslim rule vis-à-vis Jews and Christians well into the modern period, with very minor exceptions. 'The Talmud was burned in Paris, not in Cairo or Baghdad', notes the historian Mark Cohen. 'Staunch Muslim opposition to polytheism convinced Jewish thinkers like

---

[5] Maria Rosa Menocal, *Ornament of the World: How Muslims, Jews and Christians Created a Culture of Tolerance in Medieval Spain* (Boston, 2002); Richard Fletcher, *The Cross and the Crescent: Christianity and Islam from Muhammad to the Reformation* (New York, 2004), p.48.

Maimonides of Islam's unimpeachable monotheism. This essentially liberal view of Islam echoed Islam's own respect for the Jewish "People of the Book".[6]

Principles

The essential message of the Quran with regard to prior revelations is one of inclusion and respect. Certainly there are verses which are critical of earlier practices. Yet the spirit of what the Quran envisions is summed up here:

> We have revealed unto you the Scripture with the Truth, to confirm and protect the Scripture which came before it ... For each We have appointed a Law and a Way. Had God willed, He could have made you one community. But that He might try you by that which He has given you [He has made you as you are]. So vie with one another in good works. Unto God you will all return, and He will inform you of that wherein you differed. (5:48)

In this verse, two vital principles are established. First, the Quran affirms the legitimacy and value of *all* divine revelations. Indeed, the plurality of these revelations stems from the divine will on the plane of human communities. Second, the plurality of faith communities is intended to stimulate respectful engagement and mutual enrichment. Hence, differences of opinion are inevitable consequences of the very plurality of meanings embodied in diverse revelations. Let us take a closer look at each of these principles.

Affirming the legitimacy of all revelations

It is ironic that media stereotypes as well as Muslim ideologues have cast Islam in the role of an exclusive claimant to revealed truth. 'Jihad' as 'sacred war' has become a slogan in this regard, as if the politics that attend such claims stem from Islam as a faith

---

[6] Mark R. Cohen, 'Islam and the Jews: Myth, Counter-Myth, History', in *Jerusalem Quarterly*, 38 (1986), p.135.

tradition. In fact, the Quran is blunt in asserting that 'there is no compulsion in religion' (2:256).[7] It is filled with the narratives found in the Hebrew and Christian Testament, including numerous affirmations of the importance of Abraham, Moses, Jesus and other prophetic figures to the unfolding Muslim message:

> Truly We inspire you, as We inspired Noah, and the prophets after him, as We inspired Abraham and Ishmael and Isaac and Jacob and the tribes, and Jesus and Job and Jonah and Aaron and Solomon, and as We bestowed unto David the Psalms; *and Messengers We have mentioned to you before, and Messengers We have not mentioned to you* (4:163–4). (emphasis added)[8]

Both universal revelation and human diversity are seen not as accidents of human experience but as expressions of divine wisdom. If God is absolutely one yet immeasurably infinite, the human race too is one in its essence yet infinitely variegated in its forms. 'And among His signs is the creation of the heavens and the earth, and the differences of your languages and colours. Indeed, herein are signs for those who know', says the Quran (30:22).

The *fitra*, or primordial nature, is the inalienable substance of each human being and this essence of human identity takes priority over all external forms of identity such as race and nation, culture or even religion: 'So set your purpose firmly for the faith as an original monotheist, [in accordance with] the *fitra* of God, by which He created mankind. There can be no altering the creation of God. That is the right religion, but most people know it not'

---

[7] On the inadmissibility of compelling non-Muslims to affirm belief in Islam, see Hashim Kamali, *Freedom of Expression in Islam* (Cambridge, 1997), pp.88–93.

[8] Many other verses fashion and reinforce this open-minded approach: 'For every community there is a Messenger' (10:47); 'And We never sent a messenger save with the language of his people, so that he might make [Our message] clear to them' (14:4); 'And We sent no Messenger before you but We inspired him [saying]: There is no God save Me, so worship Me' (21:25); 'Naught is said unto you [Muhammad] but what was said unto the Messengers before you' (41:43).

(30:30). As seen earlier, the only criterion by which hierarchical distinction can be established among human beings is *taqwa*, the sense of the divine presence in the human conscience.

In the same vein, the diversity of religious rites is generously affirmed. 'Unto each community We have given sacred rites (*mansakan*) which they are to perform; so let them not dispute with you about the matter, but summon them unto your Lord (22:67).' When faced with alien religious rites and beliefs such as those of the Buddhists and Hindus, the response of Muslim scholars in the eighth century was to have a 'good opinion' (*husn al-zann*) and advise that they be treated as 'People of the Book'; we shall return to this below. It is no surprise, then, that the Prophet is told to say in the Quran that his mission is no 'innovation' in the cycle of revelation. He only reiterates the central message of all revelations, a message that comprises diverse modes and facets but which remains one and the same in its essence.

Plurality as mutual social and spiritual enrichment

A major source of intolerance is the exclusivist notion that one's religion alone grants access to salvation, all others being false religions leading nowhere. This is captured in the Roman Catholic formula *extra ecclesiam nulla salus* (no salvation outside the Church). Rather than respond with an exclusivism of their own, Muslims are told to elevate the dialogue and call for reasoned appeal. Indeed, the Quranic position is to affirm that the path to salvation is accessible to all human beings, whatever their religious affiliation (2:62, 5:69).

> And they say: 'None enters Paradise unless he be a Jew or a Christian'. These are their vain desires. Say: 'Bring your proof if you are truthful'. Nay, but whosoever submits his purpose to God, and he is virtuous, his reward is with his Lord. No fear shall come upon them, neither shall they grieve. (2:111–12)

In another verse we read: 'It will not be in accordance with your desires, nor with the desires of the People of the Book' (4:123).

One sees here that insofar as the Muslim 'desires' that salvation be restricted to Muslims in the specific, communal sense, he falls into the kind of illogical exclusivism for which Christians and Jews are criticised. The very same term is used for the 'desires' (*amani*) of the Christians, Jews and Muslims. In other words, one form of prejudice is not to be confronted with another, but with a measured recognition that divine justice stands far above religious chauvinism.

In the traditional sources, the trait most often used to define the essence of the Prophet's personality is *hilm* or forbearance, compounded by wisdom and gentleness. The tolerance accorded to the Other by the Prophet is an expression not only of knowledge of the universality of revelation, but also of the divine generosity from which this universality arises. Tolerance here goes far beyond formal acceptance of the Other. It is the ethical form assumed by one's conformity to the standards set in the Quran, and in emulation of the prophetic nature, most notably the trait of *hilm*. 'It was a mercy from God that you are gently disposed to them', observes the Quran; 'had you been fierce and hard-hearted, they would have fled from you' (3:159).

Moreover, the Prophet only had the duty to deliver the scriptural message, not to impose it: 'Call unto the way of your Lord with wisdom and fair exhortation, and hold discourse with them [the People of the Book] in the finest manner' (16:125). The Muslim is called upon to bear witness to his faith, certainly, but the manner of doing so should be marked by grace and wisdom. This kind of dialogue presupposes tolerant acceptance of the right of the Other to differ, and it can bear fruit in the common quest for a wisdom which rises above confessional boundaries.

Action

In Thomas Arnold's still unsurpassed historical account of the spread of Islam, *The Preaching of Islam*, it is evident that the manifestation of tolerance was a critical factor in making the faith so attractive to non-Muslims. He cites abundant evidence in this regard, and the following example is particularly telling. The

Christians of the Persian province of Khurasan embraced Islam en masse within the first century of Muslim rule over Persia. This elicited a bitter complaint from the Nestorian Patriarch, Isho-yabh III, to Simeon, Metropolitan of Rev-Ardashir, Primate of Persia:

> Alas, alas! Out of so many thousands who bore the name of Christians, not even one single victim was consecrated unto God by the shedding of his blood for the true faith . . . [the Arabs] attack not the Christian faith, but on the contrary, they favour our religion, do honour to our priests and the saints of our Lord and confer benefits on churches and monasteries. Why then have your people of Merv abandoned their faith for the sake of these Arabs? (pp.81–2).

The nature of the early Muslim polity was derived from the Prophet's embodiment of the Quranic revelation. His acts of states-manship should not be seen in isolation as a series of historical events only, but also as symbolic acts which uphold the inviolability of the religious rights of the Other and the necessity of exercising a generous tolerance. The seminal and most graphic expression of this vision is found in the following well-attested episode in the life of the Prophet. In the ninth year after the Hijra (631), a prominent Christian delegation from Najran, an important centre of Christianity in the Yemen, came to engage the Prophet in theological debate in Medina. The main point of contention was the nature of Christ: was he one of God's Messengers or the unique Son of God?

What matters here is not the disagreements voiced, nor the means by which the debate was resolved, but the fact that when these Christians requested to leave the city to perform their liturgy, the Prophet invited them to accomplish their rites in his own mosque. According to Ibn Ishaq, who gives the standard account of this remarkable event, the Yemenis here performed the Byzantine Christian rite.[9] Hence, they were enacting a form of the rites that

---

[9] A. Guillaume, tr., *The Life of Muhammad: A Translation of Ibn Ishaq's Sirat Rasul Allah* (Oxford, 1968), pp.270–77.

incorporated the fully developed trinitarian theology of the Orthodox councils, emphasising the definitive creed of the divine sonship of Christ – doctrines explicitly criticised in the Quran. Nonetheless, the Prophet invited the Christians to accomplish their rites in his own mosque. Disagreement on the plane of dogma is one thing, tolerance – indeed encouragement – of the enactment of that dogma is another.

One should also mention here the tolerance that is inscribed within the first Muslim constitution, that of Medina. A polity defined by inclusivity and plurality is envisioned in that historic document. The right to freedom of worship was assumed, given the open recognition of all three religious groups who were party to the agreement: Muslims, Jews and polytheists – the last comprising the majority at this time. Each group enjoyed unfettered religious and legal autonomy, and the Jews, it should be noted, were not required at this stage to pay any kind of poll-tax. The Muslims were indeed recognised as forming a distinct group within the polity, but this did not compromise the principle of mutual defence at the root of the agreement: 'Each must help the other against anyone who attacks the people of this document. They must seek mutual advice and consultation, and loyalty is a protection against treachery.'[10]

Tolerance also requires, of course, tolerating opinions contrary to one's own. Evidence of this in the early Muslim polity is offered by the conduct of Imam Ali b. Abi Talib as caliph (656–61) toward the Kharijites, who were among his fiercest political opponents. They enjoyed full rights to express their dissent, even when this extended to calling Ali a *kafir* (infidel). 'If they oppose me through speech, I will hold discourse and argue with them'; and 'I will only resort to arms when they fight me.'[11]

Amid intense Kharijite opposition to his rule, Imam Ali

---

[10] F.E. Peters, *Judaism, Christianity, and Islam* (Princeton, 1990), vol.1, p.217.

[11] Cited in Muhammad Tayy, 'Ru'yat al-Imam 'Alī' [The vision of Imam Ali], in Mehdi Golshani, ed., *Proceedings of the Congress on Imam Ali and Justice, Unity and Security* (Tehran, 2002), pp.63–4.

continued paying them their salaries from the public treasury. The Imam addressed the Kharijites on several occasions with words such as these: 'You have three prerogatives in regard to us: we shall not prevent you from praying in the mosques; nor shall we stop payment of the *fay'* [salaries] due to you from the treasury; nor shall we initiate hostilities against you until you fight us.' Only when vociferous opposition turned to open insurrection did payments from the treasury cease. This tolerant episode is all the more remarkable in taking place at a time of constant strife – when it is tempting to invoke various 'emergency' measures that justify the curtailment of the rights and freedoms of citizens, so common nowadays.

Indeed, when state policy under the Abbasid caliph Mamun (r. 813–33) imposed a 'theology of reason' upon the community of scholars and citizens in an episode known as the *mihna* or inquisition, it failed. Mamun had his own reasons for subscribing to what was seen as a progressive movement of rationalism led by the Mutazila, which held that the Quran was a historical creation rather than an eternally present reality. Traditionalist scholars would have none of this, asserting that the Quran was quite simply the eternal word of God. When in the last year of his reign Mamun turned the Mutazili perspective into a test of loyalty for judges, officials and the *ulama*, their revolt (and especially that of the traditionalists) gradually became irresistible. The *mihna* was formally declared over in 861. It is ironic that this episode of intolerance was conducted in the name of 'reason', reminding us that such persecution has not been the sole preserve of any single ideological tradition.

Dhimmis: tolerance in practice?

The issue today referred to as 'dhimmitude', a term coined from the Arabic *dhimmi* in reference to religious minorities granted protection by the Muslim state in return for the payment of a poll-tax or *jizya*, merits special mention. The word *dhimmi* comes from a root meaning 'blame': any violation of the religious, social or legal rights of the protected minority was subject to the 'censure' (*dhimma*) of the Muslim authorities who were charged with the protection of these rights.[12]

The institution of the *dhimma* was established by the Prophet in a series of agreements with tribes and groups in the Arabian Peninsula. The principle embodied in these agreements was followed by the Prophet's immediate successors, and it set a standard by which all subsequent regimes could be judged. One of the most momentous and far-reaching of such acts by the Prophet's successors was undertaken by the second caliph, 'Umar, in his conquest of Jerusalem in 638. On entering the city he was invited to perform his prayers in the Church of the Holy Sepulchre, but decided instead to pray outside, for fear his action would be taken as a pretext to convert the church into a mosque. Not only did 'Umar guarantee security and freedom of worship to the Christian inhabitants, but he showed equal reverence to the holy sites of the Jews, personally taking part in the cleaning of the Temple Mount, which had been converted into a rubbish dump under the Byzantines. When Jews returned to the Old City, he interceded on their behalf against the Christians who were opposed to the Jewish resettlement. The agreement contracted between himself and the inhabitants of Jerusalem was as follows:

> This is the assurance of safety [*aman*] which the servant of God 'Umar, the Commander of the Faithful, has granted to the people of Jerusalem. He has given them an assurance of safety for themselves, for their property, their churches, their crosses, the sick and healthy of the city, and for all the rituals that belong to their religion. Their churches will not be inhabited [by Muslims], nor will they be destroyed. Neither they, nor the land on which they stand,

---

[12] E.W. Lane defines *dhimma* as 'A compact, a covenant, a contract, a league, a treaty, an engagement, a bond, or an obligation . . . because the breaking thereof necessitates blame'; *Arabic–English Lexicon* (Cambridge, 1984), vol. 1, p.976.

nor their crosses, nor their property will be damaged. They will not be forcibly converted.[13]

One should note the following important statement by the Caliph-imam Ali b. Abi Talib, disclosing the essence of the *dhimma* institution: 'Those who have contracted the agreement of *dhimma* have done so only in order that their lives and their properties should be as inviolable as our own.' He further established absolute equality between Muslims and the protected minorities by saying that the compensation for the killing of a Muslim was the same as that for a Jew or Christian.[14] This chimes well with Imam Ali's injunction to one of his deputies, Malik al-Ashtar, when appointing him governor of Egypt: 'Infuse your heart with mercy for the people in your charge, have love for them and be kind to them. Be not like a ravenous beast of prey above them, seeking to devour them. For they are of two types: either your brother in religion or your like in creation.'[15]

The protected minorities are by no means confined to the 'People of the Book' (*ahl al-kitab*), that is, the Christians and Jews alone; this category was in practice extended to include all revealed religions. The inclusion of Hinduism and Buddhism into this juridical category, at the outset of Muslim expansion into India in the eighth century, is instructive. During the short but successful campaign of the young Umayyad general, Muhammad b. Qasim, in Sind, launched in 711, petitions were received from the indigenous Buddhists and Hindus in the city of Brahmanabad regarding the restoration of their temples. He consulted his superior, the governor of Kufa, Hajjaj b. Yusuf, who in turn consulted his religious scholars. The result of these deliberations was the formulation of

---

[13] Al-Tabari, *The History of al-Tabari*, tr. Y. Friedmann (Albany, NY, 1985), vol. 12, p.191. See also Norman Stillman, *The Jews of Arab Lands: A History and Source Book* (Philadelphia, 1979), pp.154–5.

[14] Muhammad Tayy, 'Ru'yat al-Imam 'Ali , *Proceedings of Congress*, p.71.

[15] Quoted in my *Justice and Remembrance: Introducing the Spirituality of Imam 'Ali* (London, 2006), p.220. A full annotated translation of this immensely influential letter is provided as Appendix 2 (pp.219–36).

an official position which was to set a decisive precedent of religious tolerance for the ensuing centuries of Muslim rule in India. Hajjaj wrote to Muhammad b. Qasim a letter which was translated into what became known as the 'Brahmanabad settlement':

> The request of the chiefs of Brahmanabad about the building of Budh and other temples, and toleration in religious matters, is just and reasonable. I do not see what further rights we can have over them beyond the usual tax. They have paid homage to us and have undertaken to pay the fixed tribute [*jizya*] to the Caliph. Because they have become *dhimmi*s we have no right whatsoever to interfere in their lives and property. Do permit them to follow their own religion. No one should prevent them.[16]

Later Muslim rulers were to vary in their degree of fidelity to this precedent in India. But the point being made here is more normative. What is to be stressed is that Buddhists and Hindus (and other religious communities, such as the Zoroastrians) were, in principle, to be granted the same religious and legal recognition as the Jews and the Christians, or the 'People of the Book'.

The principle of tolerance within Islam cannot be restricted in its application to the institution of the *dhimma*. As Khaled Abou El Fadl notes, the Prophet did not collect the *jizya* from every non-Muslim tribe that submitted to the Muslim states. Some tribes were actually paid from the Muslim treasury, because they were deemed within the category of 'those whose hearts are to be reconciled' (9:60). The caliph 'Umar entered into a peace settlement with Arab Christian tribes who objected to paying the *jizya*; they were permitted to pay a tax which was referred to as *zakat*, the same kind of tax paid by Muslims.[17]

It is clear, then, that the institution of *dhimma* is a complex result of history and law, politics and ethics, universal principles

---

[16] Gobind Khushalani, *Chachnamah Retold: An Account of the Arab Conquest of Sindh* (New Delhi, 2006), p.156.
[17] Khaled Abou El Fadl, *The Place of Tolerance in Islam* (Boston, 2002), p.22.

and particular conditions. It was a juridical application of the principle of tolerance in a context governed by the exigencies of imperial politics. There is little doubt that the 'protected' status of religious minorities under Muslim rule generally fell short of modern standards of religious equality and tolerance. Yet through much of history, the status enjoyed by such minorities was far in advance of anything that could be expected by minorities in Christendom. One shudders to think of the fate which awaited any Muslim who tried to build a mosque in lands ruled by Christians.

This tolerant tradition was exemplified as recently as the 19th century, amid the onset of European colonial rule in the Middle East, as well as intolerant impulses on the part of some Muslims themselves. It involves an extraordinary episode in the life of the Emir Abd al-Qadir al-Jazairi, who had been defeated by the French after a gallant defence of his Algerian homeland from 1830 to 1847. The Emir, then in exile in Damascus, witnessed a shameful attack on the Christian quarter. With his band of Maghrebi followers, Abd al-Qadir sought out the terrified Christians, giving them refuge in his own home. News of this spread and on the morning of 10 July 1860 an angry crowd gathered outside the Emir's house, demanding that he hand over the Christians. Alone, he went out to confront them; after a series of exchanges, it appeared that the Emir and his entourage would have to fight to defend the Christians. His words to his men were: 'My Maghrebis, may your hearts rejoice, for I call God to witness. We are going to fight for a cause as holy as that for which we fought before!' The mob dispersed and fled in fear.[18]

It is estimated that, in the end, no fewer than 15,000 Christians were saved by the Emir and his followers. This number included all the ambassadors and consuls of the European powers together with their families. Abd al-Qadir received the highest possible medals and honours from all the leading western powers. He was

---

[18] This incident is recorded in Boualem Bessaïeh, 'Abdelkader à Damas et le sauvetage de douze mille chrétiens', in *Itinéraires: Revue semestrielle* (Fondation Abdelkader), 6 (2003), p.90.

willing to sacrifice his life and that of his entourage in order to uphold a principle expressed in the Quran, regarded by most commentators as the first to be revealed in relation to warfare, granting Muslims the right to fight back in self-defence. 'Permission is given to those who are being fought, for they have been wronged . . . Had God not driven back some by means of others, then indeed monasteries, churches, synagogues and mosques, wherein the name of God is oft-invoked, would assuredly have been destroyed' (22:39–40).

Conclusion

Religious tolerance is one of the wellsprings of today's secular separation of church and state. Muslim ethics, in precept and practice, has played an important role in the historical process by which the principle of religious tolerance has become enshrined as a central tenet in the western tradition of political philosophy and conduct of state. This is too readily overlooked amid spates of intolerance in the contemporary Muslim world, which are often ascribed to the 'backwardness' of Islam. In particular, its holistic view of *tawhid*, in which the oneness of the sacred ideally fashions and infuses the entire domain labelled as 'the secular' in western discourse, is often singled out as a barrier to a 'modern' civic approach to tolerance that is typical of the West.

This view is not only simplistic, it also obscures an irony at once historical and theological. Tolerance has in practice been a trait of Muslim society right up to its decline in the pre-modern period. The decline was accelerated by the assault of western colonialism and its brand of modernity, with the ensuing backlash of fiery brands of Muslim nationalism and then fundamentalism, all of which eroded the spiritual vitality of Islam's humane traditions. In contrast, the *intolerance* which characterised Christendom for much of its history only began to be 'deconstructed' in this same period, with the advent of western secularism. Thus, the rise of religious tolerance in the West appears to be correlated to the declining influence of Christian values in public life in modernity. By contrast in the Muslim world, it is the decline of the influence of Islamic values that has engendered that peculiar inferiority complex of which religious intolerance is a major symptom. Through the emasculation of this spiritual heritage, all sorts of ideological counterfeits – most notably militant radical Islamism – have sought to disguise the resulting impotence: the outward socio-legal forms of religion lack transformative power in the measure that they are deprived of their spiritual, intellectual and ethical substance.

Muslims should be invited to retrieve the principle of tolerance which truly characterises the spirit and history of their tradition, and to use this as a yardstick by which to critically judge contemporary attitudes and behaviour. Tolerance is 'neither of the East nor of the West'; no religion or culture can claim a monopoly on this universal ethic. Its practice does not at all require Muslims to imitate the philosophical teachings of the West. Yet there is no reason why they should not benefit from and acknowledge the positive aspects of practical tolerance enacted by western nations in public law, human rights and political governance. Indeed, the roots of these, as has been seen, often drew inspiration from Muslim practice.

Without tolerance, diversity is jeopardised; without diversity, the very nature of humanity is violated. If the diversity of religions and cultures expresses the wisdom of divine revelation, then tolerance of the differences which will always accompany that diversity becomes not just an ethical duty but also an intellectual obligation: for tolerance is a mode of engaging creatively with the wisdom underlying the very existence of diversity. It thus becomes an invitation to respect, and also reflect, the wisdom of the Creator. By accepting this invitation, Muslims may fashion a contemporary civic culture worthy of their heritage.

Further Reading

Burckhardt, Titus. *Moorish Culture in Spain*. London, 1972.
Ess, Josef van. *The Flowering of Muslim Theology*, tr. J.M. Todd. Cambridge, MA, 2006.
Heyd, David, ed. *Toleration: An Elusive Virtue*. Princeton, 1996.

Ikram, S.M. *History of Muslim Civilization in India and Pakistan.* Lahore, 1989.

Kiser, John. *Commander of the Faithful: The Life and Times of Emir Abd el-Kader.* London, 2008.

Lewis, Bernard. *Semites and Anti-Semites: An Inquiry into Conflict and Prejudice.* London, 1986.

Lings, Martin. *Muhammad: His Life Based on the Earliest Sources.* Cambridge, 1984.

Peters, F.E. 'A Modernist Interpretation of *Jihad*: Mahmud Shaltut's Treatise, *Koran and Fighting*', in his *Jihad in Classical and Modern Islam.* Leiden, 1977.

Shah-Kazemi, Reza. *The Other in the Light of the One: The Universality of the Qur'an and Interfaith Dialogue.* Cambridge, 2006.

Sharafuddin, Mohammed. *Islam and Romantic Orientalism.* London, 1996.

11

Nonviolence

Ramin Jahanbegloo

In the past decade, Islam has come to be associated more than ever with images of extremism and violence. Osama bin Laden and Saddam Hussein are stock characters in this association in the wake of September 11, 2001 and the 'war on terror'. Lost in all this are rich layers of Muslim experience of nonviolent change and civility, both past and present. Yet Islam is not alone in having to come to terms with the interplay of secular and sacred that accounts for ethical choices among individuals and societies.

Violence in the name of religion is a subject which reminds us of the ambiguities that attach themselves to the lived experience of the sacred. Even as it inspires and shapes a sense of community that gives meaning to the lives of its members, the sacred may be appropriated for deeply divisive and damaging ends. Religious intolerance and persecution have been common throughout history; most faiths have been caught up in them at one time or another. For Richard Dawkins, a prominent British commentator on science and secularism, religion leads quite logically to violence and all kinds of horrors. This does not mean that every religious believer will take that path, but that a religious way of thinking invites us to be violent. In an interview a few years ago, Dawkins was asked whether he could think of anything good about religion – 'one positive, if minor, thing religion has done' for the good. With no hesitation, Dawkins replied, 'I really don't think I can think of anything; I really can't.'[1]

Historically, religious ideas have been used to justify both war and peace, violence and reconciliation. What remains an open question is: can religion make anybody good or nonviolent who would otherwise be malicious and violent? The relationship of religious belief to social and political action is profoundly obscure. One cannot predict with certainty which religious beliefs will lead to violence, and which to compassion in any particular mind. Perhaps what we need to grasp is how to accept belief as belief, not as directive: how to consider it with critical judgement and not an idolater's compliance. This is about the capacity to distinguish in one's religious outlook between belief that is accepting of different ways of seeing the world (and the Divine), and that which is attached to exclusive ways of seeing and being. The latter is a short step removed from rationalising violence as itself a sacred act.

The events of September 11 have led to an insistent linkage between sacred violence and Islam. For Bernard Lewis, an influential western scholar, 'a long and bitter struggle lies ahead' if bin Laden persuades Muslims to accept his views and leadership. Moreover, 'Al Qaeda and related groups will clash with the other neighbours of Islam – Russia, China, India – who may prove less squeamish than the Americans in using their power against Muslims and their sanctities', says Lewis; if bin Laden has his way, 'a dark future awaits the world, especially the part of it that embraces Islam'.[2]

Yet Islam hardly glorifies violence – and quite explicitly exalts its opposite. History offers much evidence of Muslim tolerance and civil engagement with other faith and cultural traditions. Cordoba has become a byword for the pluralism of the *convivencia*

---

[1] 'Religion: For Dummies', interview with Laura Sheahen, *Beliefnet*: http://www.beliefnet.com/story/136/story_13688_1.html. See also his claims about scripture and violence in *The God Delusion* (London, 2006), chapters 7–8.

[2] Bernard Lewis, 'The Revolt of Islam', *New Yorker* (19 November 2001).

in which Christians, Jews and Muslims fostered a thriving civilisation in Andalusia. While not perfect, pluralist Muslim rule there between the eighth and 15th centuries was well in advance of the rest of Europe well into the early modern period.[3] Nor was it an isolated episode, as Reza Shah-Kazemi's chapter in this volume makes clear, even as we recognise serious lapses in this history of tolerance. What I address here is the distinctive contribution that Islam brings to the idea and practice of nonviolence. How has this faith tradition approached violence, and shaped the ethical practice of Muslims over time? What direction might a nonviolent Muslim ethos take in the globalised future of a post-September 11 world? I draw attention to modern exemplars whose strategies of nonviolent social and political change have plenty to teach us.

Foundations

The ethics of nonviolence in Islam stem from the same basic sources as law and sharia: namely the Quran and the sunna (traditions) of the Prophet. Although it is not a treatise of ethics, law or philosophy, the Quran like other scriptural texts lends itself to multiple readings. What makes scripture compelling across time and space, whether in Islam or other traditions, is the conviction that the moral code is both timeless and dynamic. Faith in a Supreme Being is coupled with the gift of the intellect, which allows scriptural principles to be applied to ever-changing circumstances. In all this, peace or *salam* is both a spiritual and material quality of paramount importance.

'O you who believe, enter the peace, all of you', proclaims the Quran (2:208). It warns against corruption (*fasad*) from this state of peace – and against aggression. Muslims are invited repeatedly to strive in the path of God on behalf of the weak and against the oppressors (*zalimun*). Hence, the authentic struggle or the 'greater jihad' (*al-jihad al-akbar*) is a constant internal striving against one's baser self. The 'lesser jihad' (*al-jihad al-asghar*) involves

---

[3] Maria-Rosa Menocal, *The Ornament of the World: How Muslims, Jews and Christians Created a Culture of Tolerance in Medieval Spain* (Boston, 2002).

the physical defence of the faith, subject to highly restrictive conditions on when and how it is legitimate to do so. Islam's ethical vision is unambiguous. Peace has primacy, war is an evil that requires strong moral justification and must end at the first opportunity: 'If they incline to peace, you should incline to it and trust in God' (8:61). Above all, the sanctity of life is to be respected: 'Do not kill the soul that God has made sacred, except by right' (6:151).

Not surprisingly, then, restraint or *sabr* becomes a primary Quranic virtue in the face of provocation, for individuals and communities. Repeatedly, those who are steadfast and forgiving in the face of provocation are held up for reward. Only as a last resort and within the narrow provisions of self-defence is recourse to physical force allowed. Historically, it was in Medina where the umma had settled into a formal community after its persecution in Mecca that the Prophet first received permission to physically defend the community. Thus, if the Quranic verses on the use of violence and nonviolent resistance appear to contradict one another, this is explained by the specific context of the verses. Indeed, Muhammad shows himself 'a reluctant practitioner', and is quick to seek an end to hostilities, often against the urging of his Companions.[4]

With Muhammad's passing in 632, four of his Companions consecutively ascended to the leadership of the umma as the 'rightly-guided caliphs'. Their authority derived from having been most familiar with his teaching, methods and practice. But this did not spare the community strife and violence over the leadership of what was to become a rapidly expanding political domain. Abu Bakr's accession as the first caliph (r. 632–4) saw the beginnings of a Muslim empire, with forces being sent to Syria and Iraq which were successfully conquered. This policy

---

[4] Sohail H. Hashmi, 'Interpreting the Islamic Ethics of War and Peace', in Terry Nardin, ed. *The Ethics of War and Peace* (Princeton, 1996), pp.141–74; John Kelsay, *Islam and War: A Study in Comparative Ethics* (Louisville, KY, 1993), pp.46–7; Reza Aslan, *No god but God: The Origins, Evolution and Future of Islam* (London, 2006), pp.84–7.

was followed by his successors Umar b. al-Khattab (r. 634–44) and Uthman b. Affan (r. 644–56) who sought to retain the unity of the empire by appointing members of his clan. A civil war ensued, often called the *Fitna* and regarded as marking the end of a unified Islamic nation. It afflicted the reign of the fourth caliph, Ali b. Abi Talib (r. 656–61), who strove in vain for a conciliatory resolution to warring claims, including those on his own behalf. At issue was legitimate succession to the Prophet; the outcome was to unfold most sharply in the schism between Sunni and Shia Muslims. From Muhammad's death to the Mongol invasions and the sacking of Baghdad in 1258 and beyond, caliphs and dynasties presided over the Muslim world in Asia, Africa and Europe – some benevolent and others tyrannical. Violence was associated with the politics of empire as it has always been in human history. Where did 'Islam' stand in all this as a faith tradition?

The privileging of both divine and social justice (*adl*) generates the twin imperatives of pursuing *salam* and resorting to its defence in Islamic ethics. 'In the Quran there are over two hundred admonitions against injustice', notes Majid Khadduri, 'expressed in such words as *zulm, ithm, dalal,* and others, and no less than almost a hundred expressions embodying the notions of justice, either directly in such words as *adl, qist, mizan,* and others as noted before, or in a variety of indirect expressions.'[5] The various manifestations of justice coupled with the paramount commitment to *salam* or peace and forbearance, signal quite clearly the preferred strategy in Islam. It is one of striving ceaselessly for positive social change with minimal recourse to physical force with all its undesirable consequences.

Hence the foundational legacy – in terms of social and political history as well as the ethical principles that stem from Islam as faith tradition – offers critical teaching here. Not only are the ideals of *salam* robust, they are livable, as shown repeatedly in historical experience. Deviations from the ideals have been

---

[5] Majid Khadduri, *The Islamic Conception of Justice* (New York, 1984), p.10.

conspicuous too, from the earliest times. But they stand out as departures from a large body of actual Muslim practice and ethical ideals. Nonviolent resistance against injustice, which has come to be closely associated with a 'Gandhian ethos', has strong resonance within Islam.

Modern Exemplars

In our time, nonviolence as a practical approach to deep political and social change – often in the face of great odds – owes much to the thought and practice of Mohandas K. Gandhi (1869–1948). Gandhi coined the term *satyagraha* during his civil disobedience campaigns in South Africa. For him, *satyagraha* was about a relentless search for truth (*satya*) and a firm determination (*agraha*) to reach it. It was not only a tactic to be used in acute political struggle, but a universal solvent for injustice and harm – which made it a more complex idea than western concepts of 'passive resistance' and 'civil disobedience'. On the basis of his experiences and experiments over time, Gandhi developed his approach as a form of active ethical resistance to all the social, political, economic and psychological pressures that confront individuals and communities.[6] *Satyagraha* was like a banyan tree with innumerable branches, which Gandhi believed could be appropriated by men and women of all faith traditions in the cause of civic harmony. Indeed, the civil rights campaigns of Martin Luther King and Nelson Mandela were avowedly influenced by *satyagraha*. Of immediate concern, however, were the communal tensions in colonial India and its aftermath. Like Gandhi, key Muslim leaders also reached for resources in their own tradition on which to build a nonviolent approach, while wrestling to expose and repudiate the forces of violence inherent in those traditions.

Khan Abdul Ghaffar Khan (1890–1988) was one such leader. More recently in this tradition, Muslims can also look to the civic leadership of Fethullah Gülen (1941–). Both rejected violence when

---

[6] See Mohandas K. Gandhi, *An Autobiography: The Story of my Experiments with Truth*, trans. Madadev Desai (Boston, 1993).

it was a tempting recourse for others in similar contexts. Moreover, both sought to work creatively with Muslims as well as non-Muslims outside their own milieu to build civic solidarity, which made for change that was transformative. This legacy is vital in bridging the divide between secular and religious activists in the Muslim world, and in fostering a genuinely civil and pluralist Muslim public space.

Khan Abdul Ghaffar Khan is perhaps better known as a Pashtun nationalist rather than as a proponent of nonviolent Islam in India's struggle for independence from Britain.[7] Yet he began forming his philosophy of nonviolent civil action before coming into contact with Gandhi, inspired by his own Islamic ideals that favoured a secular politics. 'I did not learn secularism from Bapu [Gandhi]', noted Ghaffar Khan, 'I found it in the Quran.'[8] Gandhi's ideals, by contrast, drew upon the Bhagavad Gita, the New Testament and the writings of Thoreau, Ruskin and Tolstoy. For Ghaffar Khan, the values of truth, love and service were central to his idea of a spiritualised public space where each faith could play an important role. Harmony among Hindus and Muslims was a key aspect of this vision, in which ethnic identities flourished in 'mutual toleration'.

The *Khudai Khidmatgar* or 'Servants of God' movement that Ghaffar Khan founded in the 1920s attracted over 100,000 recruits, fully committed to peaceful resistance to colonial rule. It is all the more remarkable that the *Khidmatgar* found success in a region of South-Central Asia which is stereotypically thought of as the home of a 'warrior ethic'. When fired upon by British soldiers during their protests, their disciplined restraint held firm: *sabr* was called for, violence was inherently unacceptable. Ghaffar Khan's quest for harmonious rather than conflictual change was tied to his conviction that all great faith traditions shared an underlying unity of purpose; his Islam was an inclusive teaching that was

---

[7] See Eknath Easwaran, 'A Man to Match his Mountains: Badshah Khan', in *Nonviolent Soldier of Islam* (Petaluma, CA, 1984).

[8] Quoted in Shrinivas Rao S. Sohoni, 'Badshah Khan: Islam and Non-violence', in *Khan Abdul Ghaffar Khan: A Centennial Tribute* (Delhi, 1995), p.48.

ultimately about spirituality and the collective welfare. It followed that 'secularism' for Ghaffar Khan was not about excluding religion from the public domain, but exercising equal respect for all faith traditions. Dissociating the *state* from religion was indeed necessary. So was the protection of minority rights under the constitution, and the avoidance of communalism. This was also how Gandhi understood secularism, as the framework in which civility could best thrive.

Fethullah Gülen is a Turkish scholar of Islam and a social activist. Born in Erzurum in eastern Turkey in 1938, Gülen began his career as a government preacher and, in 1958, took up a teaching position at a mosque in Edirne. Four years later, he transferred to Izmir where his nonviolent movement began, inspired by the pluralist progressivism of Said Nursi (1868–1960), a revered scholar. During the era of military rule starting in 1971, Gülen was arrested for clandestine religious activities and spent seven months in prison. Throughout his career Gülen has lectured on such subjects as the Quran and contemporary science, and social justice in Islam. Unlike many other Islamic activists and scholars, Gülen opposes the idea of the state applying the sharia as law. He advocates an 'Anatolian Islam' based on tolerance, and excluding harsh restrictions or fanaticism.

For Gülen, tolerance and dialogue are the keys to civic peace and progressive social change even in the face of oppressive forces. 'We can build confidence and peace in this country', he says of Turkey, 'if we treat each other with tolerance.'[9] Hence, 'no one should condemn the other for being a member of a religion or scold him for being an atheist'.[10] On women's freedom in Turkey today, Gülen argues that veiling is a legitimate modern choice: 'no one can suppress the progress of women through the clothes they have to wear'. Quite simply, 'no one should be subject to criticism for his or her clothing or thoughts'. Gülen's movement seeks to

---

[9] Alistair Bell, 'Turkish Islamic leader defies radical label', *Reuters* (7 August 1995). See generally, Mehran Kamrava, *The New Voices of Islam: Reforming Politics and Modernity* (London, 2006), Chapter 4.

[10] *The Turkish Daily News* (18 February 1995).

revitalise traditional values as part of modernising efforts by reshaping a legitimate link between the state and religion, while emphasising the close relationship between peaceful tolerance and successful democratic life. Scientific rationalism and technology are embraced, as they were a century ago by Said Nursi when the Ottomans were confronted by European modernity. Nursi firmly rejected the notion that such rationalism was outside the realm of religious tradition.

'Islamic movements' today are often associated with political militancy, anti-secularism and a narrow religiosity. The Gülen movement is not alone in eschewing this trend. Other prominent examples include Indonesia's Nahdatul Ulama movement as envisioned by Abdurrahman Wahid (1940–), and the Senegalese Muridiyya brotherhood founded by Ahmadou Bamba (1850–1927).[11] With members numbering in the tens of millions, their commitment to nonviolent social progress is not merely tactical but woven into an outlook that couples secular and sacred ideals. Like the Gülen movement, their capacity to provide a distinctly Islamic civil voice amid fears about the erosion of identity in a globalised world is no less significant than their insistence on peaceful ways of doing so.

Toward Civil Society

Political Islam is largely an ideological response to the hegemony which the West has acquired in our time. The success political Islam has enjoyed says much about the failure of the secular state in providing a space where democratic culture and faith traditions can both thrive, and thereby capture the Muslim public imagination. Post-colonial secular governments have often been aggressive in their projects of modernisation, lacking in sensitivity toward religion and forcefully authoritarian in their politics. This does not mean that Muslim societies are somehow averse to democracy and pluralism, as the 'clash of civilisations' thesis would have

---

[11] For an overview of faith-based initiatives in this regard, see Glenn D. Paige et al., eds, *Islam and Nonviolence* (Honolulu, 2001).

us believe. Inclusive governance and the rule of law have flourished before in Muslim societies – and they cannot, in any case,
be imposed from above or outside, as contemporary Iraq has
shown.

For indigenous civil society to emerge as the space where pluralist
democracy can take root, a shift is needed in the exercise of citizenship. That is, citizenship of an 'adversarial' nature (and prone
to violence) must give way to one that is 'socially engaged', where
citizens have a genuine stake. Such a shift only happens when a
society's past and future are bridged by a meaningful narrative of
identity and values – inclusive in its scope toward *all* its citizens
– that helps navigate a troubled present. When this fails to happen,
and a 'tribal' narrative is offered instead, violence is often the
result.

Religion may contribute vitally to this inclusive need with its
resources of memory, spirituality and bonding. That religion can
play a divisive as well as a conciliatory role has much to do with
the nature of sacred texts, and the social setting in which they are
read. All religious texts are open to multiple levels of reading, by
readers who vary in their capacities and dispositions. A 'hard
reading' of a text like the Bible or the Quran seeks to appropriate
sacred truths on behalf of a particular collective identity, usually
translated into the idea of a 'chosen people'. It is a short step from
there to the kind of self-righteousness that fuels 'holy wars'. Here,
'religion' as the sense of union and unity (from the Latin *ligare*)
is turned into a rallying point against an Other that is the subject
of hatred and violence. Indeed, hard readings end up generating
hard politics. All faith traditions have their share of believers for
whom hard religion is the only serious kind. Charles Taylor, one
of our most influential observers in this regard, sees it thus:

> One becomes aware of how easily our reaching for the religious
> or the spiritual can be abused, and turned towards appalling hatred
> and destruction. The fact of such hatred is obvious; we see it every
> day on television. But we need to understand better how this terrible
> deviation arises. Some atheists duck this difficult task by the essen-
> tialist claim that religion of itself leads to violence. Some believers

try a similar evasion by blaming certain other religions for this. This essentialism flies in the face of the fact that large-scale violence has been done in the name of all religions, and also of atheist ideologies, like Marxism or Fascism. Religious violence in our day has a lot in common with the violence inspired by nationalism. Indeed, the two often fuse. At the same time, it clearly has to do with our need to feel that we are pure and good by projecting all evil on to the Other.[12]

We return, then, to the need for a social narrative that is meaningful not only in terms of having legitimacy (something that can be achieved simply by appealing to the base instincts that make a mob dangerous), but of being 'responsible' on behalf of the common good. Whether secular or religious, a narrative that lacks ethical commitment is less likely to take civility seriously. This is no less true of forms of social violence at large, from criminal gangs to family violence. Without the privileging of an ethic of civility, what defence can the mere fact of shared citizenship offer against the temptations of violence?

Conclusion

Ghaffar Khan's legacy reminds us that the dialogue which nonviolent Islam inspires is an inclusive civil quest. Divides of class, culture, ideology and religion cannot be wished away: they underscore the need for a civil imagination that is also ethical.[13] Indeed, a civic space without the binding fabric of shared ethical values is hard to sustain. This is not about forsaking secular culture – which is what makes a generous ethical space more likely. Nor

---

[12] Charles Margrave Taylor, 'The 2008 Commemorative Prize Kyoto Lectures', accessible at http://www.inamori-f.or.jp/laureates/k24_c_charles/lct_e.html. See further Taylor's reflections in this regard in his discussions of dilemmas in religious belief, in *A Secular Age* (Cambridge, MA, 2007), chapters 17 and 18.

[13] See Amyn B. Sajoo, ed. *Muslim Modernities: Expressions of the Civil Imagination* (London, 2008), especially chapters 9 and 10.

should secular culture mean the exclusion of religious motivation and argument from the public sphere. Between secular and theological absolutism is the middle ground of pluralist civil society and inclusive governance. It is here that local narratives which reject violence in favour of *salam, sabr* and *adl* can take root.

It is important to resist the claim that civil and political modernity depend on the primacy of secular reason over Muslim narratives. The latter is not just a stock of historical ideas and longings. It is a process of 'coming to know' for individuals and communities, a lived experience that cannot be reduced to secular and rational discourses without stripping away meaningful facets of identity. The result of this stripping away of roots and ethical attachments is frequently a greater readiness to embrace versions of modernity that are only about techno-materialist values that have little of substance to say about deeper human quests and solidarities. How else to account for the reversals today in the 'naked public square' (to recall Richard Neuhaus' lament in the 1980s on religion being isolated in private spaces) of so many western and westernising societies?[14] For those who insist on tying public religion to political violence, one may point to the frightful record of mass slaughter in the name of secular ideologies through much of the 20th century, as Charles Taylor has noted.

Nonviolent Islam could give fresh life to a healthy secularism in Muslim societies. It may help steer public space away from state-dominated as well as other forms of political Islam, with their foolish utopias. Yet an ethical secularism that allows public religious life to thrive can contribute enormously to a genuine civic pluralism, and indeed civility, with regard to social violence more generally. Realising the ideals of nonviolence is a perennial struggle for Islamic communities the world over, and integral to the struggle for democratic life. There are rich foundations and legacies to build on in making this shift to an ethical civic culture in a post-September 11 universe. Yet if democracy is understood

---

[14] Richard John Neuhaus, *The Naked Public Square: Religion and Democracy in America* (Grand Rapids, MI, 1984).

less as an ideal than a process, then the plural ways of arriving at it become a vital part of democracy itself.

Further Reading

Appleby, R. Scott. *The Ambivalence of the Sacred: Religion, Violence, and Reconciliation.* New York and Oxford, 2000.

Bondurant, Joan V. *Conquest of Violence: The Gandhian Philosophy of Conflict.* Princeton, 1988.

Gerard, Rene. *Violence and the Sacred*, tr. Patrick Gregory. Baltimore, MD, 1977.

Hashmi, Sohail, ed. *Islamic Political Ethics: Civil Society, Pluralism, and Conflict.* Princeton, NJ, 2002.

Kamrava, Mehran. *The New Voices of Islam: Reforming Politics and Modernity.* London, 2006.

Kelsay, John and James T. Johnson, eds. *Just War and Jihad: Historical and Theoretical Perspectives on War and Peace in Western and Islamic Traditions.* Westport, CT, 1991.

Maalouf, Amin. *In the Name of Identity: Violence and the Need to Belong*, tr. Barbara Bray. New York, 2000.

Nardin, Terry, ed. *The Ethics of War and Peace: Religious and Secular Perspectives.* Princeton, 1996.

Paige, Glenn D., Chaiwat Satha-Anand (Qader Muheideen) and Sara Gilliatt, eds. *Islam and Nonviolence.* Honolulu, 2001.

Sen, Amartya. *Identity and Violence: The Illusion of Destiny.* New York and London, 2006.

Smith-Christopher, Daniel L. "'That was Then . . .': Debating Nonviolence within the Textual Traditions of Judaism, Christianity, and Islam', in Joseph Runzo and Nancy Martin, eds, *Ethics in the World Religions.* Oxford, 2001, pp.251–69.

Index